CONNECTING LIVES:

INTERBELIEF DIALOGUE IN CONTEMPORARY IRELAND

CONNECTING
LIVES

Interbelief Dialogue in Contemporary Ireland

EDITED BY PATRICIA KIERAN

VERITAS

Published 2019 by
Veritas Publications
7–8 Lower Abbey Street
Dublin 1
Ireland
publications@veritas.ie
www.veritas.ie

ISBN 978 1 84730 761 3

10 9 8 7 6 5 4 3 2 1

A catalogue record for this book is available from the British Library.

Designed by Pádraig McCormack, Veritas Publications
Printed in Ireland by SPRINT-print Ltd

In memory of Prof. Michael Hayes (1957–2017), who opened the first interbelief dialogue seminar at MIC, and to members of all interbelief networks in Ireland, North and South, especially the Mid-West Interfaith Network, Dublin City Interfaith Forum, Kilkenny Interfaith Friendship Group, Three Faiths Forum and Northern Ireland Inter-Faith Forum.

CONTENTS

Be patient toward all that is unsolved in your heart and try to love the questions themselves, like locked rooms and like books that are now written in a very foreign tongue. Do not now seek the answers, which cannot be given you because you would not be able to live them. And the point is, to live everything. Live the questions now. Perhaps you will then gradually, without noticing it, live along some distant day into the answer.

Rainer Maria Rilke

FOREWORD

In a fractured world, where 'unfriending' those with different viewpoints is sometimes the norm, this book, which reminds us of the significant benefits of interbelief dialogue and friendship, could not be more timely or more important.

I was raised in an American community where virtually everyone observed Orthodox Judaism. When I moved overseas I was excited to learn about other people and their cultures. When I moved to Ireland and I was the only Jew living in my area, I was quickly thrust into the role of Jewish representative at interfaith events.

And I ran with it. An Eid al-Fitr celebration with my Muslim friends, a joint Jewish High Holydays–*Eid al-Adḥa* celebration, an interfaith Passover Seder, a Chanukkah menorah lighting (and potato latke eating) in a Dominican priory – I couldn't get enough. I got a high every time I noticed something another tradition shared with my Jewish tradition. The 'You do that too?' moments always made me light up.

Yet I felt something was missing. In one interfaith meeting, I wondered aloud whether we were really accomplishing all we could. I said, 'The people who attend our events don't really need our events, because they already have the mindset of coexistence and mutual respect, while the people who still don't have that mindset aren't attending our events.' The leader of the group nodded her head and said, 'We're preaching to the converted.'

Rabbi Hiyya bar Abba said: Even a father and son or a teacher and student who are involved in Torah study in the same study hall become o-y'vim [adversaries] of each other. Yet they do not move from there until they become ohavim [beloveds] of each other. (Babylonian Talmud: Kiddushin 30b)

A yeshiva study hall is quite unlike any other. Students of all ages study in pairs, sometimes arguing with each other, often vociferously and even more often loudly, about how to understand a certain passage of the Talmud. 'Hillel is saying X' is countered with 'No! Hillel is saying Y!' with accompanying thumb gestures for emphasis.

It took a dear Catholic friend to remind me of the yeshiva approach described above. She connected this approach to the tension that perhaps needs to occur in the interbelief context in order for real barriers to be broken down.

'Iron sharpens iron, so a man sharpens the countenance of his family' (Proverbs 27:17). Rabbi Chama bar Chanina said: 'A knife becomes sharpened only at the side of another. So too, a Torah scholar can become sharpened only by another.' (Midrash: Genesis Rabbah 69:2)

The students in the Jewish houses of learning are looking at the same passage of the Talmud and seeing it in different ways. They go through the discomfort and angst of hearing the other person look at that very same passage and not see it the way they see it. The discomfort is real, and, by definition, uncomfortable. Rather than avoiding the discomfort and focusing on what they agree on, they tackle the difference in viewpoints head on and challenge each other. The result, if done with the right intentions, can be *greater* understanding of the other and even, as Rabbi Hiyya bar Abba said, love.

The arguments in the yeshiva study hall do not always end with agreement. But the key is they come right back the next day to the same study session, with the same study partner with whom they wrangled the previous day. They don't say, 'He has different views from mine, so I need to move on from him.' They have had time to process the previous day's learning, and they have had a chance for at least some of what the other person said to be accepted in their mind as reasonable. At least something from the other person's viewpoint has influenced their own and thus helped them understand the world in a new way, something that never would have occurred if not for that uncomfortable 'sharpening of knives' in which the two engaged in the previous day.

Perhaps, therefore, one way to foster greater mutual understanding and even admiration when bringing together people of different beliefs, whether the different beliefs be religious, philosophical or political, would be to have those involved look at the very same event or theme (the way the yeshiva students look at the same passage in the Talmud); have each person share how he or she views that event or theme; engage in honest, even vigorous (and respectful) dialogue and tackle the differences head on, so that everyone fully understands each other's viewpoint; and then, most importantly, keep bringing those same people together.

It would seem the last part – to keep getting together despite, or indeed because of, the differences in viewpoints – requires an appreciation of just how much one can gain from seeing how the other views things differently. My hope, and expectation, is that this book will help more people develop such an appreciation.

Etan Blass
6 November 2018

ACKNOWLEDGEMENTS

Special thanks are due to the Anna Lindh Foundation and the NCCA who supported the Interbelief Dialogue (IBD) in Contemporary Ireland Seminar on 17 February 2016.

This IBD seminar would not have taken place without the generous support and participation of a whole range of groups and individuals including members of the Anna Lindh Foundation (ALF), the Dublin City Interfaith Forum, the Mid-West Interfaith Network (MWIN), Kilkenny Interfaith Friendship Group, the Chester Beatty Library, the Glencree Peace and Reconciliation Centre, Doras Luimni and community members from Direct Provision Centres. Indeed, a debt of gratitude is owed to the many members and leaders of faith and belief traditions who participated in the seminar and shared their stories through dialogue. It is also important to thank the football players from SARI and MIC, the musicians from the Sikh community in Shannon, musicians and singers from Elikya, artists from the Congolese Women's Group and the members of the public who participated in the IBD day.

In particular the editor would like to acknowledge the support and encouragement of Mary Immaculate College Writer's Retreat in providing a space to help complete this project. A debt of gratitude is due to Prof. Michael Healy, Dean of Research and Graduate Studies, as well as Dr Elaine Murtagh, Dr Ailbhe Kenny and Dr Dorothy Morrissey. Special gratitude is due to Dr Carol O'Sullivan, Head of the Department of Learning, Society and Religious Education and wonderful colleagues including Dr Daniel O'Connell, Dr Maurice Harmon, Dr Fiona Dineen, Dr Noírín Ní Riain, Ms Lylian Fotabong, Ms Rachel Ryan, Ms Brighid Golden, Dr Ann Higgins, Dr Fionnuala Tynan and Dr Mary Kelly. Dialogue with Prof. Aislinn O'Donnell (NUIM) and Prof. Marie Parker-Jenkins (UL), and Anne Ryan has been pivotal in the editor's own research journey. The editor would also like to acknowledge the contributions of pre-service teachers, past and present, at MIC who inspired her to work on this book and whose constructive dialogue, critique and insights into teaching and learning about religions and beliefs has been a formative influence. Veritas Publications and in particular its editors have been gracious and expert with their comments, suggestions and advice. A special gratitude is also due to Donna Doherty, Commissioning Editor, Daragh Reddin and Leeann Gallagher for their professional and detailed editorial work.

Finally, the editor would like to thank Kevin McDonagh, her father-in-law, for a lifetime of lively and passionate dialogue about religion and beliefs in Ireland. As always, she owes a big thank you to her five children, John, Brigid, Patrick, Michael and Meabh, and to her husband John McDonagh for keeping the dialogue vibrant, real and great fun.

ABBREVIATIONS

AI	Atheist Ireland
B.Ed.	Bachelor of Education Degree
BM	British Museum
CBL	Chester Beatty Library
CDP	Community Development Project
DEIS	Delivering Equality of Opportunity in Schools
DES	Department of Education and Skills
DCIF	Dublin City Interfaith Forum
EE	Ethical Education
EFA	Education for All
EI	Emotional Intelligence
EU	European Union
ERBE	Education About Religion and Beliefs, and Ethics
ESAI	Educational Studies Association of Ireland
ESRI	Economic and Social Research Institute
Guidelines	Guidelines for Intercultural Education in the Primary School
FAI	Football Association of Ireland
FC	Football Club
FIFA	Fédération Internationale de Football Association
HAI	Humanist Association of Ireland
HSE	Health Service Executive
IBD	Interbelief Dialogue
IRD	Interreligious Dialogue
ICC	Irish Council of Churches

IDEA	International Institute for Democracy and Electoral Assistance
IHEU	International Humanist and Ethical Union
ICCI	Islamic Cultural Centre of Ireland
IMF	International Monetary Fund
INTO	Irish National Teachers' Organisation
IPPN	Irish Primary Principals' Network
MIC	Mary Immaculate College
MP	Member of Parliament
MRBI	Market Research Bureau Ireland
MWIN	Mid-West Interfaith Network
NAPAR	National Action Plan Against Racism
NCCA	National Council for Curriculum and Assessment
OECD	Organisation for Economic Cooperation and Development
PISA	Programme for International Student Assessment
PSC	*Primary School Curriculum* (1999)
RE	Religious Education
REMC	Religious Education in a Multicultural Society
RI	Religious Instruction
RME	Religious and Moral Education
SARI	Sport Against Racism Ireland
SEN	Special Educational Needs
SIF	Strategic Initiative Funding
SPHE	Social Personal and Health Education
STEM	Science, Technology, Engineering and Mathematics
TCD	Trinity College Dublin
TD	Teachta Dála
UEFA	Union of European Football Associations
UNESCO	United Nations Educational, Scientific and Cultural Organisation
VHCCI	Vedic Hindu Cultural Centre Ireland
VSO	Voluntary Service Overseas
WHO	World Health Organisation

INTRODUCTION

Patricia Kieran

The purpose of dialogue is 'to be understood and to understand'.

David Lochhead

Doctor Bill Shaw comments that travelling through North Belfast is like traversing a patchwork of Protestant and Catholic villages separated by walls that are longer and higher than the former Berlin wall. Bill is a Presbyterian minister from the 174 Trust and he observes that walls, whether real or metaphorical, can enable people to live with stereotypical myths. In Belfast, peace walls separate Protestant and Catholic communities that have lived side by side for generations. Sometimes these communities have little interaction apart from the legacy of living with hurt and remembered violence. Incredibly Bill says that up until the age of seventeen, when he got a Saturday job in a department store in Belfast, he never met or spoke to a Catholic. However, his friendship with a Catholic boy liberated them both to build a meaningful relationship. The simple act of peer-to-peer everyday chat was at the heart of their mutual transformation. Friendly talk in a divided city changed the way they viewed themselves and others. Prior to this friendship, Bill lived with stereotypical images of Catholics. Dialogue with a friend became the beginning of an ongoing journey. In his mid-thirties, after graduation, ordination and installation in a congregation, he says, 'I began to look at my Scriptures in a different way, through the eyes of my neighbours and to ask myself, "How do I practise my faith in a manner that is not offensive?"'

The Nature of Interbelief Dialogue

Dialogue at its most basic level involves reciprocal communication with others. This can occur in a multitude of ways through formal or informal means, involving verbal or non-verbal dialogue at a local, national or global level. It can be structured or spontaneous. Informal spontaneous dialogue usually takes place where people are gathered together. It is not scheduled or rehearsed. It just happens. It is the dialogue of life as it occurs at the supermarket till, waiting for children at the school gate, or queuing in a post office. Horst Georg Pöhlmann describes his first spontaneous informal interreligious dialogue, which took place with a stranger on a train in India. 'After ten minutes of small talk about the electrification of Indian railways, he [another passenger] suddenly asked me ... "Are you living in God?" A debate about God and the Gods followed which went on for hours.'[1] Pöhlmann's dialogue quickly developed into a more reflective theological dialogue which involved the explicit exchange of religious and philosophical ideas. Indeed, Jo O'Donovan notes that 'dialogue is not necessarily all about beliefs and differences, but also about being human together.'[2]

There is no one blueprint for dialogue. Dialogue is pluriform and can be messy. On the island of Ireland dialogue about different beliefs comes with a very particular memory of the Troubles and sectarianism. Paradoxically, this violent backdrop is also a testimony to the potency of dialogue for transformative peace and reconciliation.

The Limerick Interbelief Dialogue Seminar

The inspiration for this book came from a seminar on interbelief dialogue (IBD) in contemporary Ireland that took place in February 2016 in Mary Immaculate College, Limerick.[3] The event was organised to highlight the relevance of beliefs (both religious and philosophical convictions) to everyday life and to invite people to listen to and communicate respectfully with others of different beliefs. It brought together a host of national and international experts and members from a variety of faith groups and belief traditions. These included faith leaders, university students and educators, members of interfaith groups, leaders of secular groups, members of the general public as well as artists, musical performers and sporting teams.[4] Over five hundred people participated in this IBD seminar. Some participants were skilled and experienced dialogue partners. For others, it was their first time to engage in any explicit form of dialogue about religion and beliefs. The dialogue began with baby steps. In the course of the seminar participants were invited to explore how the Irish educational system might support interbelief dialogue in schools. The National Council for Curriculum and Assessment's (NCCA) proposed introduction of a new Education about Religions and Beliefs and Ethics programme (ERBE) in primary schools highlights the need to engage with and understand the diversity of religion and belief in Ireland. It is implausible, however, to expect educators to facilitate effective dialogue among children if they have never engaged in the process of interbelief dialogue themselves and if such dialogue is not taking place elsewhere in society.

This Limerick seminar deliberately attempted to scaffold multifaceted dialogue and to affirm that while dialogue is complex and involves risk, it has the potential to lead to a renewed understanding of self, others and (for many) the divine. Dialogue potentially involves a deeply rewarding, creative and transformative engagement that can change lives. Interbelief dialogue is not a talking shop. At the Limerick IBD seminar the local Sikh community dialogued through sharing their Sacred Song and drumming. Christian Gospel composers contributed to the dialogue by performing music inspired by their faith. An exhibition of Congolese artists' work evoked aesthetic reflection, appreciation and dialogue among the community of participants. Sport scaffolded kinaesthetic dialogue as Sport Against Racism Ireland's (SARI) Hijabs and Hat Tricks team played an indoor soccer match against Mary Immaculate College's Students' Union soccer team. Talking about things that matter to communities of diverse beliefs was just one form of dialogue in a diverse ongoing dialogue process.

Why Interbelief Dialogue Really Matters

So why was it necessary to organise a large seminar on interbelief dialogue? The inspiration for the seminar came from a throw-away comment in a conversation with a teacher. Several years ago, an experienced teacher told me that there were a number of children in her primary-school class who came from minority belief traditions. 'What traditions do they belong to?' I asked. She shook her head, 'I don't know.' Intrigued, I probed, 'Didn't you find out?' She replied, 'I wouldn't like to embarrass their parents or make the children feel excluded by asking.' I was puzzled by this well-meaning response and it remained with me. Fear of inadvertently causing offence, of saying the wrong thing and highlighting difference, resulted in her compromise of silence and the children's belief traditions remained invisible. In a well-meaning attempt to be inclusive she excluded any reference to what was particular, personal and perhaps deeply relevant to these children's lives. In one sense it is not surprising that a teacher might feel this way and perhaps many people shy away from talking about religious or secular beliefs precisely because they feel they are trespassing on something deeply personal and private. Ireland is a multi-belief society and the heterogeneity of religion and belief is part of everyday life. Cosgrove notes that in recent years in the Republic of Ireland context:

ways of being which classify themselves as non-religious or which consciously resist religion (new and 'alternative' spiritualities, atheism, humanism, agnosticism, etc.) have become more widespread. World religions – Islam, Buddhism, Hinduism and so on – have arrived, with migrants and through conversion; while established churches face the simultaneously enlivening and unsettling arrival both of African churches and of large numbers of new parishioners with sometimes very different orientations to what is nominally the same denomination. Beyond these, new religious movements (NRMs) are flourishing, and what is sometimes called the 'New Age Movement' (NAM) – bringing very large numbers of Irish people in contact with yoga, meditation, traditional Chinese medicine, reiki and other forms of 'alternative' and/or 'complementary healing'.[5]

Over a decade ago J.R. Walsh noted that 'most Irish people are genuinely worried about and suspicious of some of the new religions'.[6] For some, encountering someone of a different religious or belief tradition is a source of awkward embarrassment and unpredictability. In this context teachers might feel 'vulnerable', 'uncomfortable' and 'fearful' of dialogue involving personal beliefs.[7] Sometimes the sanctuary of homogeneity is preferable to the risky vulnerability of engaging with an unknown other. Most teachers in Ireland come from the majority culture[8] and recent research suggests that both at primary and post-primary level entrants to the teaching profession are overwhelmingly white and Irish.[9] A level of teacher discomfort with issues pertaining to beliefs and values is not unique to Ireland. In the UK Julia Ipgrave's work highlights that teachers can feel exposed when their pupils have a greater understanding of myriad religious and belief traditions.[10] In 2012 the Swedish Schools Inspectorate highlighted that many teachers felt challenged and insecure when dealing with complex issues relating to children's values.[11]

Different Understandings of Dialogue

There is little scholarly literature on the topic of dialogue among people of diverse faiths and beliefs in Ireland.[12] Dialogue is fundamentally about relationships. It has a rich history. In ancient Greece, philosophers championed an interactive conversational process as the optimal way of exploring life's deepest questions. Plato wrote more than thirty dialogues and Platonic dialogue consisted of a protagonist (often Socrates) engaging in a question-and-answer process involving two or more participants in a discussion of philosophical and ethical issues. In the contemporary world, forms of a communal interactive dialogue can be found in myriad disciplines. The theoretical physicist David Bohm (1917–1992) explores dialogue as a multifaceted process extending far beyond 'typical notions of conversational parlance or exchange'. For Bohm, dialogue is a form of enquiry relevant not just to science but to all disciplines as it 'calls into question deeply held assumptions regarding culture, meaning, and identity ... what it means to be human'.[13]

The Brazilian playwright Augusto Boal (1931–2009) posits that dialogue is a natural, universal, healthy dynamic that unites humans. He sees that all people desire and are capable of dialogue. Boal's work suggests that when dialogue is absent from human life, the consequence is often oppressive monologue. His Theatre of the Oppressed is a transformative tool which turns spectators into active participants as they dialogue with performers, suggesting alternative ways of engaging with the narrative, and become 'spect-actors'.[14] Boal suggests, 'While some people make theatre, we all *are* theatre.'[15]

In the field of educational discourse, the Cambridge Dialogue Education Research Group, inspired by the work of Neil Mercer and Christine Howe, view dialogue as a 'distinctive human achievement'.[16] Mercer views dialogue as negotiation between different perspectives, sharing, testing and evaluating ideas and jointly creating new ways of making sense. In this educational dialogue one is attuned to others, open to a critical questioning of self and others and sometimes a change of mind:

> *Dialogue is the continuous co-construction of new meanings that emerge through the gap between different incommensurable perspectives. It builds commitment to engagement across difference and equitable participation. Dialogue is internal/external, spans time and space – it is cumulative over time and makes links to previous/future events or wider context beyond the immediate interaction. Dialogicality is a quality of communication not limited to talk; it includes non-verbal human communication and multimodal forms of dialogue, including interaction with text (multimodal and traditional written forms), and within technology environments, especially with digital artefacts – during the flow of verbal dialogue.*[17]

Dialogue enables people to own their own world views and values, while exploring and evaluating different perspectives, and offers the possibility of working towards reconciliation with others of different lifestyles and values. The fluidity of dialogue, its creative potential for open-ended engagement with different contributions, its facility for making room for comparisons and contrasts while negotiating some form of consensus or disagreement, means that as a process it is ideally suited to people from different belief traditions. However, interbelief dialogue is not just an application of educational dialogue in a belief context. In this volume Julia Ipgrave emphasises that dialogue from a religious perspective is not simply a reciprocal cognitive process of engagement or merely a negotiation and clarification of ideas. For Ipgrave, personal religious faith is misunderstood or even trivialised if it is treated as something that can be decided by argumentation. Dialogue is not simply verbal or conceptual. It involves memories, hopes, imagination, values and a sense of identity and belonging at the deepest level. It has its own structures, rhythms and ways of engaging as well as pluriform manifestations. Sometimes the deepest moments of dialogue involve the language of gesture, a look or indeed silence.

Why IBD?

In the area of religions and beliefs, 'dialogue' is something of a buzzword in contemporary politics and education. Indeed, the Catholic Primary RE Curriculum (2015) and *Grow in Love* RE programme for Catholic schools prioritised interreligious education. The 2016 *Goodness Me, Goodness You* (GMGY) curriculum for Community National Schools encourages interbelief dialogue and suggests that, for children, the teacher is both a facilitator and role model of respectful interbelief dialogue in the classroom. There is a growing political and cultural realisation that religious and personal beliefs are deeply relevant in contemporary Irish society.[18] At a global and international level there have been multiple initiatives, organisations, research centres, resources and developments fostering interreligious and interbelief dialogue.[19] Some of these initiatives include: the World Parliament of Religions;[20] the Harvard Pluralism Project;[21] UNESCO's Interreligious Dialogue Programme; the United Nations General Assembly on Interreligious Dialogue; the World Conference on Religion and Peace; the European Council of Religious Leaders; and the United Nations Alliance of Civilisations. The benefits of such IRD have been richly acclaimed and Dermot Lane notes that there seems to be no end to the popularity and prevalence of books on 'faith meets faith' so that interreligious 'dialogue looks set to be a defining feature of the first century of the third millennium'.[22] Swiss Catholic theologian Hans Küng gets to the heart of why dialogue is a necessity, not an option, when he says, 'There will be no peace among the nations without peace among the religions. There will be no peace among the religions without dialogue among the religions.'[23]

The Issue of Language and Terminology

In any discussion about dialogue and beliefs there is a bewildering array of terms used as a prefix to the word dialogue. These include the terms interbelief, interfaith, multifaith, inter-church, interreligious and inter-path dialogue among others. At the outset, it is vital not to get bogged down and to negotiate a way through this web of terminology where the words 'faith', 'religion' and 'belief' can sometimes be used as if they are identical and interchangeable while in other contexts they are used in radically different ways. Harvard University's Pluralism Project uses the term 'transbelief dialogue' to include secular, religious, atheist and theist dialogue. The Limerick IBD seminar facilitated dialogue from all of these groups but did not use Harvard's term and opted for the term 'interbelief dialogue' to describe its approach. Other groups, such as the Cambridge Inter-faith Programme (CIP)[24] as well as the Catholic Archdiocese of Chicago, use the term 'interfaith dialogue' to speak of dialogue internal to the three monotheistic faiths (Jewish, Christian, Muslim). The Limerick IBD seminar involved more than these three monotheistic faiths in its dialogue process. Other groups prefer the term 'interreligious dialogue' to denote Christian engagement with other religious traditions such as Buddhism and Hinduism.[25] Indeed the Vatican suggests that interreligious dialogue involves constructive Christian relations with people of other religions[26] and the World Council of Churches (WCC) differentiates between what it calls 'interreligious dialogue' as a dialogue internal to the Christian churches (elsewhere referred to as 'inter-church dialogue') and 'interfaith dialogue', which involves engagement between Christianity and other religions of the world.[27] However, the Limerick IBD process facilitated dialogue between religious and non-religious members and so none of these terms were perceived as appropriate for its approach. While this variety of terminologies can be confusing, it is vital at the outset to articulate how the term 'interbelief dialogue' is being used in this volume. In this book, 'interbelief dialogue' denotes positive communication, cooperation and energetic collaboration among people of religious faiths and secular, humanist, agnostic and atheist convictional stances. The broad usage of the term 'belief' signifies the involvement of people of both religious and non-religious convictional stances in dialogue. This understanding of the term 'belief' is consistent with the Toledo Guiding Principles[28] and is relevant to the Irish educational system at a time of increasing migration and diversity.[29] Contemporary Irish society is a multi-belief society that is home to a range of beliefs incorporating many from the world's largest religious groups (e.g. Buddhists, Christians, Hindus, Jews, Muslims, Sikhs and many others) as well as philosophical world views and convictions (e.g. agnosticism, atheism, humanism, and secularism). Some of the less well-known beliefs in Ireland include Jains, Bahá'ís, traditional African religions, Confucianists,[30] a growing Amish community, Zoroastrians as well as Neo-Pagan and Druidic groups among many others.[31] It is important to remember that within each tradition there is a heterogeneity of viewpoints and lifestyles, practising, cultural and non-practising members who are liberal, orthodox, moderate, conservative and everything in between. Furthermore, this book presents a partial and incomplete sample of the voices present at the IBD seminar in Limerick who come from myriad traditions. The chapters of this book do not claim to represent a total, 'official' or comprehensive account of the multifarious belief traditions represented in the Republic of Ireland. This would be an impossible task. Chapters in the volume come from each of the keynote speakers at the conference, Julia Ipgrave, Patrick Sullivan, Mary O'Sullivan. The remaining chapters were written by participants who made significant contributions to the event. Further, each writer who contributed a chapter in this volume expressed their own personal views and opinions which are not to be confused with the opinions of the editor and the publisher.

The Nature of IBD

Dialogue is a form of engagement which has the potential to resist stereotypical or simplistic notions of the other. Interaction with the other does not automatically constitute a form of interbelief dialogue. Dialogue can be extremely difficult and frustrating and at times seemingly impossible. Where there is a closed heart and mind some forms of interaction with others may only serve to reinforce prejudice. Dialogue as understood in this volume is a process of reciprocal engagement at a level deep enough to be open to the possibility of being changed positively by that interaction. In the early twentieth century the philosopher Martin Buber could see the power of dialogue to move beyond binaries and his writings hold that genuine dialogue is at the heart of what it is to be human.[32]

> That peoples can no longer carry on authentic dialogue with one another is not only the most acute symptom of the pathology of our time, it is also that which most urgently makes a demand of us. I believe, despite all, that the peoples in this hour can enter into dialogue, into a genuine dialogue with one another. In a genuine dialogue each of the partners, even when he stands in opposition to the other, heeds, affirms, and confirms his opponent as an existing other. Only so can conflict certainly not be eliminated from the world, but be humanly arbitrated and led towards its overcoming.[33]

Dialogue is not blind to the distinctness and complexity of people's lives. It will not accept any kind of superficial homogeneity. It takes difference seriously. Buber qualifies genuine dialogue as a recognition of the other's right to otherness. Dialogue is not monologue. It necessitates some form of reciprocal interaction. It involves listening with respect and communicating with integrity. It is an invitation to be rooted in one's own life but also able to meet, see, hear and recognise those who live differently. Dialogue is a vital part of a multi-belief world that understands that we are not all the same but we can disagree without being disagreeable. In dialogue, each participant makes a serious effort to take the concerns of others into consideration, even when disagreement persists, and no dialogue participant is forced to give up their identity.[34] It does not attempt to bleach society by removing all reference to belief commitments or to relegate religious or personal conviction to the private sphere. It means that each recognises enough of the other's valid human claims that they will act differently toward the other. Reflecting upon the nature of dialogue in a belief-plural world, Diane Eck states:

> *[P]luralism is not relativism, but the encounter of commitments. The new paradigm of pluralism does not require us to leave our identities and our commitments behind, for pluralism is the encounter of commitments. It means holding our deepest differences, even our religious differences, not in isolation, but in relationship to one another ... pluralism is based on dialogue. The language of pluralism is that of dialogue and encounter, give and take, criticism and self-criticism. Dialogue means both speaking and listening, and that process reveals both common understandings and real differences. Dialogue does not mean everyone at the 'table' will agree with one another. Pluralism involves the commitment to being at the table – with one's commitments.*[35]

People of diverse beliefs came to the IBD seminar in Limerick with their real lives. Participants owned their differences and levels of commitments to dialogue. Interbelief dialogue acknowledges that differences are often painfully difficult to negotiate but they can enrich us as individuals, as societies and as members of the human race.

IBD and the Religious Traditions of the World

Dialogue is not just interaction between one group and other external groups. It is more complex. Within belief traditions there can be internal and external dialogue. For instance, within Buddhism there are many people who consider themselves to be atheists while others might be theist. Within Unitarian Universalism some are agnostics while others are humanist and so interbelief dialogue is internal to these traditions. Within non-religious traditions there is an ancient history of dialogue. When it comes to dialogue with those outside the tradition many beliefs encourage followers to engage with non-members in a hospitable, open and positive manner. Religious traditions often originate from a context of engagement with pre-existing spiritual traditions and cultures (admittedly this is not always a peaceable and positive engagement). It should come as no surprise that a great number of religious traditions and their followers are deeply committed to interreligious and interbelief engagement. Indeed, Horst Georg Pöhlmann contends that dialogue emerges naturally from religions and is as old as the religions themselves. He suggests that most religions have come into being through engagement and dialogue with other religions.[36] As an illustration he suggests that Christianity came into being as a consequence of a dialogue internal to Judaism. In the Punjab, in the fifteenth century, Sikhism was born as a distinct religion that brought together many of the devotional traditions of Hinduism and Islam. While belief systems may be separate and distinct, they also contain common elements. Different versions of the golden rule – the principle of treating others as you would wish to be treated – are common to many religions and ethical traditions.[37] Most religions have within themselves the seeds of tolerance and compassion for others regardless of affiliation. The ancient Hindu Vedas actively encourage engagement with those outside the tradition. They state, 'Let us have concord with our own people and concord with those who are strangers to us.'[38] The Buddha told his followers to shower their companions with compassion as 'friendship is the only cure for hatred, the only guarantee of peace'. Wisely, he said, 'There are no chains like hate ... dwelling on your brother's faults multiplies your own.' In the Judeo-Christian tradition the book of Micah presents a powerful vision of the Lord bringing about a peaceful co-existence between people of different faiths where swords will be beaten into ploughshares, with everyone sitting under their own vines and fig trees without fear. 'For all the peoples walk, each in the name of its god' (Mic 4:3–5). Walter Brueggemann suggests that this poem 'is an *act of assurance*, that God will not stop until the world has been healed and brought to its senses'.[39] In the Christian tradition the parable of the Good Samaritan (Lk 10:25–37) is a radical call to cross boundaries and view the stranger hitherto considered as an 'outsider' as the very model of what it is to be a good neighbour. The parable ends with the exhortation to 'go and do likewise'. The International Institute of Islamic Thought suggests that interfaith dialogue means holding onto one's own faith while simultaneously trying to understand another's faith.[40] During his life, the Prophet Muhammad invited a group of Christians to stay in his mosque, where they prayed. In 628 CE the prophet ratified a charter protecting the religious freedom of the monks of St Catherine Monastery in Mount Sinai:

> *This is a letter from Mohammad ibn Abdallah, as a covenant to those who adopt Christianity. We are with them, they are my citizens, we will defend them. No compulsion is to be on them. Neither their judges to be removed from their jobs nor their monks from their monasteries. No one is to destroy their house of worship, or to damage it, or*

to take anything from it to a Muslim's house. No one is to force them to fight (for Muslims). Muslims are to fight for them. If a Christian woman is married to a Muslim man, it should not take place without her approval. She is not to be prevented from attending her church to pray. No one from my nation is to disobey this covenant till Last Day.[41]

In the nineteenth century, while imprisoned, Bahá'u'lláh, the founder of the Bahá'í faith, wrote to encourage people to 'consort with the followers of all religions in a spirit of friendliness and fellowship'.[42]

Within the Catholic tradition dialogue involves courageous fidelity to one's own faith and culture combined with engagement with the beliefs of the other:

Such dialogue is not just talking but it includes all interreligious relationships with both individuals and communities. It seeks common ethical values which are the foundations of justice and peace. The aim of this dialogue is not to abandon one's own inherited faith and practices but to rediscover them in a deeper way through encounter with the other.[43]

The Necessity and Challenge of Dialogue in the Contemporary World

Despite the many positive developments around belief and dialogue in the contemporary world, there is a disconcerting and increased association of religion with acts of terrorism, violence, hate crime and a polarising and intolerant fundamentalism. Allied to this are worrying levels of xenophobia, Islamophobia, anti-Semitism, hatred and persecution of non-religious groups, as well as the targeting of religious minorities with hate crimes and racist attacks. In Ireland President Michael D. Higgins has warned against stereotyping and its resulting 'ghettoising of ethnic groups and the erection of cultural barriers built on fear, prejudice, or ignorance'.[44] The Pew Report on the *Rising Tide of Restrictions on Religion* (2012) states that three-quarters of the world's approximately seven billion people live in countries with high government restrictions on religion or high social hostilities involving religion.[45] The report points to increases in crimes, malicious acts and violence motivated by religious hatred or bias, as well as increased government interference with worship or other religious practices. The UN estimates that 600 million young people live in conflict areas in the world[46] and a United Nations (UN) publication advised that the number of displaced persons – persons living in a country other than where they were born – 'reached 244 million in 2015 for the world as a whole, an increase of 71 million, or 41 per cent, compared to 2000'.[47] Fear of immigrants and calls for tighter border control has led to increased suspicion of ethnic and religious groups.

The Logistics and Challenges of IBD

In this context of hatred and bigotry some criticise dialogue as a talking shop involving 'mutual affirmation, appreciation, and admiration'. In this frame of mind interreligious dialogue is 'merely a way of being nice to one another'. In chapter eighteen Eamon Rafter states that dialogue should not be confused with other narrative and discursive practices like 'debate' or 'developing an argument to score points and find flaws'. Dialogue is not a contest with winners and losers. Thomas Thangaraj stresses that it goes way beyond verbalisation. For him, 'It is a form of *engagement* with the other, not simply pleasant *talk*.'[48] Fundamentally IBD is not about criticising or converting one's dialogue partners, rather it is about coming together and striving for mutual understanding and collaboration. The first step of IBD involves a very basic coming together. In chapter four Sr Mary O'Sullivan notes that when people of different beliefs simply gather in the same place their gathering can often become an antechamber to dialogue. The very act of being among people who are different brings the realisation that we do not use the same language or view the world in an identical fashion. However, in the midst of this difference IBD builds upon the desire to connect with the other and to be open to journeying with, learning from and with the other.

Arguably there is no level playing field in interbelief dialogue and it is vital to stress that IBD can be frustrating, difficult and open to misunderstanding. Being among people who are different has the potential to evoke negative responses including fear, ridicule, misunderstanding and hostility. Dialogue is not always easy or immediate. As Jo O'Donovan notes, 'Each religion or conviction will tend to evaluate and judge the other in the light of its own non-negotiables.'[49] That is why IBD needs to take place in a secure, respectful, safe environment. IBD takes time. There is no quick fix. Each act of dialogue has its own rhythm and tone. At the IBD seminar in Limerick a dialogue facilitator helped to scaffold interactions by negotiating communally agreed procedures for engagement before people spoke about their beliefs. Everybody was invited to speak but nobody was forced to speak. Silence and active listening were seen as valuable forms of participation and communication. Participants spoke about personal beliefs and agreed not to interrupt, criticise or try to convert others. Agreed guidelines such as these are a key ingredient in providing a safe space for different forms of dialogue. This book attempts to capture key themes emerging from the IBD seminar as well as the contribution of the keynote presenters and selected input from other participants.

The Book's Structure
The first section of this book, 'Interbelief Dialogue in an Educational Context', explores the nature and relevance of interbelief dialogue in schools and public spaces. Chapter one is

written by Julia Ipgrave, who pioneered a dialogical approach to educating children about beliefs in the UK. Her work highlights that dialogue in the classroom is not premised on an exchange of rational argument by unemotional, disembodied cogitos. It is as deeply personal and as varied in nature as the participants taking part. Dialogue entails being empowered to understand and speak about one's own tradition with confidence while simultaneously listening to and respectfully engaging with those of different conviction and learning. Ipgrave's chapter identifies four key players in dialogue: 'I', 'We', 'You' and 'God'.

In chapter two, Patrick Sullivan identifies the centrality of IBD in the proposed education about religions and beliefs curriculum for Ireland. He gives an overview and critique of some approaches taken in international contexts and argues that respectful, accurate, empathetic and critical dialogue about religions and beliefs is a key skill for citizenship in a culturally diverse world. Chapter three, written by Jenny Siung, focuses on the key skills of empathy, perspective taking, curious engagement and sensitivity as aspects of IBD which are scaffolded by public spaces such as the Chester Beatty Library and other museums.

...

In the second section, 'Dialogue of Life: Interbelief Dialogue Through Participants' Eyes', members of select diverse belief and religious communities in the island of Ireland write personally about the opportunities and challenges of living their religious faith or philosophical conviction in a multi-belief world. Writers reflect on how their own belief is shaped by dialogue with others. This section opens with a dialogue facilitator, Sr Mary O'Sullivan from the Centre for Dialogue and Prayer at Oświęcim/Auschwitz, outlining the dimensions for dialogue that are offered for visitors to Auschwitz. Each dimension begins with silence and listening to others. She reflects on her many years of experience facilitating dialogue. In chapter five,

Adrian Cristea presents a contextually rooted account of the origin and nature of interreligious dialogue as it is supported by the activities of the pioneering Dublin City Interfaith Forum. He describes how the Dublin City Interfaith Charter set out to encourage dialogue between people of different beliefs and faiths in all spheres, to eradicate misunderstanding, intolerance and exclusion, and extend openness and understanding between different faith communities.

As a Bahá'í and member of the Mid-West Interfaith Network (MWIN), working day to day to support collaboration and mutual understanding between people of diverse beliefs, Trisha Rainsford, in chapter six, presents her views on opportunities for solidarity and encounter with others through her imaginative retelling of the narrative of the blind men and the elephant. She suggests that IBD is not fundamentally about beliefs concerning the existence or non-existence of God, belief in prayer, the soul, political ideologies of any description, belief in life after death or the central figures in any or all religions and philosophical traditions. In IBD, none of these are deal-breakers. However, belief in the fact that the person in front of you is as complex and nuanced in their human reality as you are, is crucial. In the MWIN people are less interested in defining where they are going than in learning how to do every journey together.

In chapter seven, Bishop Brendan Leahy, a member of the Catholic hierarchy with a deep commitment to dialogue and a wealth of experience and expertise in ecumenical and interreligious dialogue, outlines the centrality of dialogue to the Catholic tradition. He explores a Catholic understanding of four types of dialogue. These are: the dialogue of life centred on the everyday joys, challenges and sorrows of life, especially in the context of the fundamental realities of family, language and culture; the dialogue of works, which encourages participants to collaborate in the holistic development of all men and women through social engagement and action for justice; theological dialogue, which focuses on participants' knowledge of the beliefs of their various religious traditions and their mutual interaction in sharing the teachings and wisdom of their traditions; the dialogue of religious experience based on the lived encounter of various faiths, not on intellectual abstractions, but rather on the actual lives of the faithful.[50]

Keith Scott, in chapter eight, notes that 'no individual or community comes into any kind of conversation as a blank sheet' and he reflects theologically on the Church of Ireland's understanding and practices of dialogue. His many years of involvement in interreligious dialogue in an international context give him a deep appreciation of its relevance for a fractured world.

Siobhán Wheeler, in chapter nine, gives a profound and personal account of her Methodist faith, which acts as an impetus for social and theological engagement with different cultures, beliefs and ethnicities. For her, dialogue with others is a vibrant and vital part of what it is to be a person of faith in contemporary society.

A common concern with the nature of education in Ireland and a commitment to secular schooling has brought three seemingly separate communities – atheist, Muslim and Evangelical Christian – into creative interbelief dialogue. Three chapters document innovative dialogue between Atheist Ireland, the Ahmadiyya Muslim Community and the Evangelical Alliance of Ireland.

In chapter ten, Michael Nugent and Jane Donnelly give a comprehensive overview of the work of Atheist Ireland. They outline the exciting coming together of atheists and theists in dialogue as they promote mutual respect and ethical secularism. Imam Ibrahim M. Noonan of the Ahmadiyya Muslim Community speaks about the origin and nature of the Ahmadiyya Muslim faith in chapter eleven. He gives an insightful and moving account of the experience of discrimination and marginalisation that he and many of his community have experienced in Ireland and elsewhere. His chapter argues that dialogue is key in challenging and deconstructing prejudice and misunderstanding.

Pastor Nick Park from the Evangelical Alliance Ireland argues, in chapter twelve, that secular education is good for children, good for religion, and good for society. He reflects deeply on his experience as a religious leader and writes about the importance of having a politically neutral and secular state which provides a level playing field for all religious and belief traditions. He is not in favour of doctrinal secularism, which he sees as anti-religious in nature and which wants to banish religion from the public square. Instead, his chapter advocates a political secularism where the state is entirely neutral with respect to religion.

In chapter thirteen, Tina Storey skilfully outlines her understanding and experience of what it means to be a humanist. She underlines the relevance of humanism for contemporary Irish society. She explores the history of humanism and identifies how a humanist might approach interbelief engagement in Ireland.

Chapter fourteen highlights the power of sport to combat racism and prejudice. Written by Ken McCue, it tells the fascinating story of how sport can be a transformative and dynamic form of interbelief dialogue. McCue documents the birth of a grass-roots movement called Sport Against Racism Ireland (SARI) that resulted in the formation of Hijabs and Hat Tricks (H & H), which successfully challenged and ended FIFA's ban on female footballers wearing head coverings. He suggests that playing together leads to staying together and argues that sport provides a highly effective and enjoyable place and space for interbelief dialogue that connects diverse voices and challenges racism, sexism and discrimination.

Finally, in the concluding chapter of this section, Nadia Moussad gives an autobiographical and moving account of the abiding theme of interbelief and intercultural dialogue in her life. Drawing on her rich experience of different cultures and belief traditions from her earliest days in Morocco, to her teenage years in France, to her student and working life in Germany and finally her family, academic and professional life in Ireland, she emphasises the difficulties and challenges as well as the rewards, happiness and hope associated with dialogue. For her, dialogue is an occasion to celebrate the different ways of being human.

...

The final section focuses on the 'Challenges and Opportunities of Interbelief Dialogue'. In these chapters, contributors reflect upon people's engagement with many different forms of dialogue. Chapter sixteen is a poignant and remarkable autobiographical chapter by Tomi Reichental, a survivor of Bergen-Belsen concentration camp. Reichental recounts the story of anti-Semitic violence and hatred leading to the Holocaust. He tells us that mass murder did not start with gas chambers, but with whispers. He recounts the horrors of Kristallnacht in 1938, the adoption of the 'final solution' at the Wannsee Conference in 1942 and the mass deportation of Slovak Jewry to the extermination camps. His chapter tells us what life was like for a little boy living in Slovenia before, during and after his deportation to Bergen-Belsen. Despite the unspeakable horror of the Holocaust and the fact that six million people died, numbered among them thirty members of his family, Reichental is passionately committed to dialogue and reconciliation. He writes from the personal experience of having gone to meet and be reconciled with those who imprisoned him. He works tirelessly as an advocate for education and compassion and warns us that we cannot stand by indifferently in the face of hatred and injustice.

In chapter seventeen, a powerful chapter on Islamophobia, James Carr presents the findings of his research into anti-Muslim hostility and discrimination. His research on the experiences of

Muslim men and women in Ireland reveals that just over half of survey participants indicated that they experienced some form of hostility, including verbal abuse, physical assault, damage to property, graffiti, theft, threats and harassment. This research sheds light on the experiences of anti-Muslim hostility and discrimination in the Irish context in order to inform societal dialogue and effect change at the level of official anti-racism policies and practices.

The final chapter gives an overview of the opportunities, challenges and process of Eamon Rafter's dialogue-based work with the Glencree Centre for Peace and Reconciliation. Rafter outlines reasons why dialogue is difficult or even impossible in some circumstances, while also insisting emphatically that it is a key step on the pathway to peace. Dialogue has no predetermined outcome. It is an unpredictable and open-ended engagement with others. Rafter understands dialogue, not as 'listening for ammunition', 'defending a position' or the 'insistence that one person is right and the other therefore wrong' but as a complex, positive, interpersonal, voluntary process which emerges from that engagement. This chapter is honest about the potential of dialogue and the places it can take us to while also acknowledging that they are not always what we might have hoped for. The contribution of dialogue based on trust, openness, respect and determination in the cessation of the Troubles is a reminder of the transformative potential of dialogue.

Dialogue is not the solution to all the problems of the world but in its many forms it brings the possibility of sharing a common journey which can be faced together.

SECTION ONE

Interbelief Dialogue in an Educational Context

CHAPTER ONE

Interreligious Encounter and Dialogue in Schools

Julia Ipgrave

This chapter suggests that interreligious encounter can support the growth of religious literacy among students. While examining the extent of schools' responsibilities for developing pupils' knowledge and understanding of the world to which they belong, it overviews the nature of dialogue appropriate to the scholastic religious and educational setting. In outlining the contemporary context of religious plurality, it highlights four key players in interreligious dialogue ('I', 'We', 'You' and 'God'). The chapter considers three key elements for interreligious dialogue in schools: the sociological fact of religious (and non-religious) diversity leading to *interreligious encounter*; *dialogue*, the proposed response to this diversity; and the responsibility of *schools* for managing this response.

In Europe the educational world is currently buzzing with conversations about the increased ethnic and religious diversity within our classrooms. An early product of this activity was the Council of Europe's *White Paper on Intercultural Dialogue* that, against a background of some anxiety about current developments, advocates dialogue as a way of combatting cultural and religious divides.[1] It strongly recommends the development of skills for active citizenship and intercultural dialogue.[2] For the Irish context, the 2016 interbelief dialogue seminar represents a positive recognition not just of the challenges of these demographic developments but of the possibilities they present for engaging with new perspectives and building new relationships.

My own field of educational research activity is the United Kingdom, but some of the issues with which I engage have wider relevance. In Ireland, as in the UK, a high proportion of children are born to families who have recently migrated to the country. From the youngest pupils upwards, the ethnic and religious diversity of the country's schools are increasing. Even where a variety of faith traditions is less obvious, there are other forms of religious diversity, such as practising and non-practising backgrounds and religious and non-religious positions. This pluralised context provides challenges for the teacher concerned to offer an education that respects and builds on pupils' backgrounds. It also provides opportunities for the pupils to meet and make friends with people different from themselves. Electronic or face-to-face dialogue links with pupils in schools with different religious demographics can expand this opportunity still further.[3] Confidence in their own identity and ability to relate to others are issues of pupils' personal and social development.

The challenges are not confined to classroom encounter. The times in which young people are growing up, and the world in which they are being educated to take part, are characterised by an increasingly complex interplay of religion-related issues and heightened anxiety about their impact on community relations. Few can be unaware of the increased prominence of religion in public discourse – in media, politics and public policy. At the same time (from different starting points) the Republic of Ireland and the UK, along with many other European countries, have been subject to contrary, secularising trends. For many, the religious frames of meaning that guided their forebears have lost their significance and ties with traditional religious institutions have been broken. French sociologist Danièle Hervieu-Léger writes of ruptures in the chain of memory[4] and British sociologist of religion Grace Davie has drawn attention to the paradox: just as 'religion has re-entered the public square and demands a response' so the wider population has increasing difficulty dealing with these issues as it is 'rapidly losing the concepts, knowledge and vocabulary that are necessary to talk about religion'.[5] This religious illiteracy is an educational issue, and the fact that it has been couched in terms of inability to *talk* about religion, underlines the importance of the focus on dialogue. Davie's reference to knowledge and vocabulary here shows an interest in the content and language of dialogue (not just the practice); an interest that links dialogue to schools' responsibilities for developing their pupils' knowledge and understanding of the world to which they belong.

One might begin with an exploration of interreligious encounter in classroom and wider society, with the need for positive relationships and a view of dialogue as an educational response; however, dialogue is not just response, it is also an influential pedagogy that has been gathering in momentum over the last twenty years and more and has been closely linked to the promotion of higher order thinking. The work of Neil Mercer and others has dominated this trend in England. Their *Thinking Together* pedagogy for group discussion was incorporated into the national strategy for primary school teaching.[6] Mercer's pedagogy views dialogue as negotiation between different perspectives, as sharing, testing and evaluating ideas and jointly creating new ways of making sense. The subject matter of religious education – the variety of religious positions, its interest in different interconnected levels of meaning – makes it particularly fruitful ground for the development of thinking skills through the practice of dialogue.[7] Dialogue as it comes into religious education has a cognitive as well as a relational dimension, something that makes it particularly attractive to teachers concerned to support pupils in both aspects of their development.

There exists some tension between the cognitive and relational aspects, however. Critical dialogical skills have been applied with added rigour to the subject of religious education in England and Wales, supported by direction from the schools' inspectorate that, post 9/11, pupils should be encouraged to adopt a more critical approach to the religions they are studying.[8] In a 2004 debate about the future of religious education in England, for example, a spokesperson for the British Humanist Association (BHA) advocated a 'thinking RE' based on rational argumentation involving analysing, evaluating and criticising beliefs and philosophies. It was acknowledged, however, that 'some students may take criticisms personally'.[9] Similarly, a 2007 report by Ofsted, the schools' inspection body, underlined the importance of questioning, criticising and evaluating in terms similar to the BHA.[10] It did recognise that where religion is the theme, passions and emotions are involved – but it did not draw out the implications. The fact that students might take criticisms personally requires more considered reflection.

While religious diversity might make the religious education lesson a particularly appropriate forum for dialogue, the nature of the relationship between the participants of that activity and the subjects they are discussing means the ordinary rules of classroom dialogue are not sufficient. Part of the problem seems to be the correlation of dialogue with rational argumentation when this is just one form of dialogue that, when applied to interreligious encounter, risks limiting the richness of the conversations and treading on sensibilities. The stipulation that dialogue should 'distinguish between personal criticism and criticism of ideas' does not cover cases where those ideas are constitutive of identity, bound to a personal faith, to a sense of relationship with (and of loyalty to) a personal God, to family, to community, to tradition – beliefs should not be treated as ideas in isolation from these identity and relational factors. It is for this reason that I recommend looking outside the normal practices of school dialogue to the traditions of interfaith dialogue in wider society and drawing on the experience and wisdom of those who have been engaged in such activity for a long time and have long had in mind the particular interests, sensitivities and possibilities involved. I intend to begin this process in this chapter and, as I do so I will organise my thoughts around four key players recognised in such dialogue: 'I', 'We', 'You' and 'God'.

'I'

One of the platforms of interfaith dialogue is the stability of each participant's own religious identity and beliefs. As one Muslim guide to interfaith dialogue states, 'Interfaith dialogue means to hold on to one's faith while simultaneously trying to understand another's faith.'[11] This contrasts sharply with Mercer's formula for classroom dialogue where instead of 'holding on' and protecting their own identities and interests, pupils are encouraged to 'let go' and move on to 'new and better ways'.[12] The concept of stability of identity is not to deny that in some cases interfaith dialogue has led to changes in an individual participant's religious position – even to conversion – but the principle remains that this should not be a primary aim or sought-for outcome of the activity. It might seem obvious that religious conversion should not be the aim of interreligious dialogue in schools either but, in the English system at least, it is important to guard against a form of neo-confessional secularism that has crept into some schools in recent years as a partner of the critical approach described above. Educationalist Michael Hand, for example, has argued that pupils should be actively encouraged 'to question the religious beliefs they bring with them to the classroom' so 'they are genuinely free to adopt whatever position on religious matters they judge to be best supported by the evidence'.[13] Some teachers I have interviewed have spoken of 'liberating' pupils from the religious certainties they bring from home.

Challenging pupils' religious identities and beliefs in this way seems to me to be beyond the remit of the school. It shows ignorance of the contexts of tradition, of community and of prayer in which faith develops. Personal religious faith is misunderstood or even trivialised if it is treated as something that can be decided by classroom argumentation. It also shows disregard for the nature and degree of the personal loss young people might feel should the foundation of their faith be thus shaken. I am reminded of the young Muslim teenager who confided that it was her faith that gave her a reason for getting up each morning, of the younger Muslim girl whose love for the Prophet caused her to cry with emotion as she recounted his kindness and his suffering, of the Christian girl who spoke of experiencing God's spirit in her, comforting her when she is upset. These were all powerful examples of 'I' experiences of religion. The depth of feeling expressed in these instances is a warning against the casual treatment of pupils' religious belief within classroom dialogue. It also indicates the extent of the religious learning that might take place there, should children be invited and feel confident to share their personal perspectives.

Focusing on what young people know, experience and believe from their own perspective, rather than arguing about the truth or otherwise of a religious proposition, is a way to value their identity and respect their integrity. It does not mean critical thinking is out of place in religious dialogue. Selecting words, illustrations, stories, symbols and metaphors to express their ideas, analysing them to uncover deeper meaning, exploring links between their beliefs, practices, experiences, feelings and values, can enable young people to exercise and articulate a high level a critical thinking that builds on rather than overthrows personal faith.

Some children may need prompting to raise the level of their thinking. For the child who talks about his visits to Quran school at the end of each school day, the prompt question might be, 'Why is it so important to you to learn to say the words of the Quran by heart?' For the child sharing his excitement about Christmas, a prompt question might be, 'You say Jesus is a special baby – what makes him so special for you?' In this way the pupils not only 'hold on' to their identity but deepen their understanding of that to which they are 'holding on' and improve their capacity to articulate that understanding.

'We'

Readers may be familiar with dialogue guidelines for children and young people that stress the importance of using 'I' language rather than 'we' language. There are good reasons for this. 'I' language recognises the status of each young person as an individual with their own thoughts, opinions and beliefs. It acknowledges the internal diversity of any religious tradition that means what the young person says about her religious position and practice cannot be taken as representative of all of that tradition. Indeed, the young person may have very limited experience or knowledge of the faith she professes. I have just argued that the 'I' is powerful and should be given due recognition. Yet I would want to add that the 'we' too has an important place in interreligious dialogue. Insisting on 'I' neglects the communal experience so important to the religious lives of many. A Jewish family coming together for their Shabbat meal, Christians gathering around the fire at dawn on Easter morning, Muslims going on pilgrimage to Makkah, are all 'we' experiences.

Interfaith dialogue is not just interpersonal, it is intercommunal and that is part of its purpose. When faith leaders get together at a national or international level or when at a local level ordinary Sikhs, Hindus, Muslims, Christians and people without a religious faith get together, the meeting is not just about the people who are actually present in the dialogue. Their getting together sends a signal to other believers and society in general that it is possible for people of different religions and belief communities to be in dialogue with one another.

It is not just a dialogue between individuals but between communities – but it is more than that too. Each participant in that interfaith dialogue is bringing to it their own dialogue with the tradition to which they belong. Their own faith heritage has a strong influence on their lives in some way or other. School pupils bring those internal conversations to the interreligious dialogue of the class. The young person will often have limited knowledge of their own faith tradition. There may be a disconnect between them and their family's heritage. They may be unaware of the religious origins of customs, local sites or personal names that are part of their everyday lives and identities. In these cases, the teacher can encourage them to find out more, to carry out research, to ask questions to parents and grandparents so that alongside the individualised 'I' there is also the 'I' that is embedded in the 'we' of community and tradition.

'You'
'You' is being addressed by me but is not me. Respecting 'you' is respecting the 'otherness of other'. This is a principle frequently found in guidance for interfaith dialogue. It can be found, for example, in the guidelines of the Inter Faith Network UK in the statement, 'Dialogue and cooperation can only prosper if they are rooted in respectful relationships which do not blur or undermine the distinctiveness of different religious traditions.'[14] Many find this idea of maintaining distinctiveness and otherness uncomfortable – there is an impulse towards sameness. This was the case in dialogue sessions I facilitated with a mixed group of Hindu and Christian primary-aged children. The logic of friendship appeared to them to require commonalty of belief. In particular the Christians wanted their friends to move towards a more monotheistic position, 'But one day will your ... temple stick to one god, one day, any day?' And they wanted to know which Hindu god's name could be applied to the one god they knew. The persistence of the Christian children in their

attempts to make one god of all the Hindu gods, though kindly meant, had a domineering character. This resulted from a desire to fit their partners' religion into their own framework and an inability to accept their dialogue partners as 'you'. In another conversation a Christian boy made an Islamically unacceptable translation of 'Allah' into Christian terms, though he admitted to problems translating Hinduism into his own language, 'So I don't like say all the things that you're calling Shiva. I know like Allah as Jesus because I believe Jesus is just one god and you call Allah one god.' Translatability between the languages of the dialogue participants is clearly an issue and in some cases it is not possible. This boy has admitted defeat in the case of Shiva and mistranslated Allah.

A third boy, picking up the difficulties of translation, suggested the only answer to the divisions between religions was for everyone to get together and agree a new language for a new religion, 'All the religious people get together and find different languages and everything, and actually find a word that's appropriate for being a religion, then people can get along.' This boy's proposed solution was not a hundred miles away from the late John Hull's argument that dialogue was seriously impeded by the distinctiveness of different traditions, stating that without mutuality there can be no dialogue.[15] Hull called for a bold RE prepared to deconstruct historic religious traditions and find an underlying global faith; however, this proposed solution sets up a stumbling block for others, probably for most Christians and Muslims. The Muslim interfaith guide cited earlier saw as a major obstacle to involvement, the perception that 'the underlying purpose [of interfaith dialogue] is to create a new religion for everyone'.[16] A Christian interfaith worker made the same point when she told me that she could not have gotten involved in interfaith activity if she had thought it meant subscribing to an 'all religions are the same' philosophy.

The challenge is to learn to be comfortable with difference and not find it threatening either to one's own religion or to one's relationship with dialogue partners. Young children can be prepared for this by encouraging them to identify and discuss differences between faiths which can easily become obscured by overemphasis on similarities. This is particularly important when using thematic approaches to religious education. While recognising similarities between Hanukkah and Christmas (celebrations, miracles, lighting of candles) children need to be clear about their differences. One has meaning within the particular history of a chosen people, the other presents the specifically Christian doctrine of incarnation. Often thrown together as Festivals of Light, neither is reducible to the other, nor are they reducible to a universalising concept of celebrating light that would be a distortion of both traditions. Drawing a contrast between what might superficially appear to be different manifestations of the same phenomena, highlights what is distinctive about both and deepens knowledge and understanding of the other. It is a contribution to restoration of the religious literacy we are said to have lost.

'God'

I have talked about the different human actors in dialogue, whether 'I', 'we' or 'you', but those engaged in interfaith dialogue are often aware of another dialogue partner. A passage from the Anglican Communion statement on interfaith dialogue, *Generous Love*, illustrates this:

> *Believing ourselves to be in a dialogue with God enabled through the words of the Bible, it can be a profoundly humbling and creative experience for us to read the Bible alongside Muslims who likewise believe themselves to be addressed by the one God through the text of the Quran.*[17]

Here the dialogue partners are conscious of the God and 'I' and God and 'you' dialogues. The idea that God or an 'other-power' is involved in dialogue with humans is common across religions. The Quran is sometimes described as a book of dialogue between Allah and his creation. The wisdom of Krishna in the *Bhagavad Gita* is revealed through his dialogue with Arjuna. When the Shin Buddhist pronounces the name of Amida, it is through other-power not self-power that she does so.[18]

It is valuable for teachers to be aware that for some pupils God will be understood to be a presence in the classroom. I remember in one interview a seven-year-old girl indicated where in the classroom God was standing. Occasional hesitations about engaging with the ideas of other religions sometimes reflect not stubbornness or prejudice but children's uncertainty about whether such activity is pleasing to God. Generally, however, I have found among primary school children in particular a happy readiness to introduce God into the conversation and to talk about him in a way that reflects their relationship with him: 'I love Jesus'; 'I know my God's good'; 'My God made me'. I have found an intellectual interest in God's workings that builds on this relationship as the children wonder: 'I want to know why God this ...' or ' ... why God that ...'; 'I want to know what God's thinking about this ...'; 'When I get to heaven ... there's a big question I'm going to ask God'. These children can truly be said to be engaged in what theologian John Macquarrie called 'God-talk' and indeed in that subset of God-talk he classifies theology as the language that arises 'when religious faith becomes reflective'.[19] There is a shift in the interreligious dialogue here from talking to dialogue partners about self and community, experiences, beliefs and practices, to talking together, from different perspectives, about God. There is a problem with this move, however. Though the existence of the other actors in the dialogue, 'I', 'we' and 'you', is not called into question there are many who would dispute the existence of God, the fourth in the interreligious dialogue quartet. So far this exploration of interreligious dialogue has emphasised the importance of personal integrity, of holding firm to one's own identity, of making explicit our place in community, and of respecting the distinctiveness of the other. How now do we talk together about a dialogue partner that some of us don't believe in?

In England in recent years many secondary schools have adopted a way of talking about God in religious education that gives equal weight to non-religious perspectives. This is a philosophical approach that goes back to the first principles of whether or not God exists. As one student described it to me, 'What they do is talk mostly about arguments for and arguments against God, miracles and stuff like that.'

The reasons for this move are strong. They involve the desire to respect and include the positions of the non-religious in discussions and to put the religious and non-religious on equal footing; however, the outcomes have not been entirely positive. Some non-religious students I have encountered have demonstrated over-reliance on the positivist proofs and scientism of the so-called 'new atheists'[20] and have been arguing against the existence of a pejorative, controlling God far removed from the experience of many religious believers. Religious students, on the other hand, have often responded defensively to these arguments with a rejection of their methods on the one hand stating it is just 'science, science, science', and on the other a simplistic fideism of 'I just believe, I believe and know ...' Intellectual reflection gets lost in the middle of these unyielding positions. Much of the students' God-talk stalls at the question of whether or not God exists. Faith in God becomes not the promised platform for further intellectual engagement, but the point of dispute. If classroom dialogue is about one's own opinions and beliefs, then not believing in God means not talking further about him. This reluctance constitutes a lost opportunity for accessing a whole area of learning and thinking, for exploring in more depth the religion of one's heritage and for increasing understanding of the Other. In order to address this loss, I would recommend for these students a temporary suspension of disbelief in their dialogues so they can pick up the threads of theological thought on a platform of the supposition of God's existence. A starting point for such dialogue could be, 'If God exists (or if there is a power that transcends) then how, what, why ...?' Alternatively, 'If God is all loving *and* all powerful then, how, what, why ...?' The 'if God' formula means momentarily employing another's language and grammar to explore a logic that is not one's own and gain some understanding of those whose language it is and (in the interests of empathy) what it might be like to talk in the language of religion.

Conclusion

How might this sophisticated suspension of belief translate to children who feel uncomfortable with God-talk? How can they engage in such talk themselves in a way that respects the personal meaning of God to the believer yet does not force them into expressions of belief or disbelief? One strategy is to use religious texts and stories where God is present as a character, as stimulus for dialogue. The story of Jonah, for example, provides an excellent starting point for discussions of God's justice and mercy. The material is familiar but the opportunity for dialogue could be enhanced. Without making judgements on the truth or otherwise of the story, both religious and non-religious children can engage in dialogue about God's character and purposes for humankind.

So, to return to the concern with which this chapter began, I propose that if attention is given in the religious education class to our four dialogue players, they can guide educators in the development of different elements that, brought together, support the growth of religious literacy among students. The 'I' is learning to articulate one's own experiences and ideas about religion; 'we' is making connections between one's own experiences and ideas and wider tradition; 'you' is listening to the language of others, comparing and contrasting; and 'God' is learning to talk about God and about transcendence.

CHAPTER TWO

Interbelief Learning and Dialogue in the Proposed Curriculum on Education about Religions and Beliefs (ERB) and Ethics

Patrick Sullivan

The question of what children should learn in school and for what purpose is rarely straightforward. This question is the focus of the National Council for Curriculum and Assessment's (NCCA) work. In recent years the NCCA has contributed a number of significant milestones to the development of primary education in Ireland. The development of *Aistear: The Early Childhood Curriculum Framework* (NCCA, 2009) set a new direction for the experiences of children in early childhood settings and infant classrooms in primary school. The recently completed integrated *Primary Language Curriculum* (DES, 2015) breaks new ground in connecting children's language learning across their first, second and other language contexts. Most recently, the development of a purposed curriculum in education about religions and beliefs (ERB) and ethics breaks further new ground in primary education.

The origins of the proposed curriculum in ERB and ethics can be traced back to the Forum on Patronage and Pluralism in the Primary Sector. Launched in April 2011 by Minister Ruairí Quinn TD, this forum was established to recognise and begin to respond to the need for appropriate forms of primary school patronage for Ireland's increasingly diverse society. The independent advisory group, comprising of Prof. John Coolahan (Chair), Dr Caroline Hussey and Ms Fionnuala Kilfeather, conducted public meetings and sought submissions from the main stakeholder groups, as well as the general public as part of its work. In all, the group received two hundred and forty-seven written submissions relating to a wide range of issues and concerns raised in discussions during the forum. In its recommendations, the forum acknowledged that the state has a responsibility to ensure that all children attending primary school have the right to receive a state-provided education in religions, beliefs and ethics and so the NCCA were charged with the task of developing advice on how this could be achieved.

In line with the request, the NCCA developed proposals for the curriculum. This involved conducting national and international research, discussion groups with experts, meetings with interest groups as well as work with partners in education and patrons of primary schools. On 3 November 2015, the NCCA published the proposals and engaged in an extensive consultation until March 2016.

The development of the proposed curriculum has invited considerable comment and debate since its recommendation by the forum.[1] The consultation itself received the highest response rate of any NCCA consultation, with over two thousand two hundred questionnaire responses and one hundred and seventy-four written submissions. Throughout the development of the proposed curriculum, a number of issues have been conflated in the discourse surrounding it. Some of these issues include: the unique composition of the Irish primary sector; current debates on patronage and school choice; newly emerging communities in Ireland; the perceived erosion of patronal control of primary schools and the experience of overload in the *Primary School Curriculum*. The conflation of these issues gave rise to additional sensitivities over and above the general cut and thrust of debates about curriculum change in Ireland.

While such discourse can inform and contribute to the development of a curriculum in ERB and ethics, it can also serve to distract from the core purpose of the *Primary School Curriculum* which is 'designed to nurture the child in all dimensions of his or her life – spiritual, moral, cognitive, emotional, imaginative, aesthetic, social and physical'.[2] The proposals for a curriculum in ERB and ethics were established to enable the development of the child in all of their capacities. The proposals described that through participation in the curriculum a child can actively engage in and promote communication and dialogue between people of different cultural, religious and belief backgrounds. Children can also share ideas about the world, promoting relationships and friendships. Through a child's reflection on their own beliefs and values, and on those of others, they can grow in respect for themselves and come to understand something about the beliefs that are important to others. The opportunity to promote such teaching and learning by providing a time and space during the school day for such learning is a significant development in the Irish education system.

Curriculum and the Process of Development
In its simplest terms curriculum can be described as 'the collection of stories which one generation chooses to tell the next'.[3] Indeed, Ireland is famed throughout the world for the art of storytelling, with the *seancaithe* and *scéalaí* (storytellers) passing stories down through the generations. In the traditional sense storytelling is an interactive art. Within this understanding, the person receiving the story plays an important role in the storytelling process. Those who receive the story actively participate in co-constructing their knowledge and culture with their peers through engagement in the shared space of the story. A story is not just the recitation of a literary

narrative, instead it is endlessly recreated in its telling. The receiver of the story then is an essential part of the storytelling process. For stories to live, they need the hearts, minds and ears of the receiver.

Stories, of course, change and evolve over time and so must curriculum. As we begin to look again at the stories (curriculum) we have chosen for our children and reflect upon which may serve them best in the future, Pinar's understanding of curriculum as a form of social psychoanalysis for societies may help to shed light on the process of its development.[4] For Pinar, the active reflection that is required means that 'curriculum becomes a verb, an action, a social practice, a private meaning, and a public hope. Curriculum is not just the site of our labour, it becomes the product of our labour, changing as we are changed by it.'[5]

Pinar stretches our thinking beyond the limits of curriculum as an object and opens our view to action and process. In this way curriculum becomes socially constructed, dynamic and culturally shaped; however, questions loom. For instance, what is the purpose of the curriculum? Who undertakes this work? Who is listened to? What is their bias? How is the curriculum negotiated?

The Rationale for Curriculum
In the international context the development of curriculum or programmes of study similar to Ireland's ERB and ethics curriculum have often been motivated by security concerns. Sometimes such curricula are chiefly concerned with reducing the risk of radicalisation and the promotion of community cohesion. This may be an understandable consideration given the current ethnic, cultural and religious tensions within and across Western and global societies. However, while a curriculum may contribute to some inclusive school practices, it would seem unlikely that any curriculum could or should address the security concerns of a nation. Speaking about *Prevent*, part of the UK's broader counterterrorist

programme, Aislinn O'Donnell argues that 'education must not be subordinated to security and intelligence agendas on pragmatic, educational and ethical grounds'.[6] Security issues are outside the remit of the educational system and subject to a myriad of complex factors. Another rationale often referred to in the development of curricula focusing on religions, beliefs and ethics is that they cater for the needs of a diverse population. This is also prevalent in research, which often positions diversity as a challenge to be overcome. This has the unintended consequence of placing newly settled communities in a vulnerable position as it problematises religions and beliefs. For instance, the development of a curriculum in ERB and ethics could be perceived erroneously as 'solving the issue of diversity in Irish primary schools'. Such discourse problematises the visibility of diversity in Irish society. Yet Irish classrooms have changed greatly in recent years. Schools are welcoming places for more diverse populations than ever. In the 2011 national census more than twenty-eight belief systems (both secular and religious) were represented and in the 2016 census the number of those with no religion grew by 73.6 per cent.[7] While the inclusion of newly settled communities in Ireland has posed challenges for schools, these are arguably due to inertia and long-standing systemic structures in the education system that have fostered a sense of business as usual.[8]

Thankfully, in Ireland the development of the proposed curriculum in ERB and ethics does not hold such aforementioned aims. Instead the proposals are concerned with the child, their world and their experience of it. The curriculum recognises that an important aspect of a child's education involves learning about and understanding the lives, values and traditions of friends, classmates and members of the wider community. This type of learning is closely aligned with a child's sense of their own identity and belonging. By encouraging experiential learning, the creation of inclusive school environments and positive relationships between the child and their teacher, the proposed curriculum aims to nurture the child's sense of who they are, what they understand of their world and how they can contribute to it.

Scottish philosopher John Macmurray describes the priority of education as:

> learning to live in personal relation to other people. Let us call it learning to live in community. I call this the first priority because failure in this is fundamental failure, which cannot be compensated for by success in other fields; because our ability to enter into fully personal relations with others is the measure of our humanity. For inhumanity is precisely the perversion of human relations.[9]

In a world where much educational policy is driven by the Global Educational Reform Movement[10] or by economic forces, ERB and ethics seems to run counter to this. It is not about accountability, standardisation, privatisation, economics or about preparing children solely for the world of work. It would seem to be about something altogether more important than these. It is about human flourishing and enabling children to develop as moral and ethical beings, with the capacity to connect with and realise meaningful relationships with people in their communities, and the creation a better world. In recognising such aspirations, it also has to be recognised that curriculum alone cannot achieve any of these. Indeed, the educational context and the processes within the school and classroom become crucial considerations.

Relationship between Teacher and Child

We all want to feel cared for and valued by the significant people in our lives. Children are no different. Children spend up to a third of their waking hours in the care of their primary school teacher. With this in mind, the types of relationship between teacher and child that affirm a child's sense of identity and promote a feeling of belonging to the school community become vital aspects of teaching and learning. Demonstrating care and investing emotionally in the educational process is one of the most powerful ways to build positive relationships between teacher and child.[11] A relational pedagogy of teaching and learning consistent with a sociocultural perspective supports the idea that enquiry learning and co-constructing knowledge are processes of meaning-making that take place during intelligent and informed interactions. This approach may also be described as a nurturing pedagogy which emphasises children's feelings and dispositions such as motivation, confidence, perseverance, and how they see themselves as learners.[12] As Wells states, 'Knowledge building takes place between people doing things together.'[13]

The *Primary School Curriculum* (1999) is premised on the principle that collaborative learning provides many advantages so that 'children are stimulated by hearing the ideas and opinions of others, and by having the opportunity to react to them. Collaborative work exposes children to the individual perceptions that others may have of a problem or a situation.'[14] The *Primary School Curriculum* also emphasises the importance of the teacher using information he/she gathers about the child, to ensure that learning opportunities and activities are effective in advancing the child's learning. This approach requires teachers to take a more active participatory, as opposed to a didactic, role in supporting children's learning. In this context learning occurs through complex and dynamic exchanges between children, their actions to make sense of the world and the social and cultural processes in everyday activities.[15] This process is premised on a relational foundation and encourages both adults and children to have an active role in the teaching and learning process. Within this dynamic, children can take on the role of leaders of learning in techniques such as peer-tutoring. In this child-led approach the teacher is no longer the sole source of knowledge, instead the child is enabled to share their understanding of the world and their perspective on matters relating to their own religion and beliefs, thus promoting interbelief conversation and learning.

Child Voice

The role of the child's voice in education has become a metaphor for children's engagement and participation in issues that matter to their learning. While many educators agree that the inclusion of the child's voice and their sense of agency in educational matters is important, there is significantly less agreement on developmentally appropriate ways to do this. Consequently, the 'acoustics of the school' – in other words, who is heard in decision-making processes – has become an important consideration.[16] Likewise 'who is not heard in the school?' is significant. While the voice of the child is widely regarded as important in the educational process, providing the time and space for learners to share their ideas and beliefs about the world may not be as easy to achieve as one may think. Fielding, for example, suggests that it 'requires a transformation of what it means to be a student; what it means to be a teacher. In effect, it requires the intermingling and interdependence of both.'[17]

For Fielding, the role of the teacher changes from the custodian of knowledge to an 'enabler' of reciprocal relationships in the classroom. This approach requires the teacher to be a facilitator in the child's learning process; to listen effectively and facilitate good questioning among children. In the context of learning about children's religions, beliefs and ethics it is important that the teacher remain open-minded, fair, balanced and non-judgemental.

Working in partnership with children, calls for a pedagogical shift for the teacher – from teaching to learning.[18] Indeed, in this context it seems as though teachers are 'developing a pedagogy of listening',[19] where they spend more time listening to children and helping them build on one another's ideas rather than directing classroom activities. In this dynamic, teachers when dealing with their own 'unknowingness' become co-learners, fostering a disposition of openness and flexibility.

Interbelief Conversation in ERB and Ethics

Building upon representations of the child in the *Primary School Curriculum* and in *Aistear: The Early Childhood Curriculum Framework*, the image of the child in the proposed ERB and ethics curriculum is of a curious, capable, confident and caring individual.[20] The curriculum also recognises children as being fully human and as such they exhibit flaws that are a feature of the human condition. Children are understood as social actors who actively participate in and co-construct their knowledge, identity and culture with peers and adults. In Ireland children encounter and interact with a variety of cultural, ethnic, religious, belief and linguistic groupings. As children grow and develop through their encounters with diverse groups, differing opinions and perspectives can become more complex and tensions may occur. Children's engagement with these tensions is an important feature of a pluralist society. Presenting the child as a 'caring' individual recognises their ability to relate to those with whom they disagree and thus negotiate such tensions.

Children are 'experts in their experience' and as such are capable of leading their learning when discussing aspects of their experience. In this context teachers have a key role in fostering positive dispositions in the classroom to ensure respectful engagement. Children who learn actively have positive dispositions to learning and in turn an active and stimulating environment improves neural connections which aid the later learning of skills, acquisition of knowledge and understanding of concepts.[21] This has an impact on the teacher's practice in the classroom, highlighting the importance of a stimulating, respectful environment along with active and meaningful activities which promote a positive disposition to learning.

As they nurture positive dispositions for interbelief dialogue, it is important that teachers are aware of their own value base. No teaching is value-free; therefore, teachers need to be conscious of their own convictions and beliefs and how these influence the way they encourage children to talk about their personal beliefs. Remaining mindful of the difficulties of presenting any teaching and learning in a manner that is impartial and free of bias, it is nonetheless essential that the classroom encourages secure, respectful and reciprocal relationships that value diversity among children and promote the practice of inclusion. This ensures that the rights of all children to hold a particular religious or belief perspective is respected, protected and fulfilled, and allows for the voices of all children to be heard, provided these voices are in keeping with the protocols of respectful discourse of the school and classroom.

A Challenge to Interbelief Dialogue in the Irish Context

According to Bruner, the purpose of education is not just imparting knowledge, but also to facilitate a child's thinking and problem-solving skills which can then be transferred to a range of situations.[22] He argued that education should also develop symbolic thinking in children and create autonomous learners. A growing number of studies highlight the importance of the child's own agency in relation to their beliefs; that is, the way in which even young children do not necessarily adopt their parents' beliefs uncritically. Research suggests that children develop a personalised sense of religion and belief through interaction with, but not determined by, their family and school context.[23] Nonetheless, parents, siblings, peers and teachers all contribute to the child's meaning-making as they introduce them to cultural practices and teach them new skills and ways of understanding the world.[24] From this perspective, informed by sociocultural theory, a child's understanding of the world around them and ethical development are firmly embedded in their social context. The relative roles of the home and school in the development of children's dispositions towards and participation in interbelief dialogue and learning has been the subject of much debate as evidenced in the recent consultation on the proposals for a curriculum in ERB and ethics in Ireland.

While the teaching and learning described in the proposals for ERB and ethics received broad support, the consultation brought to the fore many issues in the primary education sector that impact upon the implementation of curriculum in schools. Perhaps the most prominent challenge is posed by the very structure of the Irish primary education system. Of the 3,124 mainstream primary schools in Ireland, 96 per cent are under the patronage of denominational organisations. In recent years, with the emergence of a more diverse population, school patronage in Ireland has been the subject of much consideration at a policy level and within public discourse. The Forum on Patronage and Pluralism in the Primary Sector recommended that in line with the wishes of parents, divestment of a certain number of schools might be considered to provide multi-denominational education.[25] It has been commented upon by both the denominational and multi-denominational representatives that this process has been slow to date and so the debate continues.

While the debate regarding school patronage may be seen as separate to the development of a curriculum in ERB and ethics, the ownership and management of schools impacts on how the primary curriculum is taught by teachers and experienced by children. This is evident in the Education Act, which states that in prescribing a curriculum for schools, the minister 'shall have regard to the characteristic spirit of a school'.[26] With this provision, among others in the act, schools and patrons have the right to teach the entire *Primary School Curriculum* in accordance with the ethos of their schools. Consequently, the patronage of primary schools has a direct impact on the teaching of the *Primary School Curriculum* and may have significant implications for the types of teaching and learning described in a curriculum in ERB and ethics. For instance, the child-centred, constructivist approach advocated in the proposals for the ERB and ethics curriculum was highlighted as being a potential challenge for Catholic schools. It was suggested that this might conflict with how a child learns from within their own tradition.

> The NCCA document favours a 'child-centred' approach that leads to 'co-construct' their knowledge identity and culture with peers and adults and in turn generate their own meaning and knowledge. The idea that a 6-year-old child can simply discern about religious matters as proposed in the NCCA model is not substantiated and conflicts with the concept of a child learning from within their own tradition or community and then moving to evaluate or critique it in the later years.[27]

While this submission makes a relevant contribution to the challenge of providing age-appropriate learning in ERB and ethics, it is important to highlight that the 'child-centred', constructivist approach advocated in the proposals for a curriculum in ERB and ethics also underpins the entire *Primary School Curriculum* and is at the heart of the learning that currently takes place in Irish primary schools.[28] Some anxiety was also expressed around the basis for the ethics component of the proposals. For some respondents ethical learning could not be separated from a particular religious perspective. It was suggested that the underpinnings of the ethics component could undermine and contradict a Christian perspective.

The ethics component endorses the morality of secular liberalism wherein individual moral autonomy is considered an ultimate end in itself. Such an approach is incompatible with the emphasis Christian moral theology places on theocentric personalism, objective moral goods and norms, the virtues, and the harmony between the individual's good and the common good.[29]

The human rights perspective which has informed the proposals for the ethics component of the curriculum has been interpreted by some respondents as a potential threat to the ethos of denominational schools. It was suggested in some submissions that the ERB and ethics proposals represented liberal, secular or agnostic values and, therefore, directly challenged denominational school ethos.

It was also argued that a pluralist approach to learning about religions and beliefs might be a challenge for denominational schools. According to the Catholic Primary Schools Management Association, the pluralist approach:

encourages pupils to see their religion as one among many standpoints which have equal validity. This arguably encourages a form of religious relativism. This pedagogical process suggested by NCCA is completely at odds with the way in which religious education is taught in Catholic schools.[30]

While many denominational primary schools establish and maintain very inclusive school communities, the rights of the patron nonetheless have a significant impact on the implementation of the curriculum in primary schools. The Education Act (1998) establishes the rights of the school patron to 'promote the moral, spiritual, social and personal development of students and provide health education for them, in consultation with their parents, having regard to the characteristic spirit of the school'.[31] Section 15(2)(b) requires a board of management to 'uphold, and be accountable to the patron for so upholding, the characteristic spirit of the school as determined by the cultural, educational, moral, religious, social, linguistic and spiritual values and traditions which inform and are characteristic of the objectives and conduct of the school'. A potential for tension may be seen here between what the state describes as appropriate provision for primary school children and what patrons decide is appropriate for their schools. Of course, for the majority of the *Primary School Curriculum* this tension may not have a particular impact on the education provided to children. However, when it relates directly to a child's sense of identity and belonging, particularly in relation to their religion, beliefs and ethics, what has been envisaged by a state curriculum may transact differently depending on the ethos of the school.

Conclusion

The consultation on a curriculum for education about religions and beliefs (ERB) and ethics brought to light many contextual features that, while external to the development of curriculum, have a significant impact on how a curriculum is taught in primary schools.[32] The legislation underpinning primary education is one such feature. While the Education Act (1998) endorses the rights of the patron body it also potentially limits what is achievable through a state curriculum for ERB and ethics. This challenge is not posed by the patron bodies which have a legislative right to teach the primary curriculum in accordance with the ethos of their schools, but rather it is exacerbated by the structure of the primary school system which is predominantly faith-based. The provision of Sections 9(d), 15(2)(b), 30(2)(b), among others, are potential barriers to the type of 'objective, critical and pluralist' approaches advocated in the proposals for a curriculum in ERB and ethics. The debate relating to the tension between what the state describes as appropriate learning for children and the reality of what transacts in classrooms across school types has been long established and so the debate continues.

What emerges from the NCCA consultation is a broad support for the types of teaching and learning described in a curriculum for ERB and ethics. However, the contextual features outlined above indicate a need for a responsive curriculum that recognises the current pressures on schools in meeting the needs of their communities. As part of the consultation process, schools were invited to share examples of inclusive practice and many called for an ERB and ethics curriculum that would ensure structured, coherent and incremental learning for all primary school children while also providing time and space during the school day to support these important practices. Children have described experiential and enquiry-based learning opportunities when discussing the proposed curriculum, calling for a curriculum that relates to their experience and natural curiosity. For parents, the development of children's skills and dispositions in relation to social justice, human rights, equality, empathy and the impacts of discrimination and prejudice was seen as an important feature of the curriculum.

It would seem as if the Irish education system is at an important juncture. The discourse around school choice coupled with that of equality of opportunity for all children has seen the emergence of a cacophony of voices from a significant number of interest groups at national level. These groups have excised their views on the current system and have called for a more egalitarian primary education system. While the development of a curriculum in ERB and ethics is external to such debate, it nonetheless cannot be developed outside of this context.

The NCCA is in the process of redeveloping the entire *Primary School Curriculum*, as this work progresses consideration needs to be given to the types of teaching and learning that received broad support during the consultation on ERB and ethics, while also respecting the rights of the school patron body as enshrined in the Education Act (1998). The NCCA now has to consider how best to incorporate the types of teaching and learning that received broad support during the consultation into the *Primary School Curriculum*, without infringing on the rights of the patron body. This learning centres on the fostering of skills and dispositions, the knowledge and understandings of religions, beliefs and ethics that enable children to engage positively with the world in which they live, be respectful of those from other traditions, and have meaningful relationships with their peers. While the rights of patrons must be respected, equally so too do the rights of children. As provision for teaching and learning related to ERB and ethics continues to be developed it would seem now more than ever that partnership and collaboration between stakeholders in education needs to continue in order to progress this important work.

CHAPTER THREE

Museums as Public Spaces for Intercultural Dialogue and Learning

Jenny Siung

The Chester Beatty Library is a unique art museum and library situated in the centre of Dublin city, Ireland. Its uniqueness derives from the collections it holds, which, in an Irish context, are one of a kind. The library's rich collections originate from across Asia, the Middle East, North Africa and Europe. Through its exhibitions and learning programmes, diverse communities can share and discover different cultures as represented in the collections. Intercultural dialogue and learning play a key role in the library's mission and encourage visitors to compare, contrast and explore the historical, cultural, scientific and religious aspects of its collections. This work was celebrated in 2014 in the *Museums as Places for Intercultural Dialogue and Learning* seminar in the library[1] and a one-day symposium exploring *The Role of National Museums (Re)Negotiating National Identity* in response to the Ireland 2016 programme.[2] As Ireland celebrated its state centenary, the library asked what it meant to be Irish in 2016 in a documented vox pop, 'Chester Beatty Library Ireland 2016 – Exploring Cultural Diversity and Identity'. This was in recognition of our culturally diverse communities and the change in population.[3]

Exploring World Faiths through Museum Collections

The library's core mission is to 'promote a wider appreciation and understanding of the international cultural heritage embodied in the collections and to foster relations between Ireland and its peoples whose cultures are represented in the collections'.[4] With the relocation of the library from the suburbs to the city centre of Dublin, the director and curators decided to exhibit three of the great religions (Islam, Christianity and Buddhism) side by side, a first in a European museum. It was acknowledged as a vital resource for the understanding of the written texts and history of sacred scripture from the world's great religions. Two core themes for exhibition were developed: 'the sacred' and 'the secular'. The Sacred Traditions gallery displays religious texts and objects from the Islamic, Christian and East Asian collections with some material from the Jewish, Sikh, Hindu and Jain collections. The then director Dr Michael Ryan says the library made a conscious decision to have a balance of representation of the religions and cultures as represented in the collections.[5]

The library's entire collection consists of over eight thousand manuscripts on paper, vellum and other media with approximately four thousand fine and early printed books.[6] Key treasures include biblical and Manichean papyri, Islamic manuscripts with over three hundred complete or fragmentary copies of the Holy Quran as well as works of philosophy, liturgy and spiritual belief from China, Japan, South East Asia and non-Islamic India. The Christian collections comprise illuminated manuscripts from Egypt, the Levant, Byzantium, Western Europe, Ethiopia, Russia, Serbia and documents recording Christian missions to East Asia in the seventeenth and eighteenth centuries. The Islamic collections include over two thousand six hundred scholarly manuscripts, including Islamic law, prayer and commentary on the life of the Prophet, medicine, mathematics, science and books of pilgrimage. The collections reflect the historical aspects of world religions including Christianity, Islam and Islamic learning and spirituality, as well as East Asian traditions such as Daoism, Confucianism, Zen Buddhism, Buddhism, Jainism, Sikhism among others.[7] Two examples of temporary exhibitions within the past decade reflect the very nature of the library's approach: *Leonardo: The Codex Leicester* (2007) and *Chester Beatty's A to Z: From Amulet to Zodiac* (2014–15). Leonardo's scientific manuscript reflected his observations of water, nature and other explorations. Western science was contextualised with Arabic, Chinese and Japanese science sourced from the library's collections. Doctor Ryan made a very conscious decision to emphasise the historical and significant impact and contribution the Islamic and East Asian world made in Western scientific development.

There was a circulation of knowledge between the two worlds of Western Europe and the Middle East, explains Ryan, much of it channelled through Moorish Spain. European science, medicine and philosophy merged with Jewish and Arabic ideas and after further development during a glorious period of Middle Eastern learning returned to Europe to fuel the emerging Renaissance.

The Arabic texts were chosen for a clear purpose, says Ryan. 'We wanted to show the debt that scientists in the West owed to Arab scientists. Many of the developments seen during the Renaissance were gathering force earlier in medieval times.'[8]

This emphasis on shared heritage continues in the library's programming. The current director, Fionnuala Croke, who instigated the exhibition *Chester Beatty's A to Z: From Amulet to Zodiac* in 2014, explained the rationale for the selection in the introduction to the catalogue: 'As one browses through the galleries, the similarities – rather than the differences – between cultures become evident.' The works on display in the exhibition explored the threads that link cultures across the

Western, Islamic and East Asian worlds. Starting with A is for Amulet, the visitor was introduced to the universality of the human belief in the power of amulets. Concluding with Z is for Zodiac, the objects illustrated the fundamental human desire to understand the cosmos.[9]

Chester Beatty Library Intercultural Education Programme as a Form of Dialogue

The relocation of the library in 2000 to Dublin Castle coincided with a rise in immigration to the island of Ireland, and has created an opportunity to engage with diverse audiences. In order to share the significance and richness of the Chester Beatty Library's collections, the Education and Public Programme of the Chester Beatty Library was established in 2000. In particular, the education department seeks to engage with those communities who are represented in the collections, through a number of events and programmes ranging from cultural family days with the Thai community and Chinese New Year celebrations, to art workshops for children and adults, teen club, family activity packs, adult and teen drawing packs, music performances, films, lectures and intercultural storytelling projects in schools.[10] The library has been a key partner in a number of European and Asian intercultural dialogue projects since 2005. The Education and Public Programme of the library regularly reviews and seeks new ways to engage with its audiences.

Cultural Diversity in Irish Museums

At the 2015 Irish Museums Association conference in Belfast, a call was made for Irish museums to support and engage cultural diversity within its exhibitions and learning programmes.[11] Cultural diversity is relatively new in Ireland. Emigration, not immigration, has historically been an Irish phenomenon and with the recent global economic downturn, it has returned to Ireland. During the Celtic Tiger (1995–2007), Ireland experienced an unprecedented wave of returning Irish migrants as well as significant European and international migrants.[12] Ireland has experienced colonisation and immigration throughout its history yet in the late part of the twentieth and twenty-first century the government has been slow to develop policies relating to immigration and integration.[13] With the recent significant change in its population, a new chapter in Irish history has opened. In June 2015 the library was invited to present its experiences of working with diverse communities through its public programming with members of the Irish Museums Association. Based on the experienced gained by the education department, participants of the workshop were provided with a checklist to kick-start a dialogue on what cultural diversity means to museums in Ireland today.[14] This was followed by a second workshop as part of *The Role of National Museums in (Re)Negotiating National Identity* symposium in 2016.

Collective Conversations: Exploring a Kaleidoscope of Irish Identities at Irish Museums introduced participants to the library's intercultural education programme and the programme at the House of European History, Brussels, which opened in May 2017. Participants were introduced to the dramatic changes that have taken place in Ireland as a consequence of migration in the past fifteen years and how Irish museums can address new and existing migrant communities. Key themes included migration and identity and a number of museum objects and resources were introduced to explore how these complex themes might be developed in different museum contexts. Attendees worked with: oral histories; tried and tested learning resources from the House of European History; and European, Islamic and East Asian art historical material from the Chester Beatty Library.[15]

The Museum as an Instigator of Dialogue with Multi-Ethnic Communities

The library emphasised the importance of dialogue with multiethnic communities and shared its experience of working with

Chinese, Japanese, Thai, Middle Eastern, European and Irish indigenous groups. Groundwork and research are essential if a museum wishes to engage with communities. In other words, it is vital for museums to develop an understanding of their potential audiences. Relevant staff should be encouraged to work outside the museum, develop partnerships with potential cultural and educational organisations, meet members of communities and instigate dialogue. The fostering of these relationships is extremely important and can lead to positive results. It was strongly recommended that Irish museums must develop programmes that sit comfortably within the remit of their organisation in the formation stages of intercultural activities.[16]

Ways of Seeing I and II – A Cross Border Project Exploring Intercultural Dialogue

As part of the library's commitment to intercultural dialogue and learning, it teamed up with members of the Irish network of the Anna Lindh Foundation (ALF) and project-led two network activities. *Understanding Islam in Irish Education* was a one-day seminar with Mary Immaculate College, Limerick, Kerry Action for Development Education and Youth Work Ireland Cork in 2013.[17] A number of workshops and presentations were designed to explore and uncover how the Irish education system understands and represents Islamic faith and culture in Ireland today. The overall feedback from the 2013 seminar suggested that very few homegrown learning resources in Irish education exist although the profile of children in Irish schools has become increasingly culturally diverse. As a follow-up, the library teamed up with the Inclusion and Diversity Service, Northern Ireland (IDS) to develop a learning resource addressing world faiths as reflected in the library's and Ulster Museum's collections. *Ways of Seeing II* was launched in May 2015 and provides teachers in Northern Ireland and the Republic of Ireland with cross-curricular approaches to key world religions as a means to address cultural diversity in classrooms.[18]

Teachers are introduced to cultural diversity through museum collections and themes found in the curriculum such as world faiths, science, art, maths, literacy, language skills, history and geography. Teachers from the IDS developed the learning resource with the education department of the Chester Beatty Library as it is important to capture the voice of educators and stakeholders when addressing cross-curricular themes as reflected in the learning resource.

The second ALF activity was in response to both the aforementioned one-day seminar in 2013 and *Ways of Seeing II*. The library led a three-part series of workshops and symposia with members of the Irish network of the ALF (2015–16). The library's partners included Dublin City Interfaith Forum, Mary Immaculate College and Triskel Arts Centre. Each of the partners held one-day events addressing interfaith dialogue in contemporary Ireland and addressed third level students, educators, teachers, multi-belief communities as well as members of the Irish network of the ALF.

During the one-day seminar in Mary Immaculate College the library worked with postgraduate education students drawing on findings from a previous Anna Lindh Common Action workshop held in Tarragona, Spain, 2015. The Mary Immaculate seminar was an opportunity to explore how the *Ways of Seeing II* resource could be used with teachers, educators, NGOs, and members of the ALF network from Tunisia, Lebanon, Jordan, Algeria, Morocco, France, Belgium, Spain and Ireland.

Sacred Texts Workshop, Mary Immaculate College

In a Chester Beatty Library workshop co-presented with Jo-Anne Sunderland Bowe (Heritec, UK, British Library and British Museum), *Ways of Seeing II* was introduced as the starting point for an exploration of world faiths through the theme of sacred texts. The participants were asked the following questions:

- What does the word 'sacred' mean?
- What does the word 'texts' mean?

- When these two words are combined, what does 'sacred texts' mean?
- Who makes sacred texts?
- How are they made?
- What materials are involved in the creation of sacred texts?
- Who reads sacred texts and how are they interpreted?
- What materials are involved in the creation of sacred texts?

Examples of sacred texts were provided from both the Chester Beatty Library and the British Library (which has an online interactive site that allows visitors access to zoom in on manuscript details and turn pages as well as meet members of multi-faith communities).[19]

The group was provided with hands-on materials, including: writing utensils; a calligraphy pen made out of bamboo and feather quill; images of a scribe; natural materials including gum arabic; cochineal beetle used to make red dye; yellow ochre; a pestle and mortar to grind the materials into powder and make into paint and lapis lazuli. A handling kit reflecting Islamic faith was also presented to the group, which comprised of: a prayer mat; Quran stand; Qibla finder; prayer beads; celebratory cards; and a prayer hat worn by some men and hijab (head scarf) worn by some women.[20]

Overall the feedback from the workshop was positive with many of the participants expressing their wish to engage with similar topics as part of their pre-service teacher formation. They enjoyed the dialogical nature of the workshops and the ideas suggested as a way to teach the theme of sacred texts. Participants found learning about world faiths, in this instance Islam, as a very positive and fun experience. The workshop provided them with an imaginative, learner-centred, interactive and dialogical method that could be used with children in the classroom. More importantly, participants enjoyed the open forum of the workshop and the collaborative learning as they worked in groups and provided each other with their own insights as well as the workshop facilitators. Hands-on interactive learning was central to the workshop and generated curiosity, dialogue about sacred texts, and confidence as well as know-how when addressing cultural diversity through world faiths and museum objects.[21]

Conclusion

Museums have a crucial and enabling role to play as facilitators of dialogue in a multi-belief and multi-ethnic society. This dialogue can promote intercultural awareness and encourage social inclusion. It has been suggested that during the Celtic Tiger (1995–2007) the Irish government's multi-cultural policy encouraged assimilation rather than cultural pluralism.[22] In February 2017 the Department of Justice and Equality published an integration strategy so that migrants might be 'facilitated to play a full role in Irish society, that integration is a core principle of Irish life and that Irish society and institutions work together to promote integration'.[23] However, it is unclear whether the promotion of intercultural awareness includes arts, culture and multi-faith/cultural diversity.[24]

Any initiative which ignores or refuses to give recognition to the diverse cultural communities in contemporary Ireland comes from an unwillingness to acknowledge that Ireland has distinctive and separate identities from the 'norm' or romantic identity of Irishness as constructed by the first members of the Irish Free State. It is understandable that there are times of resistance to reconstructions of Irish identity. Máiréad Nic Craith's book *Culture and Identity Politics in Northern Ireland* suggests, 'If different cultural, ethnic and religious subcultures were to coexist and interact on equal terms within the same political community, the majority culture must give up its historical prerogative to define the official terms of the *generalised* political culture, which is to be shared by all citizens, regardless of where they come from and how they live.'[25] Shortly after its celebration of one hundred years of independence, the Irish Republic must continue to explore its historical legacy and generate new initiatives to develop its own unique identity in a postcolonial world.

Museums can offer a space for the development of multiple identities as they offer people an exciting place to understand and engage with their own and others' histories and identities by facilitating mutual understanding. Some national cultural institutions appear hesitant and unsure how to approach multi-ethnic groups. The seminars *Museums as Places for Intercultural Dialogue and Learning* (2014) and *The Role of National Museums (Re)Negotiating National Identity* (2016) described how the Chester Beatty Library initiated intercultural dialogue. Through dialogue, confidence is built both within the museum and its communities, and this has the potential to create conversations with other multi-ethnic groups. I believe Irish national museums feel hindered in engaging with new communities due to the nature of their national collections, as they view them as traditional and Irish. However, I also believe commonalities, such as storytelling, exist across cultures and Irish national museums can take a bold step and commence new dialogue in their programming.

If museums categorise multi-ethnic communities within the dominant or majority ethnic identity groups, it will limit museums in their interaction with visitors. Yet if museums initiate new approaches and remain open to critique and review their practice, it will lead to better interaction with communities. Identity – and Irish identity – is not fixed, it is constantly changing, and with the impact of globalisation, this flux must be recognised by both government and policymakers. If not, communities will become ghettoised and marginalised and create divisions within society with resulting problems such as racism, conflict and misunderstanding. Museums can facilitate dialogue and have a key role to play in ensuring this does not happen.

SECTION TWO

Dialogue of Life:
Interbelief Dialogue
Through Participants' Eyes

CHAPTER FOUR

Dialogue About Belief: Voices from the Centre for Dialogue and Prayer in Oświęcim/Auschwitz, Poland

Sr Mary O'Sullivan

I write this chapter about the nature of dialogue as it is experienced and understood in the Centre for Dialogue and Prayer in Oświęcim/Auschwitz, Poland, where I live and work. Located at the threshold of the Auschwitz-Birkenau Memorial, the Centre for Dialogue and Prayer is a Catholic institution founded in 1992 by the then archbishop of Krakow, Franciszek Cardinal Macharski, in agreement with the bishops of Europe and representatives of Jewish organisations. It is a house of hospitality open to everyone irrespective of language, nationality or religion, with conference facilities and accommodation for guests. The centre's aim is to commemorate all of the victims of Auschwitz and to contribute in a small way to the creation of mutual respect, reconciliation and peace in the world. While visiting Vienna in 1988, alluding to the work of the centre, Pope John Paul II said, 'Among numerous initiatives that are being undertaken in the spirit of the Council [Vatican II] for Jewish–Christian dialogue, I would like to mention a centre for information, education, meeting and prayer that is being prepared in Poland ... One can hope that it would bear abundant fruit and could also serve as an example for other nations.'[1] In July 2016 Pope Francis became the third pope to visit the Auschwitz-Birkenau death camps, following in the footsteps of John Paul II and Benedict XVI.

Dialogue from a Place of Mass Murder

In 1940, almost one hundred and fifty thousand Polish people arrived at Auschwitz and half of these were murdered. In 1941, after the German invasion of the Soviet Union, at least fifteen thousand Soviet prisoners of war came to Auschwitz. Almost all of these were murdered. From 1942 onwards, under the so-called 'Final Solution of the Jewish Question', approximately one million one hundred thousand Jews from all over Europe were deported to Auschwitz. Of these, more than nine hundred thousand were killed upon arrival in the gas chambers and one hundred thousand died in the camp. From 1943, around twenty-three thousand Sinti and Roma gypsies were sent to Auschwitz and only two thousand survived. Other prisoners, mostly political opponents of the Nazis from Czechoslovakia, the Soviet Union (Belarus, Russia, Ukraine), France, Yugoslavia and other countries, including Germany and Austria, as well as Bible students (Jehovah's Witnesses), homosexuals, so-called re-education, asocial and criminal prisoners were sent to Auschwitz.[2]

It is almost impossible to imagine what it meant for a prisoner to be incarcerated in Auschwitz. The survivors were all prisoners of the camp. They tell their stories because they feel an obligation to speak about the unspeakable. Most of the victims were never prisoners because the vast majority, mainly Jews, came in on trains and were sent to the gas chambers. There is no physical trace left of them. Of the more than one million Jewish people transported to Auschwitz, about two hundred thousand became prisoners in the camp because they had to work before they died. It is beyond our comprehension that one million Jewish people disappeared like this. They were just gassed, burnt and their ashes thrown away. Within Jewish memory, Auschwitz represents a big murderous hole into which the European Jewish world tragically disappeared. Only a minority of Jewish people became prisoners in the camp.[3]

Four Dimensions of Dialogue at the Centre for Dialogue and Prayer

Dialogue among any group of people can be challenging; however, dialogue in a place of mass murder, with a historical backdrop of hatred and unspeakable acts perpetrated on so many innocent victims, may seem impossible. Yet an approach to dialogue has grown slowly at the Centre for Dialogue and Prayer at the edge of Auschwitz.[4] This approach has four dimensions that are offered as suggestions to groups and individuals who visit or stay.[5] Each dimension begins with silence and listening:

1. *Listen to the voice of the earth.* Participants are invited to understand what happened in Auschwitz by learning the facts. Taking a guided tour in the Auschwitz-Birkenau Memorial Place and meeting with a survivor presents us with the facts. Even today, it is difficult to imagine what it was really like during the days when the camp was in operation. There are no graves. You do not see anybody dying or being tortured. You may not feel the atmosphere of horror and terror, but you have to try. It is difficult to develop an awareness of those who are invisible in Auschwitz and yet it is a most important task in the work of memory.[6]

2. *Listen to the voice of our hearts.* The Centre for Dialogue and Prayer tries to create a place where reflection is possible and where the environment is conducive to silence or a shared conversation with others about what happened. It is important to have time to feel how we are connected to the story of Auschwitz and to try to understand the overall truth and the implications that Auschwitz has in our own

lives. So, we need to be silent and to listen. We might ask: Where would I have been at that time and how would I have reacted? Which side would I have been on? What does it mean for me today? Where is my hope, despair, my values, my faith or belief? This reflection will always be very personal and individual. That is why groups and individuals coming to visit Auschwitz very often need time alone.

3. *Listen to the voice of the other.* Being silent and listening is an important step before dialogue. Therefore, it is important to have time for ourselves. First, we must know the story and reflect on what it means for us as individuals before we are able to dialogue. Dialogue is not always organised in a formal way though occasionally there are formal dialogue events in the Centre for Dialogue and Prayer. The fact that the centre is a place where everyone is welcomed and hopefully listened to, a place where everyone can be with their own perspective and roots and where everyone is respected, is diametrically opposite to the destructive hate-based relationships resulting in genocide and the atmosphere of terror that prevailed during the Holocaust. The Centre for Dialogue and Prayer understands that trust is the doorway to dialogue. Once there is trust, it is easier for dialogue participants to listen to one another. The centre offers guidelines for dialogue participants. These guidelines stipulate that everyone speaks about themself only. Everyone listens to the other. Nobody speaks about the other. We each carry our own wounds daily. When we come together, therefore, it feels like an encounter of wounded people. If you touch the wound, there can often be an emotional reaction. Often it is better to be silent. Sometimes you say more by saying nothing. Yet dialogue is not about running away from the wound.

4. *Listen to the voice of God.* Although it is called the Centre for Dialogue and Prayer, very often the starting point is

neither dialogue nor prayer but silence and listening. The question, 'Where was God during the Holocaust?' is wrestled with often, as is God's question to us, 'Where were you and where are you today?' In Auschwitz there are testimonies of faith and testimonies of people who lost their faith. The painful history of Christian–Jewish relationships is encountered, as well as the question of responsibility. The challenge for us involves both an examination of conscience and a confession of faith. We are challenged to reflect on our beliefs and values and say where our responsibility is today.

Basic Pointers for Dialogue
These four dimensions of dialogue form the backbone of the educational work in the Centre for Dialogue and Prayer. They have provided some basic pointers for dialogue including:

- Dialogue begins with listening, not talking.
- Listening means I respect you as 'other' in your 'otherness'. This is the foundation of dialogue and there is no attempt at converting or silencing the other.
- In the centre, respect means a place of welcome for everyone, no matter who they are, where they come from, or whether they are with or without religious belief. The centre is the antithesis of what Auschwitz was.
- Transparency of identity enables dialogue to flourish. In dialogue I personally identify that I am Catholic, a religious sister and this is my starting point. Other dialogue participants identify their distinct and personal identity. Dialogue is possible when people are open about their identity.
- Everyone is invited to speak about Auschwitz but nobody is forced or coerced to do so. Everyone respects the wounds of the other.
- Everyone speaks about themselves, not about the other. Everyone listens.

- People come to dialogue from different backgrounds and perspectives and with different family stories. Some dialogue partners may have a mother or grandfather who was murdered in Auschwitz. Others may have a father or grandmother who was in the SS. Listening in dialogue means respect for what cannot be said.
- Context matters. In the work of the centre when we listen and talk together it is about Auschwitz. Auschwitz is not Rwanda or Cambodia or Darfur. We look at Auschwitz very concretely. The victims suffered in Auschwitz and in other camps very concretely. There is a temptation to avoid this difficult encounter with Auschwitz and divert attention to other places of injustice and crime. Yet the concrete questions remain: What did we do to the Jewish people in Auschwitz? What did we do to one another? What does the memory of Auschwitz mean to me? This is all very difficult. Of course, we cannot change the past. We are at least three generations after World War II and we are not responsible for the past; however, staying in a place of trust opens the heart to listening to the other and to letting the other in to tell their story. Staying with the concreteness of Auschwitz opens us to our present responsibility and other contemporary questions emerge.
- There has to be a basic trust to begin dialogue. The actual 'coming together' of people is part of the process of building trust. Trust and coming together form the doorway, the entrance room, to dialogue. The aim is to get to the dining room of dialogue.
- Dialogue structures grow from encounter. We meet people and we begin to trust and then we see if it is possible to come together to listen and to talk. This is what happened at the interbelief dialogue seminar in Limerick in February 2016. People of different faiths and beliefs came together in trust to listen and to talk. This is how the environment of trust grows.

Our experience at the Centre for Dialogue and Prayer has taught us that the work of dialogue, peace and reconciliation cannot be done solely within one's own group. Christians cannot engage in interbelief dialogue on their own. Jews cannot do it on their own. Atheists cannot do it on their own. Buddhists cannot do it on their own. Consequently, the centre has developed positive and ongoing cooperation with the Polish Council of Christians and Jews, the International Council of Christians and Jews, Zen Peacemaker Auschwitz Retreat teams, Pax Christi International and other groups engaged in dialogue, peace and reconciliation work.

On 4 May 2016, Pope Francis met with participants of a meeting between the Royal Institute for Interfaith Studies of Amman and the Pontifical Council for Interreligious Dialogue. He said:

Dialogue is going out of ourselves, with a word, to hear the word of the other. The two words meet, two thoughts meet. It is the first step of a journey. Following this meeting of the word, hearts meet and begin a dialogue of friendship, which ends with holding hands. Word, hearts, hands. It's simple! A little child knows how to do it.[7]

The interbelief dialogue seminar in Limerick in February 2016 took the form of this word-hearts-hands dialogue process. This nascent interbelief dialogue will slowly find its own shape and development. There are new and promising initiatives for dialogue developing in contemporary Ireland. A 'dialogue of friendship, which ends with holding hands' can enrich the uniqueness of each faith and belief tradition. In the Irish context this may be the 'entrance room' to dialogue and the beginnings of the process of trust. Those of us fortunate to participate in the interbelief dialogue seminar in 2016, and all those involved in interbelief dialogue groups in Ireland, where people of diverse faiths and philosophical world views gather together in trust and openness to the other, witness and experience dialogue in action. From my own faith perspective, I understand that we are only instruments of dialogue. Let us not be afraid to leave some work to God.

CHAPTER FIVE

Dialogue in Dublin City Interfaith Forum

Adrian Cristea

Dublin is the capital city of Ireland and its name originates from the Gaelic *dubh linn*, meaning 'black pool', thus referring to the pool of dark water formed when the Poddle stream and the river Liffey merge. With a population of over one million people, the 2016 census revealed that 44 per cent of Ireland's total urban population live in Dublin.[1] As a city, Dublin has a long history which benefitted from the arrival of migrants. Indeed, it owes its very existence to migrants who settled in the area when the city was established by Scandinavians in the ninth century.[2]

Of course, these arrivals are usually referred to as invaders but invaders tend to conquer, pillage and then leave, whether willingly or after some 'persuasion'. Migrants, on the other hand, tend to arrive, settle and become part of and indeed enrich the area, contributing to commerce, art, language and so on. Migrants become residents. So, Dublin has a long history of absorbing and benefitting from the many peoples who have arrived on its shores over the centuries.[3] This process has not always been easy yet Dublin's inhabitants are capable and willing to learn and adapt when the right conditions are created.

A Brief History

Dublin, both the city and the region, is the most ethnically, culturally and religiously diverse region in Ireland. According to the 2016 census, over 17 per cent of residents in Dublin city and one in six of those residing in Fingal, are non-Irish nationals.[4] In November 2010, recognising the significance of this growing diversity and working in partnership with Dublin City Council's (DCC) Office for Integration, the Irish Council of Churches (ICC), with funding from the European Integration Fund, began implementing the project that finally led to the establishment of the Dublin City Interfaith Forum (DCIF) on 31 January 2012.

By taking this creative, thinking-outside-the-box approach, DCC and ICC helped to establish a unique organisation in which Dublin's faith communities work together with the city to support and facilitate the process of integration for both our migrant and indigenous communities.[5]

Process and Practice

Initially the most important element of the DCIF project was the development of relationships within the various faith communities and faith networks. The project officer met with faith leaders and key people within the various faith communities in Dublin city. We also attended meetings and events held by other faith groups. Dublin City Council had a number of existing relationships with faith communities. The Office for Integration, for example, was engaged through community networks and funding relationships with many diverse faith groups. The project began by building a database of faith communities and contacts.

The first of a series of interfaith workshops took place on Thursday, 29 September 2011 at the Wood Quay Venue in the Dublin City Council Civic Offices. This Wood Quay (An Ché Adhmaid) Venue is deeply symbolic as it stands on the site where the migrant Vikings settled in Dublin one thousand years previously. Approximately forty-five members, coming from six faith traditions in the city, attended the first workshop. This day-long workshop was facilitated by Dr Inderjit Bhogal OBE, a former leader of the Corrymeela Community, Northern Ireland's oldest peace and reconciliation organisation.[6] Inderjit, who has impeccable credentials in the field of interfaith work, was warmly received by members of all of the faith communities. The first workshop proved to be very valuable and was a unique opportunity for members of various communities to meet in a neutral venue, and to share stories and aspirations in a spirit of friendship and faith. The theme of the workshop was 'Local Interfaith Dialogue and its Role in Creating Inclusive Communities where all Belong and Contribute'. After introductory speeches from Gerry Folan representing Dublin City Council and Mervyn McCullough from ICC, there was a keynote address by Inderjit Bhogal that set the scene and incorporated his own story. This was followed by speeches from the Roman Catholic Archbishop of Dublin, Dr Diarmuid Martin and Shaykh Dr Umar Al-Qadri from the Islamic community.

These contextual stories were followed by a series of small group discussions during which participants broke into groups of four to discuss issues and points raised by both Inderjit and the two other main speakers. This discussion focused on the questions, 'What is an inclusive community?' and 'How can my faith community positively contribute to building an inclusive community?' These small group discussions proved effective and opened up creative new areas of dialogue and fresh insights. Members of the various faith communities consulted and had an opportunity to speak. Their input was openly welcomed and treated with due consideration and respect.

After lunch, felt-tip markers and sheets of paper were handed around so that everyone could write an adjective or verb that described the spirit of the event for them. This proved to be a very powerful experience. Participants displayed and briefly spoke about the adjective/verb they had chosen.

Words used to describe the day included: listening, respect, understanding, exchange, justice, openness, friends, integration, home, mutuality, united, warmth, open-hearted, contribution, sanctuary, justice, participation, all (In the name of God the beneficent the merciful, there should be no compulsion on religions), unity, synergy, together, welcome, cooperation, salmagundi, dialogue.

At this stage of the day there was a real sense of deep friendship and an even deeper sense of interconnectedness. Recurring key issues throughout the course of the day included: the role of religion in the public square; the role of faith in shaping identities and inclusive communities; working with each other; and the challenges of speaking to one another. The day ended with a summing up from Inderjit and a looking forward to what we as a group hoped to achieve in the process of the next workshop.

The second workshop took place in Trinity College Dublin on Thursday, 10 November 2011. Once again the facilitator was Inderjit Bhogal, and the theme was 'Setting Up the Dublin City Interfaith Forum – Process and Practice'. Thirty people from six faith traditions attended the workshop. There was an initial welcome from Adrian Cristea of ICC[7] and feedback from the first meeting by Inderjit. A process for establishing a forum and the criteria for selecting members were outlined. Inderjit offered two interfaith models, those of Humbert and Yorkshire and of Wolverhampton.[8]

Small-group questions included: What did you think of the interfaith structures presented earlier? How do you envisage an interfaith structure appropriate to the Dublin city context? What would you add and what would you change? The small-group discussions proved to be filled with a lot of energy and enthusiasm. After these discussions, we broke for coffee and returned to our groups to participate in a game involving spaghetti, string tape and a marshmallow. The game required the small groups to use the materials provided to construct the tallest structure possible in the allotted time. The game generated a lot of creative interaction and laughter. People developed a variety of operational strategies to deal with the challenges posed. This was effective on a number of levels as it showed who had the capacity to lead and who to listen as well as to cooperate at a team level. At a much more human level, it generated conversation and participation among the different individuals and religious traditions. In this context, the game was both effective and successful.

People were now getting to know one another at a deeper level and were learning about one another via a variety of conversations on daily life, personal spirituality, worship, practice and theology. In purely practical terms, this was a very successful workshop. A number of issues were raised and important decisions made. The workshop helped move things forward and agreements were reached on issues related to selection criteria, an agreement was also reached on the interfaith model that the project would adopt as well as the given name of the group: Dublin City Interfaith Forum (DCIF). The criteria mooted and provisionally agreed upon were that members of the forum should be deeply informed about their own faith, have wide respect, influence and a network within their own community, deep respect for other faiths, be from an identifiable world faith community and be committed and able to integrate actively to the integration process.

In chronological order the faith groups represented included: Bahá'í, Buddhist, Christian, Hindu, Jewish, Muslim, and Sikh. The general aims of DCIF were explored and these included to: support and strengthen the contribution of faith communities in Dublin; educate and encourage people of different faiths to dialogue; reflect and work together in matters of policy, strategy and action; challenge all forms of injustice and discrimination and contribute to a fully integrated city for all. It was agreed that the forum should be representative of gender and age, not be too large and begin by building relationships. While outlining the above aims, Inderjit also proposed 'future steps' and 'future direction' by exploring what might prove to be a productive way to move forward. In this context a pre-forum meeting involving key personnel was planned for 31 January 2012 for the inauguration of the new Dublin City Interfaith Forum.

This date marked the official launch of Dublin City Interfaith Forum by the then lord mayor of Dublin, Cllr Andrew Montague. A large number of people attended the launch and showed their support for the project. The event was then followed by the first meeting of the forum. The first event organised by DCIF took place on 22 February 2012. It consisted of a visit to the places of worship of various forum members.

Purpose of DCIF and the Interfaith Work Programme
DCIF is not a talking shop. It is a body that acts. It has no interest in or remit to discuss differences in belief, faith, philosophy and so on. Those topics are for other bodies to explore. The DCIF constitution identifies that its purpose is to:

- Support and strengthen the contribution of faith communities towards social and civic integration in Dublin city.
- Promote and support the participation of migrants in the civic, community and public life of the city.
- Challenge all forms of injustice and discrimination.
- Contribute to a fully integrated city for all.
- Promote respect for and acceptance of the diversity of faith and culture in Dublin city.
- Actively liaise with Dublin City Council and other statutory and voluntary bodies towards these ends.[9]

The main focus of the forum's activities is the Interfaith Work Programme. At the beginning of each year DCIF holds a planning meeting to establish a programme of events, activities and projects relevant to the city of Dublin from an interfaith and integration perspective. These events also provide an opportunity for participants to witness to people from many different cultural, religious and ethnic backgrounds working together, not only in harmony but in genuine friendship and ease with each other.

DCIF Activities

The forum has engaged in a variety of activities with the aim of building a deeper sense of friendship and connectedness. In February 2012 members visited some of each other's places of worship. These visits were to: the Al-Madinah Mosque; the Dublin Buddhist Centre; Dublin Central Mission; St George and St Thomas Church and the Pro-Cathedral. This was followed later in the year by visits to the Bahá'í Spiritual Assembly, the Rathgar Synagogue, the Milltown Mosque and the Sikh Gurdwara in Ringsend.

In order to further develop DCIF's work a Capacity Building and Planning Workshop was held to produce concrete proposals for future projects. These included:

- Faith in the City: a series of six public talks organised on the history, beliefs, rituals, etc. of some of our faith communities based in Dublin's north inner city.
- Ongoing meetings with An Garda Siochána to discuss security and policing issues of special interest to faith communities.
- A large and successful Interfaith Walk for Peace to mark UN International Day of Peace led by the religious leaders in the city. This has since become an annual event.[10]

The forum also provided a number of extremely successful seminars, such as the Intercultural Cities Conference in 2013. In February 2012, the forum, through DCC's Office for Integration, was invited to provide a seminar and workshops at the European Intercultural Cities' milestone event, *Making*

Diversity Work for Cities. Intercultural Cities, a Council of Europe programme, provides a platform for a wide range of cities which are managing diversity as an asset, rather than a threat. DCIF selected as its theme, 'Creating a City of Possibilities', to reflect one of the main themes of the Intercultural Cities conference, 'Diversity Advantage'. Diversity advantage refers to the positive contribution migrant communities can make to our cities. Our event provided an opportunity for delegates from cities across Europe and further afield to explore the idea that faith communities, uniquely present in each context, are a positive resource to be realised not a problem to be solved. DCIF explored themes relevant to encouraging other cities to include a similar engagement between city administrators and local faith communities in their strategies for developing intercultural cities.

Education and Information
Education is of primary importance if we are to break down the lazy habits of intolerance, prejudice, suspicion and ignorance that underpin most incidents of racial and religious hate. Such incidents are currently and alarmingly increasing in frequency. To this end, the forum devised a number of strategies to educate people about our faith communities, such as the Faith in the City programme. DCIF is developing a strategy for working with schools, which was piloted in Oatlands College, Dublin, in March 2012. This consisted of a series of short talks from each of the participating DCIF faith communities on their individual history, beliefs, etc. Not only did this give the students an opportunity to hear about different faiths but more importantly to see us working together in friendship and harmony. The forum has plans to develop further programmes and resources for the educational sector.

Another initiative was the launch, in June 2013, of our guide to places of worship in Dublin, entitled *Come and See for Yourself*. This booklet, which gives simple advice on what one would expect if they were to visit a church, mosque, temple or centre of one of our faith communities in Dublin, was distributed to public spaces around the city.[11] DCIF members continue to invite each other to events and celebrations in our communities so that we are constantly learning about each other and developing our relationships.

Spirit of Service

Faith communities have as a common ideal the spirit of service, not just to their own communities but also to the wider civil society. We often hear reference to the silent majority in contrast to the vocal minority. In the case of faith communities, I would suggest that the silent majority are 'silent' not in the sense of a disinterested or disengaged group but rather 'silent' because they are busy getting on with looking after people, providing effective and efficient services to those who are in need in society and engaging in dialogue within and between their communities. Further I would suggest that faith groups are sometimes regarded as 'silent' because of the noise of a violent tiny minority who take outrageous action while hiding behind spurious claims that they are acting in the name of some religion or other. I suggest that now is the time to choose whether to relate to the faith communities through a dysfunctional and disaffected minority voice or through the creative and engaged majority.

Diversity Advantage

A major theme for the Intercultural Cities conference involved seeing groups and communities as assets to be realised and not as problems to be solved, managed or placated. In many ways the work of DCIF since its inception has been to nurture, develop and exhibit that faith communities are potential resources for Dublin city and not something to fear, manage or placate. Faith communities are part of the city, willing and able to participate in and support civic life and integration.

Within the DCIF the focus is on all faith traditions both new and indigenous and not just on minority communities. Developing mutual understanding of the sensitivities of both the resident local and resident migrant communities is a key part of DCIF's work. It is our aim to continue to develop strategies to support integration initiatives through cooperating with local civic, health and social services to promote mutual understanding of cultural, religious and legal sensitivities so that the needs of both civil authorities and migrant communities can be addressed.

Conclusion

DCIF regards itself as a pioneer and as a pathfinder where many of its initiatives are pilot projects to test and explore the possibilities of what works, what does not work, what are the pitfalls, opportunities, potentials and best practices in the area of interfaith cooperation and civic integration. We need help and support to continue. To do this we need not just moral support but financial support. There is one key factor to the success of this project: we have had a full-time person organising and supporting our efforts. Organisations such as DCIF are inevitably made up of dedicated and therefore very, very busy people. Without the resources of a full-time coordinator we would not have succeeded. Martin Luther King Jr said, 'I have a dream, that my four little children will one day live in a nation where they will not be judged by the colour of their skin but by the content of their character.'[12] To which we could add, 'by their religious beliefs, cultural background or ethnicity'.

Despite all of the progress that we as a people have made, we live in a time of great challenge as decreasing resources make life increasingly difficult and challenging for people. Unfortunately, increasing pressures on individuals and communities more often than not lead to increasing levels of despair, anger, hatred and outrage. We are already seeing a significant increase in hate crimes. The Church of Ireland

Archbishop of Dublin, Dr Michael Jackson, commented at a DCIF event:

> *Ireland is an angry, post-theocratic state. We need to be taken seriously as leaders and servants, as those of faith, who are key players in building an Ireland of the future out of the rubble of economic greed.*

If initiatives such as DCIF are not supported, the only voices heard will be the increasingly strident militant voices of opportunistic minorities both within faith communities and within civic society, who will take the opportunity to further destabilise the situation for their own profit and the inevitable but, to them, incidental suffering of our people. Dublin City Interfaith Forum now stands at a crossroads. It can be supported to build on the unique achievements and successes delivered in the short time it has existed, or it can be allowed to falter and fail to the detriment of our city. We are not, nor do we regard ourselves as, a knight in shining armour who can rescue the situation singlehandedly; however, we can be a vital part of an ongoing set of strategies that, if supported, will provide great and significant service to this city and its people. As Dr King also said, 'We have come to remind you of the fierce urgency of now. This is no time to engage in the luxury of cooling off or to take the tranquilising drug of gradualism.'[13]

The opportunists of chaos are here, now. They wear the cloak of intolerance, of inter-communal blame, of violent solutions and the imposition of the rule of hate. You only have to look to other European countries to see where complacency can lead. The experience we have had over the last few years developing DCIF and working together to explore ways to enhance integration, mutual respect and harmony within and between our communities convinces us of the validity and utility of engagement between faith communities and civic authorities.

CHAPTER SIX

Learning from Diverse Beliefs in the Mid-West Interfaith Network

Trisha Rainsford

There is an ancient story about six blind men who are asked to describe an elephant that is standing in front of them. Having never seen an elephant each man goes forward and feels one part of the animal. When they finish they are asked to describe the elephant.

The man who felt a leg steps forward confidently. 'I have examined the elephant and I can tell you an elephant is exactly like a pillar.'

The man who had felt the elephant's tail throws up his hands in disbelief. 'You are completely mistaken,' he cries. 'I am telling you that an elephant is like a rope.'

'Don't be ridiculous,' shouts the man who had felt the elephant's trunk. 'It is clear that an elephant is like the branch of a tree.'

'How can you be so foolish?' says the man who had felt the elephant's ear. 'The elephant is a delicate creature much like a fan.'

'A fan?' shouts the man who had felt the belly of the elephant. 'Nonsense. An elephant is as solid as a wall.'

'I can't believe any of this,' declares the man who had felt the tusk of the elephant. 'I have never encountered anything more like a solid pipe than an elephant.'

The arguing carries on in earnest as each man continues to insist that his description explains the full reality of the elephant. Luckily, a wise woman comes along just at that time. The six men asked her to adjudicate. She sits in silence for a few minutes and then she speaks.

'You are all correct,' she says.

The men are furious. 'That's not possible,' the oldest of the men shouts and the others nod in agreement. 'This is an argument simply about facts. Each of us is either right or we are wrong. You can see the elephant so you can tell us who has best described it. All we ask is that you stick to the facts.'

'All right,' says the wise woman. 'I will stick rigidly to the facts. Because each of you has faithfully described the part of the elephant you encountered, all of you are correct; however, unfortunately it is the case that all of you are also wrong.'

The wise woman pauses as the six blind men struggle to understand what she is saying. 'The error you made was not in describing your own experience and understanding. The error was in thinking that your limited encounter with the elephant describes everything about the elephant. What you have failed to realise is that an elephant is made up of all the parts you described – and more. Therefore, if you truly want to learn the truth about the elephant, you need to combine your understanding and make the learning journey together.'

Communities of Interpreters

This story illustrates something that I am far from the first person to realise – that if I want to know about anything, I need to be open to different perspectives. Indeed, I am not even the first person to realise that it is possible to hold my own truth while engaging with diverse perspectives. This is the best way forward. However, somewhere along the line as a human race we seem to have lost sight of how this works. We live in a society that has come to think that belief is necessarily divisive. It is easy to see how this might appear to be the case. In an attempt to counteract this, we often try for a 'belief-free' version of society in the hope of creating harmony and understanding.

The problem with this route is that belief is such an important part of being human that it is almost impossible for us not to believe *something*. When we are against believing in God or gods or art or medicine or anything, in itself this stance becomes our new belief. In this way, an anarchist is not just a person who does not believe in having political systems run their country. Rather she or he is a believer in not having a political system. And so on.

As the twentieth century has shown, just as much damage has been done in countries where religion is outlawed as in countries where religion is fanatically enforced. Alexander Solzhenitsyn described this phenomenon as a problem of ideology:

> *Ideology – that is what gives evildoing its long-sought justification and gives the evildoer the necessary steadfastness and determination. That is the social theory which helps to make his acts seem good instead of bad in his own and others' eyes, so that he won't hear reproaches and curses but will receive praise and honours ... the agents of the Inquisition fortified their wills by invoking Christianity; the conquerors of foreign lands by extolling the grandeur of their Motherland; the colonisers by civilisation; the Nazis by race; and the Jacobins (early and late) by equality, brotherhood and the happiness of future generations.*
> *Thanks to ideology, the twentieth century was fated to experience evildoing on a scale calculated in the millions.*[1]

While many bad things have been done in the name of belief, in itself belief is not a bad thing. In fact, the human capacity to believe has accomplished many wonderful and positive things; for example, belief in freedom and self-determination has fuelled countless revolutions and whether one agrees or disagrees with the methods or the outcomes, it is this strong pulse of belief that has built many nations. A belief in human dignity and justice defeated the lucrative business of slavery and changed the common perception from one where ownership of human beings was the norm to one where ownership of human beings was – at least mostly – condemned. In 1949, after World War II, a belief in the fact that all human beings are equal and equally entitled to human rights and protection brought the nations of the world together to sign the Universal Declaration of Human Rights. Imperfect as these social movements might be, they are still the concrete physical manifestation of belief. There is no doubt that all social realities are woven from beliefs – for good or ill.

Undesirable Beliefs?

It is undeniably the case that some beliefs are not constructive or useful; however, like all naturally occurring phenomena, the trick is to learn how to harness the power inherent in the phenomenon rather than to cut it off. In the same way that electricity has the potential to be a dangerous and destructive force when not channelled properly but is of enormous benefit to humanity when used properly, the natural power that is in belief can be harnessed for the well-being of society. Valuing the beliefs and views of others not only helps us to live more harmoniously as a diverse society but also increases our chances of seeing the 'truth' in anything, as we come to see that we need other perspectives if we are ever to come close to glimpsing the tiniest fragment of truth about anything.

In the 1960s, physicist David Bohm described how this process works even in something as simple as understanding concrete reality:

> *By combining many views of the object we understand the object ... By combining many views of the circle ...*

we get the notion of the circle, by combining it with the scientific view we get another view on it ... the more views we get that we can integrate and make coherent the deeper our understanding of the reality is. Every view is limited, it's like a mirror looking this way, each one gives a limited view ...[2]

To approach anything in this way we each need to offer what we see and experience in the full and certain knowledge that there are other parts we cannot see. In other words, like the blind men feeling the elephant, while our view may be absolutely accurate and *related* to the reality, it does not by itself *define* the reality. Once we realise this, if we are interested in understanding the reality of anything, we will realise, as Bohm described, that, 'The more views we get that we can integrate and make coherent the deeper our understanding of the reality is.'

Mid-West Interfaith Network

This is a strong case for interacting with people who hold diverse beliefs. The value of dialogue among people of different beliefs is something I have learned from being a member of the Mid-West Interfaith Network (MWIN). This welcoming, grass-roots network, founded in 2010 by an Irish Catholic priest and a Syrian integration worker from a local NGO, supports different forms of collaboration and dialogue among people of diverse beliefs in the Mid-West region of Ireland. It is open to all people and it is engaged in a variety of community-based activities. Being involved in interbelief dialogue offers ample opportunity to learn about the nature of belief as it manifests in the everyday lives of ordinary people. It really helps everyone involved to come to see that for most people their beliefs – regardless of what they may be – are not like a cardigan that they can slip off if it gets too warm. Their beliefs are part of who they are as people, like their sinews and cells and DNA. Indeed, sometimes their beliefs can lead to friction.

This brings me to perhaps the most valuable lesson that I have learned from engaging with people who hold diverse beliefs. There is only one core belief necessary to make all dialogue and interaction between people productive and possible: the unshakeable belief that every single person on the planet is, quite simply, a human being. Beliefs about the existence or non-existence of God, belief in prayer, the soul, political ideologies of any description, belief in life after death or the central figures in any or all religions – none of these are deal breakers. However, belief in the fact that the person in front of you is as complex and nuanced in their human reality as you are, is essential. A strong conviction that, notwithstanding ethnicity, culture, tradition, conceptual frameworks or world view, everybody you meet – regardless of whether or not they agree with you about *anything* – is, in their essence, exactly like you, is all we really need in order to work out how to move forward together in every area of life.

It is true that working with MWIN I have learned lots about different religious traditions and practices; however, the reality is that if I wanted more information only, I could have googled most of that. Even though it is the case that being invited to worship and celebrate with others from different faith traditions is an enriching and enjoyable experience, and one I have come to greatly value, this is not where the real learning happens. It is only through interacting with others in a real and ordinary way, through engaging properly and not just tolerating difference at a superficial level but getting into the nitty-gritty, having problems and overcoming them, that I have truly come to appreciate that they are far from 'other' but are, in fact, just like me.

This is a most ordinary statement and one that most people would agree with in theory. Now there's the rub – theory. Before I joined the Mid-West Interfaith Network, I most definitely already held this belief. Looking back now I think that though I did understand it as an idea, the truth is that my understanding was intellectual, vague and untested by the robustness of real experience. Just like we all think we know about raising children before we have them.

The Oneness of Humanity

After many years of working with, laughing with and crying with the various members of the MWIN (some there for the long haul, some short-term members), I no longer know this truth about the oneness of humanity on an intellectual level only. Now I know it at a much deeper level of my being. When I meet someone who seems different to me, not just in looks or belief but maybe even a person who holds views diametrically opposed to views I hold dear, I know now that underneath all of that they are just like me. I cannot describe specifically how I have learned this as it is a learning that happens like a child grows. You do not see it happening, it just happens when you are not looking and you do not really notice until something draws your attention to it. All I do know is that I have learned this from being part of the Mid-West Interfaith Network.

Since its inception, the Mid-West Interfaith Network has had a varying membership. It has consisted of people from vastly different religious traditions – Bahá'í, Buddhist, Christian denominations, Hindu, Jewish, Muslim, Sikh, Zoroastrian, and others. It has had members of many nationalities – American, Dutch, English, French, Indian, Irish, Malaysian, Nepalese, Nigerian, Slovakian, Sudanese and Tunisian. It has been made up of men and women, clergy and laity. A Jewish member of the network once explained to a visitor that we were less interested in defining where we were going than we were in learning how to make every journey together. Like the various strands in a Celtic knot, the diverse beliefs in the Mid-West Interfaith Network have not only been tolerated but have been integral in learning how to come together in a flowing, grass-roots expression of the spiritual crossing of paths and the endurance of life, love and belief.

The group has developed organically with regular meetings where members come together to discuss their own traditions and common concerns. There is lively debate but the dialogue extends way beyond verbal encounter. Members gather to plan events and organise activities. In recent years members from different religious traditions have co-presented at national conferences on the topic of interbelief dialogue. Members have spoken on local radio about the activities undertaken by the network. These include working with local communities to organise an 'Eat, Meet and Greet' event where old and newcomer communities come together to celebrate what it means to live in a vibrant culturally and religiously diverse community. For many years members of the MWIN have participated in Limerick city's St Patrick's Day parade in order to celebrate and make visible to the wider community the enduring friendship and mutually beneficial activities that unite people of different faiths in the mid-west region. In recent years a very simple and effective informal dialogue occurred when MWIN members teamed up with local community members to pick up litter as part of the Great Limerick Clean Up. Other activities have involved the MWIN helping to organise and co-host an Eid celebration in Limerick city centre with members of the Islamic faith. MWIN members have been involved in celebrating many festivals from different faith traditions in Limerick. These include celebrating Passover with members of the Jewish community, as well as being involved in a celebration of Diwali with members of the Sikh and Hindu communities. Simple activities like MWIN members gathering on the streets at Christmas time to wish people a happy Christmas have given concrete expression to the respect, trust and good will among people of diverse religions in the region. In 2018–19, members of the network participated in interbelief dialogue cafés with local primary school children and staff in Limerick city. The members of the MWIN are just ordinary people from different faiths who come together in the spirit of openness and friendship with the aim of 'living our tomorrows together'. All of these organic, sporadic and tentative initiatives represent baby steps. Yet where there is a simple gathering characterised by openness and friendship, there is also great hope.

CHAPTER SEVEN

Catholic Perspectives on Interreligious Dialogue

Bishop Brendan Leahy

On 27 October 1986, I attended the first major gathering of the world's religious leaders for a day of prayer for peace. Pope John Paul had invited them to the Italian town of Assisi so much associated with St Francis the peacemaker. Prayer was needed as world peace was fragile. The event was an amazing occasion that left a deep impression on me. Many have commented that the Assisi gathering was like an icon of the Church as envisaged by the Second Vatican Council – a Church of dialogue, relationship and communion. The varied religious garbs and colours, rituals and prayer formulas, added to the wonderful atmosphere of hope that invaded us all in the beautiful Franciscan town.

The day was unusually cold and dark for October but just as the day's proceedings were drawing to a close, after the final release of doves of peace, the sun broke through and flooded the square in front of the Basilica where we were gathered. We had all assembled in that square after prayer rituals at the various points of the town. We had respectfully listened as each one prayed, spoke or read a meditation.[1] Gradually we had become one in hope. The sun coming out was like a sign from God: this is my beloved family in whom I am well pleased!

Assisi 1986 was a great event; however, the Catholic Church has a longer history of contact with religions than we might normally realise. It is enough to think of St Justin (c.100–165 CE) in the second century reflecting on how Christianity fitted into the bigger picture of the Roman world with its gods and philosophy. We know that in 1219 Francis of Assisi visited the Sultan al-Malik al-Kamil in Egypt. We can think of the Jesuits in China in the sixteenth century, attempting new ways of dialogue with the Chinese culture and beliefs.

Yes, we can point to many positive attempts at outreach to members of other religions. I cannot hide, however, that, unfortunately, we can also point to negative experiences of attempted repression of world religions. That is what made the Catholic Church's 1965 milestone document on the Church's relationship with other religions, *Nostra Aetate*, so remarkable. This first official statement on the topic in the Church's history affirmed that the Church's very identity is to be a Church in relationship with other religions – Jewish, Muslim, Buddhist, animist, etc. This Second Vatican Council document stated that the Catholic Church rejects nothing of what is true and holy in the world's religions and so wants to enter into discussion and collaboration with members of other religions.

From that year on, the Catholic Church worldwide entered a new phase of openness toward and contact with members, leaders and groups of the world's religions. Today the Catholic Church has a pontifical council in Rome dedicated to interreligious dialogue defined as 'all positive and constructive interreligious relations with individuals and communities of other faiths which are directed at mutual understanding and enrichment in obedience to truth and respect for freedom'.[2]

Today, more than ever, interreligious dialogue is a necessary condition for peace in the world. It is a duty for Christians as well as other religious communities. The Church is involved in many interreligious initiatives. Movements within the Church, such as the Focolare Movement and the Community of Sant'Egidio are actively engaged in interreligious dialogue.[3] The relationship with the followers of Islam has taken on great importance in recent times.[4]

What is the Basis of Dialogue?

No one enters dialogue as a neutral observer; likewise, when the Catholic Church entered into dialogue with the world's religions, it did so from a particular perspective. It has a philosophical and theological framework that guides its engagement. Catholics respect all religions but do not say they are all simply parallel pathways to God. While recognising the equal dignity of each individual person, Catholics value the distinctiveness of each religion and come to interreligious dialogue from a distinctive world view born from faith in Jesus Christ and his church.

What is this world view? Firstly, the belief that Jesus Christ is the light of the nations and that it is the Risen Jesus Christ who brings ahead the project of uniting our world in peace and friendship. He does so in and through the Church. Yet the Church is not to be reduced simply to its membership listed on the baptismal records. The Church embraces all of humanity for the simple reason that the founder of the Church, Jesus Christ, died for all. In recent times, the Church has understood more clearly its call to be an instrument of unity in the world – contributing to bringing about unity with God and the unity of the human race.[5]

In one of the most important affirmations at the Second Vatican Council, we are reminded that since Jesus laid down his life for everyone, no one is a stranger to the Church: 'For, since Christ died for all, and since the ultimate vocation of humanity is in fact one, and divine, we ought to believe that the Holy Spirit in a manner known only to God offers to everyone the possibility of being associated with the paschal mystery.'[6] In other words, God has one plan for our world that embraces the whole of humanity. Our heavenly Father sends his spirit that Jesus breathed forth on the cross to reach everyone, speak to them in their conscience, and prompt them to do good and to love others as themselves.

One of the notions that has taken hold in recent decades is the idea of the 'seeds of the Word' or 'seeds of Truth' that St Justin had already spoken about in the second century. In creating the world, God has scattered seeds of the Truth all over the world. The Church appreciates these seeds wherever they are to be found. In respectful dialogue, we learn from one another and grow in the Truth that embraces us. After all, Christians believe Truth is not about abstract ideas. Truth is a person, Jesus Christ, the son of God in whom we all exist, and move and have our being (Acts 17:28). Catholics value the aspects of Truth in many of the writings, rituals and codes of morality of other religions. Sometimes this is interpreted as meaning we should adopt a neutral pluralist position claiming the equality of all religions. Yet, as theologians such as Gavin D'Costa have pointed out, this is far from neutral.[7] Saying all religions are the same is a viewpoint based on Western liberal modernity that risks flattening out the distinctiveness of each of the world's religions.

There is a contrast between what some call epistemological and ideological pluralism. Epistemological pluralism is the recognition of the right to existence of contradictory truth claims; for example, Christianity, Islam, atheism. Ideological pluralism is the insistence that the only truth is pluralism and denies all religions their truth claims. The aim of interreligious dialogue is not to abandon one's own inherited faith and practices but to rediscover them in a deeper way through encounter with the other. This is the opposite of relativism.

Catholics believe that Jesus Christ explained himself to us as 'the way, the truth and the life' (Jn 14:6). In him, we have access to God our father in the power of the Spirit. In believing this, we also know that the risen Jesus Christ is present to all people in all situations and at all times prompting them, through the Spirit, to live the golden rule: 'Do unto others as you would have them do unto you' (Lk 6:31). Indeed, versions of this golden rule are found in all the world's religions.

Pope Francis and Interreligious Dialogue
In a summary of the Catholic Church's view of other religions Pope Francis has written:

> *Non-Christians, by God's gracious initiative, when they are faithful to their own consciences, can live 'justified by the grace of God', and thus be 'associated to the paschal mystery of Jesus Christ'. But due to the sacramental dimension of sanctifying grace, God's working in them tends to produce signs and rites, sacred expressions which in turn bring others to a communitarian experience of journeying towards God. While these lack the meaning and efficacy of the sacraments instituted by Christ, they can be channels which the Holy Spirit raises up in order to liberate non-Christians from atheistic immanentism or from purely individual religious experiences. The same Spirit everywhere brings forth various forms of practical wisdom which help people to bear suffering and to live in greater peace and harmony. As Christians, we can also benefit from these treasures built up over many centuries, which can help us better to live our own beliefs.*[8]

Four Types of Dialogue
Over the past fifty years the Catholic Church has gained much experience in the way of dialogue with world religions. It has published significant documents on the Church's understanding of its ways of dialogue. Among these are the Vatican documents: *Dialogue and Mission* (1984); *Dialogue and Proclamation* (1991); *Educating to Intercultural Dialogue in Catholic Schools Living in Harmony for a Civilisation of Love* (2013).

We can distinguish four different kinds of dialogue that Catholics engage in with members and official bodies of other religions.

Firstly, there's *the dialogue of life*. This is the everyday living contact between believers of different religions. It happens in the workplace, the school, the neighbourhood. It is made up of everyday simple experiences. I knew once of a mechanic whose name was Ulysses living in Algeria. He was a Christian, a member of the Focolare Movement there. Many came into contact with him through his work as a mechanic. They were struck simply by the attention he gave to them. He didn't distinguish between them, whether they were Muslims, rich or poor. He befriended them and they him. Gradually his Muslim friends were attracted by his way of living and in contact with him they rediscovered true values in their own religion. A dialogue of life had begun. When he died, they all felt his loss but from that a community emerged that still continues to unite Christians and Muslims in Algeria today. In the dialogue of life, we learn to accept others and their different ways of living, thinking and speaking.

Secondly, there is *the dialogue of cooperation or action*. This is when members of different religions come together to work on specific local or global projects. It happens when we cooperate on issues of social justice, peace, family, life, the environment, etc. We can think of Trócaire's works in some countries in response to natural disasters. The Religions for Peace (formerly, the World Conference of Religions for Peace) promotes such projects.[9] Through our work together on a specific task the process itself becomes an occasion of mutual listening, with all involved being purified and enriched.

Thirdly, there's *the dialogue of religious experience*. Here we can think of the Assisi meeting I mentioned above. Yet this dialogue of religious experience can take the form of international gatherings on specific themes, such as love and mercy in the Bible and the Quran. Each party offers his or her religious experience. I was involved in such a dialogue on a number of occasions through the Three Faiths Forum of Ireland when we explored together themes such as pilgrimage, revelation, peace, war by sharing the religious experience of our traditions.[10] This dialogue of religious experience can, of course, also take place in the classroom.

Fourthly, there's *the academic dialogue*. This is among experts who attend symposia or engage in academic projects of research. Papers and studies are produced on topics of academic interest and research.

God's Dialogue with Us

All dialogue requires certain attitudes and approaches to one another; likewise, in interreligious dialogue. Catholics propose we learn about dialogue first and foremost from observing the dialogue God opened up with humanity in the history of Israel culminating in Jesus Christ. From looking at how God dealt with us, we see how we can put dialogue into practice. A central theme throughout the whole Old Testament is that God loved us first. We too have to take the initiative. Dialogue needs to be proactive. God's way of dealing with us was characterised by love and mercy; likewise, dialogue with members of other religions always begins with charity. It is a love that allows freedom and is not forced. The story told in the Bible indicates how God was like a good teacher. He led us step by step in a gradual way to understanding his ways and his message. Dialogue, too, will involve a gradual development. It will go through various stages. God knew how to adopt his mystery to our human words, deeds and images. Similarly, in dialogue, we need to be able to adapt ourselves to those to whom we are talking. This means we must be clear in what we say, courteous, showing esteem, showing understanding and goodness towards others. It excludes *a priori* condemnation, as well as offensive and time-worn polemics.

God is truthful. In dialogue, we have to be truthful, bringing who we are and what we believe into the dialogue. To hide or deny the beliefs we hold in a diplomatic openness that says yes to everything in order to avoid problems would not be an exercise of genuine dialogue. In a spirit of respectful proclamation, we need to offer our perspectives and beliefs as a gift. As Pope Francis puts it, 'True openness involves remaining steadfast in one's deepest convictions, clear and joyful in one's own identity, while at the same time being open to understanding those of the other party' and knowing that dialogue can enrich each side.'[11]

Educating Towards Dialogue

Education is a key mission in the life of the Catholic Church. There are some two hundred thousand Catholic schools in the world. In the Introduction to its document, *Educating to Intercultural Dialogue in Catholic Schools Living in Harmony for a Civilisation of Love,* the Catholic Church's Congregation for Catholic Education writes that:

> *Education contains a central challenge for the future: to allow various cultural expressions to coexist and to promote dialogue so as to foster a peaceful society. These aims are achieved in various stages: (1) discovering the multicultural nature of one's own situation; (2) overcoming prejudices by living and working in harmony; and (3) educating oneself 'by means of the other' to a global vision and a sense of citizenship. Fostering encounters between different people helps to create mutual understanding, although it ought not to mean a loss of one's own identity.*[12]

From what we have already noted it is clear that Catholic schools want to avoid both fundamentalism and ideas of relativism where everything is the same. On the basis of their identity and ethos as derived from the Gospel, Catholic schools are invited to follow the pathways that lead to encountering others. In the conclusion to the *Educating to Intercultural Dialogue* document, we read about Catholic schools and their staff and students that:

They educate themselves, and they educate to dialogue, which consists in speaking with everyone and relating to everyone with respect, esteem and listening in sincerity. They should express themselves with authenticity, without obfuscating or watering down their own vision so as to acquire greater consensus. They should bear witness by means of their own presence, as well as by the coherence between what they say and what they do.[13]

Since interreligious dialogue is an essential part of our Catholic identity today it is an important element of Catholic schools, both primary and post-primary. The Catholic Church in Ireland has recently introduced a new *Catholic Preschool and Primary Religious Education Curriculum* that is particularly sensitive to interreligious and intercultural perspectives.[14]

In the introduction to the new curriculum we read, 'Interreligious education at primary level, while affirming a student's Catholic identity, will prepare young children for living alongside other Christians and people of diverse religious traditions.'[15] Catholic schools are reminded that Christians are called to 'acknowledge, preserve and promote the spiritual and moral goods found among people of other faiths'. Teaching about different religions and beliefs should be 'carried out in a fair and balanced manner in Catholic schools'. The new primary religious education programme, *Grow in Love*, strives to meet the aims, principles and outcomes of the new Catholic curriculum.

The task of interreligious education, while fascinating, is also demanding. Teaching about other religions has to be child/student-friendly and not simply an adult-size information exercise. Context is very important. As I have endeavoured to show in this chapter, Catholic schools work on the basis of an understanding of the universal significance of Jesus Christ and his church that flows into an attitude of openness in truth and in love towards the followers of non-Christian religions.

CHAPTER EIGHT

Interbelief Dialogue and the Church of Ireland

Keith Scott

No individual or community comes to any kind of conversation as a blank sheet. All human beings, whether as members of a community or as individuals, are shaped by culture, history and choices. That is as true of the Church of Ireland as of any other community. The Church of Ireland is part of the worldwide Anglican communion which defines itself as a 'fellowship, within the one holy catholic and apostolic church, of those duly constituted dioceses, provinces or regional churches in communion with the see of Canterbury'.[1]

Its basic principles of unity, known as the Chicago–Lambeth Quadrilateral,[2] uphold the Hebrew and Christian Scriptures as its source of belief and the 'Catholic Creeds' as sufficient expressions of that faith. All that this means is that it belongs to the broad Christian tradition. When the Church of Ireland comes to interbelief dialogue it, therefore, does so as a Christian community shaped by that broad tradition, shaped by whatever it means to be 'Anglican' and shaped by its own history and part in the story of Ireland. The only legitimate way to describe the Church's understanding and practise of dialogue (if any) is from a Christian perspective. In this chapter I will discuss the Church of Ireland's efforts to enter into dialogue with others of differing beliefs and world views, using language and understandings of dialogue appropriate to a Christian community. To do otherwise would not give an authentic insight into the dialogical life of the Church, nor offer a valid critique, if appropriate, of the Church's thinking and practice. I shall begin by setting out a Christian basis for dialogue.

Chicago–Lambeth Quadrilateral

The Anglican communion is an extremely disparate community of churches embracing some eighty-five million members belonging to thirty-eight autonomous national or regional churches and six extra-provincial churches and dioceses as diverse as the Mar Thoma Syrian Church of India and the Church of Ireland.[3] Inevitably, the Chicago–Lambeth Quadrilateral, which expresses the basis of the unity of communion, is carefully and deliberately 'loose'. As a basis for 'intra-faith' negotiation, that looseness has served the Anglican Church well. It has allowed the communion to embrace its startling range of autonomous churches without compromising either their autonomy or diversity.[4] It is, however, rooted in an expressed desire for cooperation on the basis 'of a common faith and order'.[5] While negotiation between Christians in order to achieve or maintain unity is highly desirable, it is not quite 'interbelief dialogue'. The whole point of interbelief dialogue is that those engaged may well have radically different beliefs, and little, or nothing at all, in common. It is difficult to imagine, for example, what could possibly constitute a 'common faith and order' between Atheist Ireland and the Church of Ireland. Yet this cannot preclude dialogue between them. In order to examine the Church of Ireland's practice of interbelief dialogue we are, therefore, going to have to reach some understanding of what interbelief dialogue might be for Irish Anglicans.

The Nature of Dialogue

David Lochhead argues that dialogue is made possible by 'otherness' rather than by having 'something in common'; thus, if dialogue is to occur, those involved are of necessity different from one another, even in ways which are mutually exclusive. Dialogue's initial goal is understanding and being understood, thereby gaining new and deeper perspectives both about one's own tradition and that of the other. The ultimate goal of dialogue is 'integration', through which one enters into the world of the other, and sees one's own world through their eyes, integrates their perceptions and understanding into one's own so that what was once alien becomes familiar. It is not a way of sharing the truths that the participants may feel they have, rather it is a way of exploring truth together. It is, thus, more properly a 'dialogical relationship' that has no end other than itself.[6]

Lochhead's understanding of dialogue is grounded in the Christian understanding of God as 'incarnate' in Christ. Orthodox Christianity thinks in terms of 'two natures in one person' without either confusion or separation. In Jesus, God encounters humanity 'from the inside' and yet remains unmistakably and entirely God without dilution. Equally the humanity of Jesus is entirely open to the divine yet remains human without dilution.

God and humanity are free to address and to be addressed, to respond in openness and love. At every moment, Jesus is the dialogue. His life and work are continual expressions of the perennial dialogue between God and the world.[7]

Lochhead explicitly rejected any *a priori* assumptions about the other with whom one enters into a dialogical relationship.[8] It, therefore, simply does not matter at the outset where the difference lies or whether 'I' think of 'you' as a worthy partner for dialogue. I simply accept that there is a 'you' who differs from 'me' and seek on the basis of the difference to enter into a dialogical relationship with 'you'. Interbelief dialogue is therefore any dialogue between those whose beliefs about the world, about the nature of ultimate reality or about the community in which those beliefs are expressed, differ.

The question of interbelief relations forced itself onto the agenda of British Christianity in the period after World War II. New migrants began to arrive in significant numbers in the industrial cities, drawn by the opportunities of an expanding economy,[9] or fleeing conflicts 'back home'. This, coupled with rising secularisation amongst the indigenous population, led to dramatic changes in the cultural composition of much of Britain. The Anglican Church, especially in the inner cities of the industrial midlands and north, was obliged to develop a response, and bishops began to appoint suitably qualified advisers, often people with overseas experience, in order to come to some sort of understanding of these new populations and their strange cultural and religious traditions.

To a very large extent, however, Ireland remained 'behind the curve' until very recently in terms of its encounter with those of non-Christian faiths. Conflict in Northern Ireland and less attractive economic circumstances in both parts of the island meant that numbers of migrants arriving in Ireland were relatively small until the early part of the twenty-first century. In as far as the Church of Ireland engaged in interbelief dialogue, it was largely confined to inter-church dialogue. This is hardly surprising; indeed, inter-church dialogue is highly desirable. Religious identity has played a crucial role in the conflicts that shaped the history of Ireland, and still plays a role in the ongoing tensions in Northern Ireland and remains a feature, albeit at a good deal less 'fraught' level, throughout Ireland. Inter-church dialogue has been and will continue to be a significant factor in attaining even a modicum of healing and reconciliation in Irish society.

Even in what might be considered the more urgent matter of building reconciliation in Ireland, however, Irish Anglicans have had a somewhat mixed record. Sectarianism is a deep and difficult trap to escape. The Church of Ireland is caught between its call to live as a sacramental sign of the New Creation in Christ and to maintain a unique identity within a strong vibrant community. Even the best-intentioned efforts can lead the Church of Ireland deeper into the trap rather than out.

Porvoo Communion

The Church of Ireland has achieved progress in inter-church relations. It has played a significant role in developing the Porvoo Communion, a full eucharistic fellowship of the Anglicans and Lutherans in Northern Europe.[10] An equally significant relationship has been developed between the Church of Ireland and the Methodist Church in Ireland. This was initiated with the covenant between the Church of Ireland and Methodist Church established in 2002 and significantly progressed when the bill providing for the full recognition and interchange of ministry between the two churches was passed by general synod in 2014.[11] The churches of the Porvoo Communion all share a 'common faith and order'; Methodism sprang from the roots of Anglicanism and again shares much with the Anglican Church, particularly the more evangelical wing. However desirable and groundbreaking they may be, these relationships are still primarily at the level of 'negotiations' towards specific ends on the basis of 'common ground'.

The Hard Gospel Project

The most radical initiative with a potential for genuine dialogue was the Hard Gospel Project. The project was initiated by a scoping study, the report of which was presented to the General Synod of the Church of Ireland at its annual meeting in 2003.[12] This challenged the synod to change its thinking in terms of maintaining the structures of the Church and instead 'incarnate the Kingdom of God and contribute to the transformation of this society'.[13] It expressed a series of hopes which gave expression to the idea that the whole project would become transformative. The Church would adopt a more dynamic, relational, and missionary world view in which it could 'deal positively with difference', both its own internal divisions as a community wracked by a gulf between northern and southern provinces, and externally with those other communities with whom it had so long been locked in hostile and rivalrous relationships.

The Hard Gospel Project subsequently addressed a series of interlinked questions:

1. 'How should we as a Christian church regard ourselves and our role in a multifaith and multicultural twenty-first century Ireland (north and south)?
2. How should we as individuals in the context of twenty-first century Ireland (north and south) regard ourselves and our responsibilities as:
   a. Individual Christians
   b. Members of the Church of Ireland
   c. Citizens of a wider community and society – living with our diverse neighbours?

The project set itself to examine how central structures should change to become more representative, how those structures may be enhanced and what new structures to promote dialogue across the internal differences within the Church of Ireland might be needed, and to identify and promote change in those areas where sectarianism and destructive patterns of relationship across differences were affecting the witness of the Church of Ireland. This last was to involve dialogue with, among others, loyal orders, ethnic minorities, women's groups, disability organisations and gender and sexuality groups.[14]

Although the Hard Gospel Project initially addressed sectarianism as one of the most fraught and pressing issues facing the Church, it required no great imaginative leap to apply the same basic approach to interfaith dialogue.[15] The Commission for Christian Unity and Dialogue had already had its remit widened in 1995 to include interfaith dialogue and the Interfaith Working Group was set up as a subgroup of the commission. It has supported a number of activities designed to promote learning about and engaging in interfaith dialogue. Each diocese was encouraged to appoint interfaith officers to engage in and promote this work and those interested were given a variety of opportunities for learning. The working group also issued guidelines for interfaith dialogue, in which there is much that is positive. Whether they properly embody the sort of dialogical relationship Lochhead envisages is open to question, yet they at least put the idea of interfaith dialogue into the Church's 'public domain'.[16]

In 2006 the Hard Gospel's *Life Beyond Boundaries* was published with an introduction by the then archbishop of Armagh, the Most Rev. Robert Eames. In the introduction the Archbishop wrote, 'But it [The Hard Gospel] calls for action, change and serious readjustment.'[17] Taking this up in 2010, Archbishop of Dublin, the Most Rev. Michael Jackson saw interfaith dialogue as an outworking of the 'Hard Gospel philosophy' and he wished to extend Archbishop Eames' thought that 'the Gospel is a hard gospel when we take it seriously. Yet the path to Calvary was not easy.' It leads beyond Calvary to Easter and Pentecost so that 'interfaith encounter and dialogue are a form of witnessing to one's own faith in the context of another person's presence as witness to his/her own faith'.

The Hard Gospel Project, the philosophy and aspiration behind it, had, therefore, opened the Church up to the idea of interbelief dialogue, as a relationship which takes seriously the otherness of the other and seeks at least to attend to the witness of the other to his or her belief. It did so by pointing the Church to a more open and missional concept of 'church'. The Church of Ireland has always been somewhat more 'Calvinist' and sectarian in its thinking than its sister churches in the Anglican communion.[18] Irish Anglicanism developed an ideology of the Anglican Protestant people as 'the Christian Nation', whose experience was often interpreted in terms of the history of the people of Israel.[19] This ideology of 'the chosen people' was expressed clearly in the sermons preached at Christ Church Cathedral and St Andrew's Church in Dublin through the period 1685–1770 on the occasion of the state 'holy day' of 23 October commemorating the deliverance of the Protestant state from the 1641 rebellion.[20] In one sermon, Nathanael Foy, bishop of Waterford, argued for 'the exact Harmony, or Agreement betwixt the Religion of the Heathens, and that of the Romish Church at this day'. The best which could be said of non-Christian traditions was that Rome was more oppressive and crueller than they.[21]

Turning Outwards
While mainstream Irish Anglicanism has long since left the more gross aspects of this ideology behind, there is nevertheless a persistent tendency to turn inward. It does not help that, like the rest of the worldwide Anglican communion, the Church of Ireland struggles with its own internal divisions focused on the current 'hot potato' issue of sexuality as well as persistent cultural differences between northern and southern provinces. The tendency to turn inward has, however, left the Church of Ireland's initiatives across the range of interbelief relationships weakened. The Hard Gospel Project was assessed by an independent assessor, Tony Macaulay.[22] The assessment was largely positive with a recognition that it was 'the most substantial denominational church initiative of its kind to have taken place in Ireland'. Its projects were well designed, with some being at the 'cutting edge' of contemporary diversity and

inclusion issues in Ireland over the previous three years.[23] The evaluation, however, expresses considerable concern over the 'mainstreaming' of the project, the embedding of its values and process within the Church long-term, which requires the turn 'outward' necessary for the Church of Ireland to fully engage in interbelief dialogue. The overall success of the project, the report argues, can be measured in the extent to which this happens, particularly as it affects the structures of the Church.[24] The assessor recognised that progress in this area had been slow and there are few current indications that this has changed. The Hard Gospel project has ended, its materials archived, with little sign that it has been taken in to the mainstream of Irish Anglican life. What might be more strictly defined as interfaith dialogue has also failed to become mainstream, or even widespread. The Interfaith Working Group seems to have come to a halt, having made no initiatives since October 2013.[25] What engagement there has been since then is due to the initiative of individuals and, as a consequence, is rather scattered.

It seems, therefore, that the Church of Ireland's concept of interbelief dialogue has grown in recent years. The Hard Gospel Project has been a significant effort at self-critical reflection on sectarianism, and the Church of Ireland has been one of the few churches to achieve this. Interfaith dialogue has also come into the public arena of the Church. In their practising of dialogue, however, the Church of Ireland suffers from the same problem that afflicts many Christian churches: that 'dialogue' is a concept to which we 'tip our hat'[26] but in practice it is marginal to the core purpose of the Church. Yet dialogue is part of the *raison d'être* of the Church, a form of 'witnessing to one's own faith' rooted in the incarnation. Modern Christian reflection on 'mission' tends to think in terms of the 'mission of God' the self-revelation of God in the Incarnation. The Church is called into this mission to be both sign and sacrament of God in Jesus Christ.[27] Dialogue is, therefore, an inextricably 'missionary' part of the self-understanding of the Church. It remains a challenge and call to the Anglican Church to engage in dialogical relationships with all those from whom it differs and so be true to its own self and to the God which it claims has called and sent it into the world.

CHAPTER NINE

A Perspective on Dialogue from a Member of the Methodist Faith

Siobhán Wheeler

> 'Provided that no one asks of me, I know; if I wish to explain it [...], I do not know.'
>
> **St Augustine**[1]

The problem Augustine encountered when attempting to define 'time' is one I recognise. I encounter the same difficulty as I attempt to determine exactly what it is that I mean by 'faith', so that I can describe what it is I live by. In matters of faith, as in everything else, we each have our individual subjective perspective and interpretation, even of that which we hold as common belief. Each believer's relationship with God is individual and personal, even while God remains God, much as all of our relationships with each other are separate and distinct. Our limited human vantage point renders us capable of seeing only certain aspects of the other and is susceptible to misinterpretation. Although a member of the Methodist Church, I speak only of my own perspective in these reflections.

Relationship with God

For me, faith is far more than a set of beliefs, a doctrine or creed; more even, than membership or identification with a particular religion or denomination. Belief is part of faith – the theoretical, intellectual part – but faith requires more than cerebral, intellectual assent. Faith is also heart-held, involving emotions as well as understanding, desire and inclination. Faith, then, is an all-encompassing wholeness of being. Faith is the defining influence on my life and how it is lived, not merely because it is logical or rational, but because it is irresistible, desirable and fulfilling in a holistic sense. Knowing God who is revealed in Jesus, and trusting him, has been the bedrock of my life, subconsciously, intuitively, informing my world view – my very being. God is the atmosphere in which I draw each breath and exhale again. This is the atmosphere that informs not just my conscience but my desires. Saint Paul in Athens reminds us that God 'is not far from each one of us. For in him we live and move and have our being' (Acts 17:27–8). This understanding of faith is based not so much on opinions and analysis as on relationship; it recognises the steadfast love and kindness of God, trusting confidently in God as loving; secure in the knowledge that I am pleasing to God; certain of his love even where my own for God, self and others is imperfectly limited and assured of God's continued love, even when I disappoint both myself and him. (As a mother, having children has helped enormously with this awareness.) This understanding of faith is based on God's transformational love that overwhelms and overflows.

Faith is not stagnant. It lives through relationship; grows, develops and matures. From my earliest moments, I have been blessed with 'a wise community of the heart'.[2] The city of Limerick, its streets and environs, were the backdrop to my childhood. Its people nurtured me in their warm embrace. Growing up in the Catholic Church, my 'official language' was that of its doctrines, but I was aware that the vernacular had many dialects; aware too of another 'language' spoken by a minority among us, that of Protestant doctrine and acutely aware of my own 'mother tongue' – a 'creole' resulting from the interactions of speakers from all of these traditions. God made me 'multilingual'. I eventually saw this as a gift. Slowly, I realised that while each 'language' is capable of expressing the deepest desires and realities of the human heart and its relationships with God and the world, particularly in the confines of its restricted traditions, multilingualism, broadening the mind's creative capacity and appreciation of the diversity of being as well as expression, permits the articulation of something new for which we have no words in our first language. So, I am both genetically and congenitally committed to ecumenism. As Bosch notes, 'The mission of the church cannot succeed without the unity of the church in the truth of the gospel.'[3] I relish those opportunities to share the taste of God and savour him in communion with one another across denominations. I am excited to sense a growing closeness and acceptance of one another among the institutional churches in Ireland and locally in Limerick. My experience has taught me that none of us has a monopoly on truth or fully knows God. Like the missionary Vincent Donovan in Africa, I can say, 'No, *we have not* found the High God ... For us, too, he is the unknown God. But we are searching for him ... Let us search for him together. Maybe, together, we will find him.'[4]

Recently, I was reminded of one of the strands in my DNA. My mother gave me a Bible – her grandfather's. He had been a Methodist local preacher. A series of circumstances led me to follow in his footsteps, beginning when worshipping as a family, in community, meant doing so in a Presbyterian setting. Mine is a 'mixed marriage', as was my grandparents' before me. To the amusement of my children, still in the Ireland of the 1980s, the term 'mixed marriage' did not refer to mixed gender or mixed ethnicity, but to intermarriage between members of different Christian denominations, specifically Catholics and Protestants. Our local church was United Presbyterian and Methodist. So, for twenty-five years I have been a member of the Methodist Church in Ireland. I am grateful for that context in which to worship God. My membership was and is a conscious choice made and renewed for a variety of reasons, but it was also only a choice to accept what God had offered me as a possibility.

John and Charles Wesley

I discovered I concurred with much about the early Methodist movement of the eighteenth century, begun by John and Charles Wesley, in which the Methodist Church of today has its origins. There is much about John Wesley's thinking and particular emphases that seems to me to be not only still valid, but still vital in today's world and worship context.

The essential doctrines of Methodism are the essentials of Christianity, and the Methodist Church forms part of the Holy Catholic Church – the Church, the Body of Christ. The Methodist movement acquired its name from the members' exceptional emphasis on detailed Bible study and devoted lifestyle. Mr Wesley himself said:

> The distinguishing marks of a Methodist are not his opinions of any sort. His assenting to this or that scheme of religion, his embracing any particular set of notions, his espousing the judgement of one man or another, are all wide of the point ... Dost thou love and serve God? It is enough. I give thee the right hand of fellowship.[5]

John and Charles Wesley knew with assurance that God is love and saw the goal of Methodism as perfect loving. They knew that God changes our hearts and, having done so, our lives, which can never be the same again. They knew that God wants to engage our whole selves, heart, mind, soul and strength. John Wesley described, in his journal, the experience of feeling his 'heart strangely warmed' by the gracious, forgiving love of God one May evening in 1738. 'God came into the centre of Wesley's life and changed a rather rigid, self-disciplined, yet always sincere person into a leader on fire for God.'[6] God so completely overwhelmed him that, 'Wesley's one consuming passion became to share with others the healing, compelling love of God in which he himself had found peace.'[7] He believed in a practical Christianity, making God visible in the world through our love; and he spoke of 'offering Christ', understanding instinctively through his personal experience that Christianity is more 'caught than taught'. He spoke of a 'steady view – a single intention of promoting [God's] glory ... [that] runs through our whole soul, fills all our heart, and is the constant spring of all our thoughts, desires and purposes.'[8] Knowing that we reflect Christ to one another, he insisted Methodists strive to be 'friends of all, and enemies of none'.[9]

Wesley was far more concerned about our walk with God than with 'orthodoxy of opinion', which he said was only:

> at very best the slender part of religion, if it can be allowed to be any part at all. Only your heart be right toward God, and that you know and love the Lord Jesus Christ; that you love your neighbour and walk as your master walked; and I desire no more ...Give me solid and substantial religion; give me an humble gentle love of God and man, a man full of mercy and good fruits.[10]

Wesley urges us to be 'social, open active Christians' who do not 'conceal this light, wherewith God has enlightened your soul [but] let it shine still more eminently in your actions, in your doing all possible good to all men; and in your suffering for righteousness sake.'[11] For the Wesley brothers, faith was both personal and social, and indeed it could never be one without being the other. Both aspects were inextricably bound and intertwined as reflected in St Paul's letter to the Galatians, which says, 'The only thing that counts is faith working through love' (Gal 5:6). In one of the six thousand hymns he composed, Charles voiced this conviction, 'Plead we thus for faith alone/Faith which by our works is shown ... Saved by faith which works by love.'[12]

Head, Hands, Heart

Methodism as a movement began at the fringes or margins of society. Its 'first impact was as a blend of religious conviction and social activism.'[13] Both Wesley brothers placed huge emphasis on justice, mercy and truth as integral to love and hence to the mission of a movement seeking the wholeness of church and society. Wesleyan mission embodied Christ for those marginalised by society, through social and sometimes political engagement, ministering to the disadvantaged, to the sick and to prisoners, accompanying the suffering and lonely and aligning with campaigns such as that of Wilberforce against slavery. The Wesley brothers saw church first of all as a community of disciples, a family, gathering in communities of love which spread and multiply. For them, church was living proof of the Gospel where ordinary people in their ordinary lives are transformed by the love of God and each other. They believed that 'in general, the Kingdom of God ... will silently increase, wherever it is set up, and spread from heart to heart, from house to house, from town to town.'[14] This understanding of familial co-dependency and belonging is still reflected today in the organisational structure of the Methodist Church which is seen as a 'connexion'. Though the eighteenth-century English requires some interpretation today, for me Wesley's words are still an irresistible invitation:

> If you walk by this rule, continually endeavouring to know, and love, and resemble, and obey the great God and Father of our Lord Jesus Christ, as the God of love, of pardoning mercy; if from this principle of loving, obedient faith, you carefully [endeavour to] abstain from all evil, and labour, as you have opportunity, to do good to all men, friends and enemies; if lastly, you unite together to encourage and help each other in thus working out your salvation, and for that end watch over one another in love – you are they whom I mean by Methodists.[15]

Annually, publicly, with 'the people called Methodists', I intentionally renew my covenant with God, who steadfastly holds to his with me. Christianity is a relationship. It is living life in connection with God, in a reciprocal, albeit uneven, relationship of love with God who first loves us. This relationship is always contemporary, lived in 'the here and now' and in the particular circumstances in which we find ourselves. Our intimate relationship with God is not exclusive, competitive or inward-looking but honest, open, inclusive, inviting and embracing. Although individual, it is always a communal relationship and church is 'always a community that has its doors open to any type of person who wants to come in'.[16]

Life is a seamless garment which cannot usefully be torn apart nor split into discrete segments. Life is a whole and God is in it all. Secular and sacred emanate from, and are bound by, his love. There is an interconnectedness of all things which not only intersect and overlap, but are fully united. 'All knowledge forms one whole, because its subject matter is one; for the universe in its length and breadth is so intimately knit together that we cannot separate off portion from portion, and operation from operation, except by mental abstraction.'[17] No one but God possesses fullness of knowledge. Retaining a fundamental humility before truth, before God, respecting and celebrating diversity in willingness to learn is imperative – and Christ-like. Jesus could always conceive of the 'impossible': for instance, a 'good' Samaritan or a 'faithful' Syro-Phoenician woman, both of whom glimpsed the essential truth of God. This truth, though staring them in the face, so blinded the 'Sons of Abraham' that they did not see clearly until assisted in doing so by these outsiders. Christians certainly have no monopoly on Christ-like behaviour as the gentleness and kindness, for instance, shown by Dr Taufiq al-Sattar, who having lost his family in an arson attack forgave the perpetrators, testifies. God is neither limited by our imagination nor our rules. He calls us, secure in his Spirit (insecurity, or arrogant blind conviction, polarises, distorts and alienates), non-defensively, to relate, to communicate, to respect and to rejoice in growing love, truth and knowledge.

The Dialogue of Life

It is a wonderful privilege for me to share with one Catholic community weekly, in *Lectio Divina* in Moyross in Limerick. Together we try to discern all the ways that the word of Scripture is being fulfilled today in our lives, as we seek to live ever more truly. This gracious community is welcoming of diversity in its midst, and has voiced the desire to see ecumenical Bible study become widespread in the diocese. Bishop Leahy urges us 'to read the signs of the times in our world today ... in the light of the Gospel ... living the Gospel with new vitality.'[18] In every age, the Gospel 'is about the crossing of boundaries, about an intercultural and interpersonal penetration that connects and sustains'.[19] If we are to spread the good news that God loves his people, all his people, then I feel that has to be a message spoken less in a literal sense than metaphorically, in all the other ways we communicate; the universal good news message of God's unwavering loving kindness revealed in loving kindness itself. For 'if it comes to a choice, we are to exercise our love of neighbour as a matter of priority! We must be ready to leave our sanctuaries of private devotion and public worship "at love's almighty call".'[20] Pope Francis concurs, advising us to remember that 'the best way to talk is not by talking about and discussing, but in doing something together, to build together, to make plans: not alone among Catholics, but with all those who have good will'.[21] In Limerick city, one such voluntary venture, with which I am connected, provides Sunday lunch for the homeless, 'disadvantaged' and lonely in the city and beyond. These weekly Sunday lunches, freely given, are a whole-city collaboration mobilising previously unknown resources. The palpable atmosphere of mutual respect, loving fellowship, goodness and kindness challenges any exclusive notions of belief and lends contemporary relevance to the word incarnate. It seems to me that there is no more eloquent expression of interbelief dialogue, in line with gospel values, than in the expression of companionship of these volunteers and diners of all faiths and none, from a multiplicity of nationalities, eating together as extended family. A potentially Babel-like confusion of humanity, these meals reflect instead a tower of compassionate empathy and essential commonality. In such dialogue, the uniqueness, value and dignity of each and every human being is celebrated. Experiences such as these come as shocking revelation. Sara Miles recounts a moment when filled with a deep desire to reach for and become part of a body, in community, she reached for a piece of broken bread and realised that Communion cannot be tasted until everyone has tasted it and so 'felt compelled to find new ways to share'.[22]

Dialogue at the Heart of a Life of Faith

Recently our city's environment has been greatly enriched by immigration from Eastern Europe, Asia, the Middle East and perhaps especially the southern hemisphere in its raw, unpretentious, non-abstract, earthiness of expression. The Limerick of my childhood has now become a multi-ethnic, multi-belief, pluralist society. I am discovering another benefit of multilingualism. The senses, having been trained to see value in multiple languages, more readily engage with successive languages, and consider the vocabulary and intonation of these for what they can contribute to the existing richness of deposit. 'We can and must welcome a pluralist society because it provides us with a wider range of experience and a wider diversity of human responses to experience, and therefore richer opportunities for testing the sufficiency of our faith than are available in a monochrome society.'[23] My personal understanding has been enhanced by connections with immigrants of all faiths through the Direct Provision system. Through friendship, together we try to alleviate some of the soul-destroying deficiencies of the asylum process.

The purpose of dialogue for the Christian is obedient witness to Jesus Christ, who is not the property of the Church but the Lord of the Church and of all people, and who is glorified as the living Holy Spirit takes all that the Father has given to humankind – all people of every creed and culture – and declares it to the Church as that which belongs to Christ as Lord. In this encounter the Church is changed, the world is changed and Christ is glorified.[24]

Dialogue is not peripheral to my life of faith; it is critical to living a life of faith in any epoch, including in contemporary Ireland. As a Methodist, I close with a final thought from Mr Wesley, whose words of wisdom I wholeheartedly endorse.

The thing which I was greatly afraid of all this time and which I resolved to use every possible method of preventing, was a narrowness of spirit, a party zeal, that miserable bigotry which makes many so ready to believe that there is any work of God but among themselves.[25]

CHAPTER TEN

Atheists and Theists in Dialogue Jointly Promoting Mutual Respect and Ethical Secularism

Michael Nugent and Jane Donnelly

Atheist Ireland and the Alliance Between Three Groups

Atheist Ireland is an advocacy group for atheism, reason and ethical secularism. We meet regularly for fun social events, interesting talks, and lobbying for religious equality. We are all volunteers. We have no paid staff or state grants and we comply with Standards in Public Office political donation laws. Atheist Ireland is a member of Atheist Alliance International.

We strongly promote the idea that atheism and reason are more reliable approaches to understanding reality and morality than faith and religion.[1] However, we respect the right of others to believe differently, as long as the state does not assist any group to impose their beliefs on others who do not share them.

That is why we are proud to work in alliance with the Evangelical Alliance of Ireland and the Ahmadiyya Muslim Community of Ireland to promote a secular education system, where state-funded schools teach children about religions and beliefs in an objective, critical and pluralist manner, while respecting the human rights of pupils, parents and teachers.

We will outline in this chapter what we mean by promoting atheism, reason and ethical secularism, and the benefits of ethical secularism to society. We will then outline in some detail the importance of genuine pluralism in Irish schools, which we believe can only be attained by a national network of state-funded schools based on human rights, and not on the ethos of private patron bodies.

Promoting Atheism and Reason

Atheist Ireland believes that faith is an unreliable way of knowing what is true and an unethical basis by which to live your life. Faith leads people to many contradictory beliefs, with no way to know which, if any, of these beliefs are true or mistaken.

We believe that reason applied to evidence is a more reliable way of knowing what is most likely to be true. Scientists test ideas against the evidence to remove human bias and scientific answers can improve with new evidence. Many people misunderstand what atheism is. Atheism can mean anything from actively believing gods do not exist, to passively not believing gods exist. Most atheists believe gods exist only as ideas in minds. Most atheists are open to new evidence that we might be mistaken. Atheism is a natural answer to the big questions of life. Most atheists believe the universe is broadly as it seems to be when we apply reason and science to the evidence of our senses. We do not need to invent gods to explain what we know or what we do not yet know.

Six Facts about Atheism and Atheist Ireland

Listed below are six facts about atheism and Atheist Ireland, which dispel some common myths:

1. Atheism is not a belief system. Yet two important beliefs do follow from atheism: that reality is not caused or revealed

by gods; and that morality and judgements are not imposed by gods. These are two significant beliefs in a world where most people believe the opposite.

2. Atheism is not a religion. Religions typically have belief systems, creeds and regulations revealed by supernatural intervening beings. Atheism has no revealed creeds, and atheists form their own beliefs. Atheist groups exist only because some religions try to impose their beliefs and rules on all of us. We promote reason, not religion.

3. Atheism does not require faith. Faith is belief that is disproportionate to the best available evidence. Atheism is proportionate to the best available evidence. There is no reasonable evidence to suggest that supernatural gods exist and a lot of reasonable evidence to suggest that humans invented the idea to explain mysteries.

4. Atheists don't have to disprove gods. The onus of proof is on a person who is making a claim to justify that claim, not for others to disprove it. Most atheists simply have no good reason to believe that gods exist, in exactly the same way as many religious people have no good reason to believe that the gods worshipped by religions other than their own exist.

5. We don't need religion for morality. Morality is a natural process of our brains, based on empathy, compassion, reciprocity, cooperation, fairness and justice. Sacred books tell you to love your neighbour and kill them. Secular democracies typically have better social outcomes. Atheists and secularists are typically less racist, sexist and dogmatic.

6. We don't want to ban religion. Atheist Ireland supports the human right to freedom of religion and belief. We just want the state to stay neutral; for example, the state should not be funding schools that promote either religion or atheism.

Promoting Ethical Secularism

Atheist Ireland supports a secular constitution, parliament, government, education system and healthcare system. We want the state to respect equally the human rights of all citizens to freedom of thought, conscience, religion and belief, equality before the law and freedom from discrimination. We promote secular state schools that teach children freedom of thought, based on human rights, and without religious segregation or indoctrination. We promote secular state hospitals based on compassion, human rights and the medical needs of patients, and not on religious ethics.

We want to remove from the constitution religious oaths for the president, judges and taoiseach and other religious-influenced clauses. We want a parliament that does not start each day with a prayer asking the Christian God to direct every word of our parliamentarians.

Atheist Ireland helps atheists and minority faith families who have experienced discrimination in the Irish school system. We have achieved inclusive tendering for third level chaplaincies. We work to end religious discrimination in civil marriages, religious oaths for judges and taoiseach, reproductive rights and the Irish blasphemy law which has been cited as an example by some Islamic states to buttress their own agendas. We lobby national politicians and government, and international human rights bodies like the UN and OSCE. We promote atheism, reason and ethical secularism through the media, talks, conferences, online newsletters, information tables, lunches and secular charities. We also respond to topical issues as they arise.

As members of the government's dialogue process with religious and non-religious groups, we had the first ever meeting between a taoiseach and an atheist advocacy group. Our lobbying at the UN and other human rights bodies has achieved important recommendations for Ireland to separate Church and state. We run a highly successful campaign for secular schooling called *Teach Don't Preach* which includes teachdontpreach.ie, Ireland's best secular schools resource.[2] We promote our Schools Equality PACT, an acronym for patronage, access, curriculum and teaching. We have got the Oireachtas Education Committee to agree that multiple patronage and multiple ethos of schools can lead to segregation and inequality. We work with other ethical human rights groups, including Atheist Northern Ireland and Atheism UK. We dialogue and work with the Evangelical Alliance of Ireland and the Ahmadiyya Muslim Community of Ireland, as three groups with different world views who are united as victims of religious discrimination in the Irish education system.

Benefits of Ethical Secularism

Secularism is a force for good in three ways. Firstly, secularism protects everybody's freedom of conscience and religion and belief by staying neutral. Secularism is not the same as atheism. Religious states promote religion. Atheist states promote atheism. Secular states promote neither.

Secondly, secularism allows religious people to focus on preparing for whatever next world they believe in, based on applying faith to their beliefs about divine revelations and it allows the state to focus on governing this world, based on applying reason to the best available evidence. Thirdly, secularism can combine with human rights standards as a foundation stone on which we can build a liberal democracy. A liberal democracy in turn can combat other threats to human rights from such ideologies as fascism, totalitarianism, communism and the unregulated free market.

Secularism has many practical advantages. Research has shown that the happiest countries are secular liberal democracies, including Scandinavian countries and northern European states.[3] In general, secular countries have lower rates of homicide, juvenile and early adult mortality, STD infection rates, teen pregnancy and abortion. Studies published by social scientist Phil Zuckerman and others have shown that atheists and secularists are typically less nationalistic, less prejudiced, less racist, less dogmatic, less ethnocentric, less closed-minded and less authoritarian. Atheists are more politically tolerant and more supportive of gender equality, women's rights and gay rights.

Internationally rigorous research has suggested that there is a pathway connecting better health systems and education systems to secular rational values. The World Values Survey, conducted by a team of interdisciplinary social scientists, suggests that as individuals move from survival values to self-expression values, which is triggered by investments in health, education, communication technologies and democracy, societies then move from traditional religious values to secular rational values.

Why We Need a State Secular Education System

There is one fundamental question that informs all discussion about pluralism and patronage in education. Your answer to that question will determine what conclusions you come to, and what conclusions are unavailable to you. That fundamental question is this: Is your aim to bring about an education system that satisfies the desires of a majority of parents and children, or perhaps to satisfy the desires of those families who happen to share your personal religious beliefs? If your aim is to bring about an education system that respects equally the human rights of all parents and all children, without sacrificing the human rights of a minority in order to satisfy the desires of a majority, you will be led to a very different conclusion.

It is understandable that many parents, and representatives of particular religions, would have as their priority that the education system satisfies their own desires and the desires of those who think like them. However, the role of the state should be to counteract a self-centred approach to the common good, and to ensure that the education system respects equally the human rights of all parents and all children. In practice, the only way to ensure this is to have as a foundation a secular state education system that is neutral on the question of religion and non-religion, and then to allow further options on top of that foundation, but not instead of it. Religious schools or atheist schools should be an added extra, if they can be afforded, for parents who want to avail of them, but having them as the foundation of the system creates only the illusion of choice. Atheist Ireland argues that it is our society that should be pluralist, not the state. Indeed, the only way to protect the rights of everybody in a pluralist society is for the state to be secular. The state has a positive obligation to ensure fairness for everybody, and not to be a partisan player that focuses on the desires of the majority ahead of the rights of everyone. Furthermore, contrary to the belief of many people in Ireland, it is not a human right to have the state fund a religious education for every family in the country.

Secular Schools Respect All Rights Equally
A secular school is not the same thing as an atheist school. While a religious school teaches that a god exists, an atheist school would teach that no gods exist, and a secular school is neutral on the question of religion. Secular schools do not teach that gods exist or do not exist. Instead, secular schools teach children in a critical, objective and pluralistic way about the different beliefs that different people have about gods, and leaves it up to parents and churches to teach specific religious beliefs outside of school hours. There are good philosophical reasons for schools to remain neutral on the question of religion. It is good for society as a whole when children are educated together. We can see from the recent history of Northern Ireland how separate schooling contributed to the problems of children understanding and respecting each other across religious divides. Secular schools bring children together. They teach them subjects that have a basis in scientific fact,

like mathematics, languages, history and critical thinking. They teach children common ethical values such as fairness, tolerance, compassion, justice and civic cooperation. They teach them about different religious beliefs and help them to understand other beliefs and respect other people. Additionally, outside of school hours, the children's parents and churches can teach them more about their own specific beliefs about the nature of reality and personal morality. More significantly, in practical terms, a foundation of secular schools is the only way to ensure that everybody has their human rights respected with regard to education. The education policy of Atheist Ireland is based on the human right to be educated without being indoctrinated and to be free from proselytism. Significantly, we would be just as opposed to children being indoctrinated in atheism as we are to their indoctrination in religion.

This policy is based on international human rights law. By ratifying the European Convention on Human Rights and various UN conventions, the Irish State has already agreed to guarantee to respect the religious and philosophical convictions of all parents in the Irish education system, and not just those of a majority. It is also consistent with the OSCE's internationally agreed Toledo Guiding Principles on teaching about religions and beliefs based on human rights.

Only Secular Schools Can Deliver Equal Rights

In theory, it could be possible to respect everybody's rights by having different schools for parents and pupils of every religion, plus schools for parents and pupils of no religion, and to have enough of each of these schools built and operating in every part of the country to make it possible to vindicate all parents' rights. However, in reality, this is financially and logistically impossible. In a pluralist society, the only way for an education system to vindicate everybody's rights to freedom of conscience, religion and belief, and to respect the convictions of all parents and not just most, is to have a foundation of a state secular education system that is neutral on the question of religion. It is simply not feasible for the state to financially support various types of schools in every area. Delivering the education system through private bodies where the state funds education on the basis of a particular majority in a given area instead of protecting the human rights of individuals, can only result in segregation, discrimination and the denial of basic human rights. Neither can the patronage system achieve respect for the religious and philosophical convictions of all parents, because human rights are guaranteed to individuals not to the religious majority in a given area. What we have in Ireland is the abuse of a dominant position. The patronage system lends its weight to identifying members of society by their religious affiliation. The patronage system coerces parents to identify with various groups in society, especially when children were refused access to the local school in the event of a shortage of places and in order to uphold a religious ethos.

Problems with State-funded Religious Ethos Schools

A religious ethos means integrating religion into the state curriculum and the general milieu of the school day. It is part of Catholic teaching that religion must be integrated into other subjects.[4] It is also part of Catholic Church teaching that religious education cannot be delivered in a neutral and objective manner. As a result of this teaching, which is protected by legislation, Section 15(2)(b) of the Education Act 1998, atheist or minority faith parents cannot exempt their child from the elements of religion that are integrated into all of the various subjects under the curriculum.

As a consequence of the integrated curriculum, there are potential areas of all subjects that could legitimately give rise to a conflict of allegiance between the school and the children's own family value system. Therefore, atheist and minority faith parents cannot guarantee that the education that their children receive is in conformity with their own convictions. Despite guarantees on parental rights under the Irish constitution, atheist and minority faith parents are denied basic human rights in the Irish education system. The *Primary School Curriculum* (1999) leaves it to each individual school to design and deliver its own religious education curriculum and this subjects atheist and minority faith parents to a heavy burden.[5] They must identify the areas of each particular subject and lesson that are not delivered in an objective, critical and pluralistic manner and then try to seek exemptions for their children. This makes necessary the disclosure of details of their philosophical convictions in order to try to opt their children out of the elements of religion that are integrated into all subjects. Not only does this breach their human right to respect for their private and family life under Article 8 of the European Convention an Human Rights but it simply cannot be achieved in practice.

It is bad enough that state-funded schools are allowed to give priority to religious beliefs over non-religious beliefs; state-funded schools with a Catholic ethos are not even happy with that level of privilege. They have made this clear in their response to the proposed new state curriculum on education about religion, beliefs and ethics. The Catholic bishops object to promoting even pluralism among religious beliefs within schools, as they believe that it goes against the philosophical basis of Catholic religious education. The Church accepts that freedom of religion is the bedrock of Western democracies, but insists that promoting pluralism within schools is against their ethos.

Conclusion

The patronage system is not a balanced system that ensures the fair and proper treatment of minorities. Atheist and minority faith parents do not enjoy the liberty to ensure that their children are afforded their basic fundamental human rights because they are coerced by force of circumstances to send their children to schools where their basic human rights are disregarded. It is simply not an option for the majority of parents to educate their children at home. Despite the European Convention on Human Rights and the various UN conventions that Ireland has ratified, the Irish State has failed to guarantee and protect these human rights.

Atheist Ireland is proud to work in alliance with the Evangelical Alliance of Ireland and the Ahmadiyya Muslim Community of Ireland to pursue the important aim of an education system that respects equally the human rights of all parents and all children, without sacrificing the human rights of a minority in order to satisfy the desires of a majority.

CHAPTER ELEVEN

The Importance of Beliefs, Respect, Secularism, Dialogue and Equal Treatment

Imam Ibrahim Ahmad Noonan

The Ahmadiyya Muslim Community is an international rapidly growing movement within Islam. It is a sect within Islam, founded in 1889, and its foundations are based on the belief that Allah (God) exists and its mission is to establish his profound truth.[1] While the Ahmadiyya Muslim Association was established in Ireland in 1993, members have been in the country since 1924. The main mosque, Masjid Maryam, is located in Galway and there are Ahmadiyya centres in Dublin, Cork, Limerick and Athlone.

Ahmadiyya Muslims attest that there is none to be worshipped but Allah, that he is one. Allah is the creator of all that exists. We believe that God is holy, free from all defects and full of all perfections. No imperfection may be found in him and there is no perfection which may not be found in him. His power is unlimited, as is his knowledge. He encompasses everything and there is nothing which encompasses him. He is the first and the last, the manifest and the hidden, the creator and master of all creation. His control has never failed in the past, nor is it failing at present, nor will it fail in the future. Free from death, he is the living, the enduring. He suffers no defect or decay. His actions are willed, not forced or constrained. He rules over the world today as he ever ruled before. His attributes are eternal, his power always evident.[2]

We believe that Muhammad (sa) is the messenger of Almighty Allah and that he is the last and final law-bearing prophet sent to humanity.[3] He is the seal of the prophets, and no prophet with a new law or new teaching will come. We believe that he was sent with the final divine teaching to humanity which came in the form of the Quran, and that Islam is the final system by which humankind can be guided towards God Almighty.

The Ahmadiyya Muslim Community follows the teachings of Islam fully as prescribed by Almighty Allah (swt) as given to humankind[4] and demonstrated by the Holy Prophet (sa).

Founding of the Ahmadiyya Muslim Community

The Ahmadiyya Muslim Community was founded in 1889 by Hadrat Mirza Ghulam Ahmad of Qadian who claimed to be the awaited messiah and Imam Mahdi (The Guided One) which the world is awaiting, whom the Holy Prophet Muhammad (sa) said would appear in the latter days, at a time when Islam's moral and ethical teachings would seem to have disappeared from the earth.[5]

Our belief is based upon the doctrine of both the Quran and the Bible,[6] that Jesus did not die on the cross, but was saved from crucifixion to enable him to complete his mission and to convey his message to the lost tribes of Israel. It is believed that Jesus travelled and settled in northern India and passed away when he was one hundred and twenty years old in Kashmir, where his grave can be found today. Hence the Ahmadiyya Muslim Community teaches that a person from among the followers of the Holy Prophet Muhammad (sa) will be raised, and will simultaneously fulfil the advent of the second coming of Jesus and the Imam Mahdi (The Guided One). The Holy Prophet foretold that a person will be a messiah, whose aim will be to call all humankind back to God Almighty. He will bring back the moral and ethical teachings of God which were taught by all the prophets of God from the Prophet Adam right up to the Prophet Muhammad.

The Ahmadiyya Muslim Community believes that the messiah and Imam Mahdi, Hadrat Mirza Ghulam Ahmad of Qadian India, was the founder of Ahmadiyya Muslim Community. He established this divine community to summon humankind towards Almighty Allah on divine command in 1889.[7]

Importance of Respecting the Right of People to Believe Differently

The Holy Quran makes it very clear that we should invite others to discuss what we have in common, using our intellect when conversing with others and debating in a cordial manner. The Ahmadiyya Muslim Community is at the forefront of this. We are a community which recognises the right to freedom of belief, and this is a fundamental aspect of justice in a free society. We believe that no one should be coerced into believing, but rather we invite others to accept the faith through amicable discussion and wisdom which we find within the pages of the Holy Quran. Allah commands us:

> *Invite (all) to the Way of thy Lord with wisdom and beautiful preaching; and argue with them in ways that are best and most gracious: for thy Lord knows best who have strayed from His Path, and who receive guidance. (Quran 16:125)*
>
> *But if they dispute with thee, say, I have submitted myself to Allah, and also those who follow me. And say to those who have been given a book and to the unlearned 'have you submitted?' If they submit, then they will surely be guided; but if they turn back, then thy duty is only to convey the message. And Allah is watchful of His servants. (Quran 3:21)*

From these verses, it is clear that the Islamic teaching is that we invite all for dialogue using wisdom and the Holy Prophets' (*sa*) mission was only to convey and not to force but to respect the choice of whoever chooses to follow whatever path they choose.

Importance of the State Acting Neutrally and Being Separate from Religion

The fundamental teaching of Islam is justice and that justice must be universal to all members of society regardless of race and colour. Respect must be given to all faiths and belief systems; therefore, the state must not interfere with the faith of any community, or of any person. Justice must be applied to all citizens of any given country. The state must ensure that the citizen's freedom of belief is well protected in their country. On the occasion of the Annual Conference of the Ahmadiyya Muslim Community, in Germany, in 2011, His Holiness Hadrat Mirza Masroor Ahmad (*aba*), the supreme head of the Ahmadiyya Muslim Community, while speaking on the importance of separation of state and religion, stated:

In one verse, the Holy Quran teaches us that: there should be no compulsion in matters of faith (Ch.2:V.257). Some of you may not be aware that this verse was revealed when the Holy Prophet of Islam (saw) had already established a government in Madinah. At the time, a covenant had already been made with the Jews and other tribes, and a functioning system of government was in place in which the Holy Prophet (saw) had already been accepted as head of state. The injunction to keep religion and government independent of each other was revealed at that time and in those circumstances, even though the difference between right and wrong had become manifest, and even though the Muslims believed their religion to be true and their teachings to be unparalleled. With this injunction it became clear that these excellent teachings were to be spread through love and affection, rather than by force or by acting unjustly towards others. Allah has said that a requirement for a just government is that it should separate religious matters from matters of state, and every citizen should be afforded his due rights.

This principle is absolute and without exception, to the extent that you must act justly even with those people who have displayed hatred towards you, and who due to this opposition have persecuted you repeatedly in every possible way. The Holy Quran states, 'O ye who believe! Be steadfast in the cause of Allah, bearing witness in equity; and let not a people's enmity incite you to act otherwise than with justice. Be always just that is nearer to righteousness.'[8]

Hence it is the belief of the Ahmadiyya Muslim Community that state and church must be separate to enable both entities to perform their responsibilities fairly and with justice without interfering with each other's work. A government's duty is to govern a country based upon justice and equality, so that all citizens are treated with impartiality and fairness regardless of creed, colour and gender.

Importance of Dialogue and the Alliance between Our Three Groups

When Michael Nugent, the chair of Atheist Ireland (AI), approached me, as a member of the Ahmadiyya Muslim Association Ireland, to consider combining forces with AI and the Evangelical Alliance Ireland (EAI), to tackle religious discrimination in the Irish education system, I must admit, I thought to myself, 'What? Atheists, Christians and Muslims coming together?' At first, I was not sure how it would work, but I knew that we must work together on common grounds as this is a fundamental teaching of Islam. This is how communities like mine, Michael Nugent's and Jane Donnelly's (AI) and Nick Park's (EAI) broke down barriers and learned to dialogue and work with each other for the common good.

Dialogue is vitally important, especially in the contemporary climate of global change as it is necessary to ensure peace, tolerance, equality and justice. Such dialogue has created an understanding between our three groups. Even with our clear differences, we have managed to develop a good friendship and deep respect for each other. What we have managed to do is show how, despite very real differences, we can work together for a good cause. Dialogue is something that society needs to adopt, where all communities are included in a dialogue that involves ensuring the upholding of justice for all members of humanity and not just a selected few. Our three groups have recognised this need, and our journey has begun to enable a better and just society free from discrimination.

Discrimination against the Ahmadiyya Community

In many parts of the world the Ahmadiyya Muslim Community faces discrimination. In Pakistan, since the Second Amendment to the 1973 Constitution of Pakistan under the government of Zulfiqar Ali Bhutto, Ahmadiyyas have been considered heretics. The constitution states:

> *A person who does not believe in the absolute and unqualified finality of the Prophethood of Muhammad (Peace be upon him), the last of the Prophets or claims to be a Prophet, in any sense of the word or of any description whatsoever, after Muhammad (Peace be upon him), or recognises such a claimant as a Prophet or religious reformer, is not a Muslim for the purposes of the Constitution or law.*[9]

Discrimination is widespread and systemic. Being an Ahmadi Muslim means being discriminated against in the armed forces, law enforcement agencies, universities, in the medical field and in the education sector.[10] In a number of well documented incidents Ahmadi Muslim communities have been the targets of violent attacks and murder. In Lahore in 2010, eighty-six Ahmadi people died and one hundred and fifty Ahmadi children and adults were injured in simultaneous attacks perpetrated by the Punjabi Taliban on the grounds that they were *wajb-ul-qatl* (deserving of death).[11]

Essentially, Ahmadis are not allowed to be in a position of influential authority in Pakistan. They also face severe persecution. This ideology of persecution has spread from Pakistan where the largest Ahmadiyya Muslim Community is located, to other countries like Bangladesh, Saudi Arabia, Algeria and many other Islamic countries. In Algeria, Human Rights Watch reported that two hundred and sixty-six Ahmadis have faced charges related to the practice of their religion since June 2016.[12] Sadly, this persecution has also taken the shape of discrimination in the form of an extreme ideology of prejudice in Europe and the western world where some members of Islamic communities refuse to recognise the rights of Ahmadi Muslims.

Discrimination is not restricted to other countries. Ahmadi Muslims have also been discriminated against in Ireland; for example, in 2017 a window in the Masjid Maryam Mosque in Galway was smashed as about one hundred people gathered for prayers for Ramadan.[13] Leaders of Catholic, Anglican, Methodist, Presbyterian and Quaker congregations in the city jointly condemned this unprovoked incident 'unequivocally and without hesitation'.[14] There have been times when members of the Ahmadi community in Ireland have attempted to give talks on the faith but they have been prevented from doing so. Since we are considered disbelievers by some who do not recognise Ahmadi Muslims as Muslim, speaking about our faith community and engaging in dialogue with others can be challenging. No Muslim has the right to declare another self-identifying Muslim or Muslim community as non-Muslim, especially in the West! There have been numerous occasions when I was told that I should not be given a platform to represent Islam as I was not a real or true Muslim. This discrimination is very real and it inhibits any form of dialogue between other groups and Ahmadi Muslims because it is based on a premise that we are a group of disbelievers and that our faith tradition is not to be engaged with. Whenever a person's right to talk about their faith is contested it is important to remember that any prohibition of talking about one's faith is contrary to Article 9 of the European Convention on Human Rights and Article 10 of the EU Charter of Fundamental Rights which protects freedom of religion or belief. Freedom of religion or belief is one of the rights listed in Articles 18 of the Universal Declaration of Human Rights (UDHR) and of the International Covenant on Civil and Political Rights (ICCPR).

Ahmadi Muslims and the Irish Education System
The position of the Ahmadi Muslim community in Ireland is that we do not support any discrimination towards any faith or belief system in schools from preschool and primary, to secondary and third level education. There should be no inequality between the various belief systems, including those faiths from the same belief families including Catholicism, Protestantism or Evangelical Christianity. The education system should not prioritise and favour any particular religious tradition or school of thought whether it be within Islam or any other belief systems such as humanism or atheism. All faiths should have equality within the education system. The basic rights of all children must be kept in mind at all times.

Ireland is belief diverse and the educational system at all levels should respond to that diversity. Children go to school to learn and not to be preached to. While religion should be taught in schools, this should be done in a manner which does not privilege any one religious tradition or belief system. So, when schools teach about faiths, it should be done without imposing a particular faith or belief system. The educating of children about the existence of other religions and belief systems should be carried out in a professional and accurate manner. By teaching children about common areas like morality, ethics and tolerance, we can create an atmosphere of togetherness and unity within diversity.

Conclusion

Dialogue is very simple, yet it has the capacity to be very profound. It comes from a place of openness to others. Entering into dialogue with AI and EAI meant taking time to meet, to listen and to engage with each other and act together. Dialogue means talking honestly and openly with others. Dialogue takes place when you move beyond initial judgement or reaction to a place of listening and respect for positions that are entirely different from yours. Dialogue invites you to engage with what you might not immediately understand. This can be quite difficult, and at times it is a very brave and risky thing to do. Sometimes there is a real creative synergy when people from different traditions and world views are united in a common cause and come together with an open mind and a willingness to understand each other and work together. It is highly surprising that three groups, one Muslim, one Christian and one atheist could form a successful alliance and campaign effectively in a manner which supports the beliefs of all three groups. This shows the power of dialogue. It is based on a willingness to engage with others, to be open to and enriched by their ideas and world views while being firmly rooted in and committed to your own tradition.

CHAPTER TWELVE

Why Secular Education is Good for Children, Good for Religion, and Good for Society

Nick Park

Evangelical Alliance Ireland exists to connect, equip and represent Irish Evangelical Christians. Evangelical characteristics include an emphasis on the ultimate authority of the Bible in faith and practice, the necessity for each individual to reach their own personal conversion experience in coming to faith in Christ, and the responsibility to witness to others so that they might make a similar faith decision. There are approximately seven hundred Evangelical churches in the Irish Republic, some of which belong to established denominations, but most of which are independent or belong to newer movements. There is also a considerable number of Evangelicals who, for one reason or another, attend non-Evangelical church congregations.

It may seem strange to some that Evangelicals would dialogue and cooperate with atheists and Ahmadi Muslims in highlighting the failings of Ireland's predominantly denominational education system, given that we have very different world views. However, we find that our communities, as minorities, encounter similar problems.

In Ireland many parents send their children to Catholic schools quite simply because there are no other viable options in their locality. Ireland's school system is overwhelmingly denominational at primary level (96 per cent) and research suggests that 'denominational schools may, if oversubscribed, give priority to students of that denomination. In areas such as Dublin, where demand for school places is very high and oversubscription is common, children of minority religious faiths and none may receive lower priority when seeking to enrol.'[1] Parents of a minority denomination or faith tradition obviously want the best quality of educational experience for their children. They want their children to learn to read and write, to understand history and geography, to grasp the fundamentals of physics or chemistry like any other child. They want their children to enjoy the rights all young people growing up in a modern western democracy are entitled to – the right to be educated. As part of these rights they may wish their children to understand the basics of various religions and the roles religions and beliefs have played in history and the development of our society. They may want their children to understand the ways in which religion has sometimes caused division and cruelty, but has also inspired great art, scientific breakthroughs and social progress.

However, parents do not want their children to be subjected to religious formation in the classroom. This is not to suggest that parents view religious education as unimportant. Precisely because some parents take seriously the roles of the family and the church in religious formation they do not wish to allocate the key role of faith nurture to the school. Many families take time each day to pray together and to discuss their faith. They also take care in choosing a church that provides Sunday school classes where children can be involved in church services.

Parents do not want their children to be segregated or ostracised. They do not want children to be made to wait at the back of the classroom during school hours while the other children are prepared for first communion or confirmation. They do not want their children to be treated as outsiders simply because they, as a family, belong to a minority religion. They do not want their children to grow up feeling that they are in any way second-class citizens who could not contribute as much as any other young person to the future of Ireland.

How Ireland's Education System Has Evolved Historically

Obviously, there are very real historical reasons why Ireland's education system has developed in such a way as to give one religious organisation a great measure of control and influence over the vast majority of the nation's schools. Ironically, one factor was a desire among parents not to allow the state to use education as a blunt instrument to force children to receive unwelcome religious indoctrination.[2]

When Catholics were subjected to persecution and discrimination under the Penal Laws (1695–1829), parents preferred to send their children to hedge schools rather than allow them to be subjected to Protestant proselytising.[3] Also, when Ireland first gained independence, the state was struggling to develop a modern infrastructure. Politicians were, quite understandably, delighted to cede much of the burden of education to the Catholic and Protestant churches rather than to incur the massive costs of building and maintaining thousands of schools. Education and religion have often gone hand in hand. In Europe and North America, the majority of the early schools and the great universities were founded by the clergy and religious of various denominations. Yet, in most of those schools and universities, a way has been found for a quality education to be provided for all without religious coercion, segregation or discrimination.

As a religious leader with links to several charities and aid organisations, I frequently travel to developing countries. Time and again, while driving early in the morning along unpaved roads marked by inadequate housing and poverty, I suddenly see lines of children in colourful, clean, even if somewhat threadbare, school uniforms. They are walking towards clusters of whitewashed buildings. They look happy and excited, knowing that they are about to receive a nutritious meal and another day of education that will assist them towards a better future.

It is noticeable that, almost invariably, many of these islands of hope are founded, operated and financed by churches. The denominational brand over the door might vary – such schools are provided by Catholics, Methodists, Anglicans, Presbyterians, Evangelicals or Pentecostals – but they stand as testimony to the positive role that churches play in providing education when a state lacks the resources to provide a quality education for all its children.

For me, the state's role in developed Western societies gets to the very heart of how we see ourselves as a nation. In developed nations, it is taken for granted that the state has a responsibility to provide basic services for its citizens. These include an adequate infrastructure of roads, electricity and telecommunications, ready access to drinking water, adequate healthcare and a good quality educational system. Such basic services may indeed come with a cost attached, but also with a safety net to ensure that no citizen is denied the basics of life in a developed nation. However, in developing nations, the state is often unable to provide such basic services. Charities, churches and aid organisations do their best to fill the gaps, but the inability of the state to meet its obligations is obvious.

The Role of the State in Western Societies

In Western societies, there is usually freedom for churches and other organisations to provide additional services, either for their members, as a service to others, or for those willing to pay for an enhanced service. Indeed, this is one of the characteristics that often distinguishes a democratic and tolerant society from a totalitarian and intrusive regime. So, for example, in most Western societies religious hospitals and schools have the freedom to operate on a private basis, sometimes even receiving funding from the state, but they do so in a supplementary way to a state system that already provides good quality healthcare and education to all citizens without prejudice or discrimination.

Ireland is somewhat unique in that it has failed, as a state, to develop its own adequate national education system for all its citizens at primary and post-primary level. Instead it has franchised its schooling, in theory to a number of (mostly) religious organisations, but in practice one denomination manages the majority of primary and secondary schools. In terms of structure, if not of educational quality, Ireland's educational model is more that of a developing nation than a modern western democracy that seeks to participate as an equal in the international community and the European Union.

How Ireland Has Changed and Continues to Change

Life in contemporary Ireland is very different to decades ago. An increasing number of citizens hold no religious affiliation, while others express their religious affiliation in many and varied ways. A people of emigrants has become a nation with a significant proportion of immigrants, and many of those immigrants are passionate in their pursuit and practise of minority religions. Certainly, a majority of our citizens still self-identify as 'Catholic' when filling their census forms, but that self-identification increasingly can look like a cultural, rather than religious, self-description. Being a Catholic in Ireland no longer automatically means that one will adhere to Catholic theology, morality or even that one will attend church services.

In short, Ireland, like most other Western societies, is experiencing a process of secularisation. This does not mean that religion is dying, or that Ireland is somehow becoming 'post-Christian'. What it does mean is that the way religion is practised is fundamentally changing. No longer will people pay lip service to a religion because it is the cultural norm, or because that is the way that they were raised.[4] This means that nominal religion is declining, and will continue to decline. Interestingly, convictional religion tends to increase in a secular society. In secular societies, people are much more likely to choose a different religious (or indeed atheistic) world view than the one in which they were raised. Others become more attached to the faith in which they were raised, but with a much higher level of commitment than the previous generation. This sometimes leads to a multiplication of smaller churches and manifestations of religion. Those who belong to such religions tend to be more passionate about their faith, and a similar passion is seen among those who reject the concept of God.

As Ireland becomes more secular, and as more people, in the words of the sociologist Grace Davie, 'belong without believing',[5] we might expect the number of religiously unaffiliated to continue to increase. Between the 2011 and 2016 census Ireland witnessed a 73.6 per cent rise in the number of those who self-identified as having 'no religion'.[6] In Ireland there has also been a sharp increase in adherents of minority religions, as well as an increase in agnostics and atheists, and these groups have become more numerous, more visible and more vocal.[7] If the current trends continue, it is reasonable to expect that the larger denominations, in particular the Catholic Church,[8] will see a decline in active membership, smaller attendances at religious services (although this may well be offset through immigration) but their members may well be more committed to the tenets of their faith. Between 2011 and 2016 the census results for Ireland showed that the Catholic population rapidly declined from 84.2 per cent to 78.3 per cent of the population. The 2016 census revealed that Orthodox Christianity was the fastest growing religion in Ireland. Islam was the third largest religion in the state with over fifty mosques and prayer centres. Over the next twenty years, it is not unreasonable to expect rising numbers of atheists, Muslims, Baptists and Pentecostals in Ireland. We should also expect mainline Protestant denominations (Methodists, Presbyterians and Church of Ireland) to experience more modest growth, and to become more racially diverse and more enthusiastic in their worship and in expressing and sharing their faith. The experience of other nations leads me to conjecture that a slimmed-down Catholic Church in Ireland might have less control over state policy, but would be more orthodox and religiously conservative, with *a-la-carte* and cultural Catholicism seeing the greatest decline.

What is clearly emerging, and may only increase as secularisation continues, is that a growing section of the population is indifferent to religion. They would not think of themselves as agnostics or atheists, but neither would religion play any meaningful role in their lives. As this demographic increases in size, they may become increasingly irritated at being expected to jump through religious hoops in order to have their children educated or to work as a teacher in a school.

How These Changes Might Influence Our Education System

You don't have to be a prophet to see how these complex and evolving factors might create tensions and frustrations when it comes to Ireland's anachronistic and overwhelmingly denominational education system. I imagine that there might be four developments as Ireland transitions to a more egalitarian secular system of education.

1. Growing numbers of culturally Catholic parents may protest against the imposition of religious requirements and attempts at faith formation when all they want is to see their children gain a good education. They will become less willing to have their children baptised into a faith that

they themselves no longer practise.[9] Interestingly, changes in legislation concerning admissions to schools mean that the 'baptism barrier' is now removed from 90 per cent of schools. Parents may also become increasingly irked by preparation for religious ceremonies being conducted during school time.

2. Non-Catholic immigrants living in Ireland may grow more assertive as they realise that integration into Irish life does not necessarily involve passively accepting the dominant role of the Catholic Church. I know a number of immigrant parents who, against their own personal religious beliefs, reluctantly allowed their children to receive first communion and to be confirmed. They knew that, for their applications for residency and Irish citizenship to succeed, they needed references from authority figures such as a school principal stating that they were integrating into Irish society. They were afraid that, if they asked for their children to be exempted from such religious ceremonies, they might be labelled as obstructive or refusing to integrate. Such parents will become more emboldened as demands increase for the state to introduce a non-discriminatory educational system.

3. Teachers will be increasingly unwilling to teach, promote or conform to a religious ethos to which they do not personally subscribe. Teachers enter their profession because they want to educate children. Some are Catholics. Some are not. Some live in partnerships that are deemed immoral by the Church. Some are atheists. They should not be expected to be hypocrites, and neither should they suffer discrimination if they seek to practise their vocation in the vast majority of state-funded schools.

4. If the state continues its present policy of tinkering with minor reforms rather than grasping the nettle and building a genuinely secular and non-discriminatory education system, we may expect those who are genuinely religious to become increasingly frustrated at what they see as a

dilution of religious education and influence in schools that still bear a denomination's name. Ironically, when religious schools are less numerous and fulfil a supplementary role to a much wider secular school system, they are likely to be granted more freedom to overtly teach their tenets. However, when religious schools constitute the bulk of a nation's primary and post-primary educational system, then more state interference is inevitable. In other words, if every child has the opportunity to attend a secular school, then those parents who send their child to a religious school could do so in the full knowledge that their child would receive a certain type of religious education and formation.

Why Secular Education is Good for Children, Religion, and Society

There is an erroneous notion, often propagated by those who want their particular brand of faith to be propped up at the taxpayer's expense, that having a genuinely secular education system in Ireland would somehow represent a promotion of atheism, or even a denial of the rights of religious parents. One of the problems with the words 'secular' and 'secularism' is that they are used in two entirely different ways. Some people understand 'secularism' as a desire to eradicate religion from public life altogether – that you can practise religion in private but should not speak about it in public. Heiner Bielefeldt, Professor of Human Rights and Human Rights Policy at the University of Erlangen, makes a very useful distinction between doctrinal secularism and political secularism.

Doctrinal secularism is anti-religious in nature and wants to see religion banished altogether from the public arena. In many ways this kind of aggressive secularism functions like a dogmatic religion itself. Political secularism on the other hand is the idea that the state should be entirely neutral with respect to religion, and that religion should be afforded no special privileges and subject to no special restrictions. In a politically secular society, all religious groups, and those of no religion, operate on a level playing field and compete in the marketplace of ideas. As Bielefeldt puts it, political secularism 'gives religious communities their independence from unwanted state intervention, and makes possible that people across religious boundaries enjoy equal rights and an equal status as citizens'.[10]

As a Christian leader, I believe passionately that a secular educational system benefits all of us. It is good for children and families because it puts the religious formation of children back where it belongs – in the hands of parents. If parents wish to seek the help of churches in that process then they are free to do so. It is good for teachers because they are not forced into dishonesty or hypocrisy. It is good for religion itself because faiths thrive when they are shared by those who believe their tenets most passionately. If I wanted to devise a strategy to destroy a religion, I cannot think of anything more effective than making its teaching a compulsory act, often implemented by those with little or no interest, and inflicted upon bored schoolchildren. Such a practice virtually guarantees that religious belief is divorced from real life and becomes perfunctory and irrelevant.

It is good for society because diversity is championed, and children learn the kind of tolerance and mutual respect that can never flourish under educational apartheid. This will become more crucial as those who are religious become more committed to their individual beliefs.

There is room in a comprehensive secular education system for religious schools to play a supplementary role, be that as private fee-paying schools or receiving some sort of state subsidy. Also, religions should be permitted to use classrooms in state schools for religious formation outside of school hours on a voluntary basis, on the same basis as chess clubs, vegetarian societies or debating societies. Again, religion should not be subjected to unfair discrimination or restriction.

Unfortunately, successive governments in Ireland have not demonstrated any willingness to behave like a developed Western democracy and provide a secular non-discriminatory education system that treats all our children as equals. Tinkering with the 'baptism barrier', or negotiating with ecclesiastical authorities to amend the religious education curriculum are exercises in futility. Sooner or later the state must act decisively. This will undoubtedly be expensive and will initially be painful for some, but delaying will only serve to multiply such expense and turmoil.

CHAPTER THIRTEEN

A Humanist Perspective on Dialogue about Religions and Beliefs

Tina Storey

I have been a humanist since 2004 and I am a celebrant trained and accredited by the Humanist Association of Ireland (HAI) since 2013. This chapter explores what humanism is while presenting some of the merits of a humanistic attitude. It also highlights some problems experienced by non-religious people while providing educators and others with some pointers to engage in meaningful dialogue with those of no religion. Unless otherwise cited, the views expressed are my own and do not represent the views of the HAI or any other non-religious body.

Humanism – What's That?

Humanism is not a religion. It is a world view which says that reason and science are the best ways to understand the world around us and that dignity and compassion should be the basis for how you act toward someone else. Albert Einstein, acclaimed scientist, Nobel Prize winner in physics in 1921 and originator of the theory of relativity, wrote that:

> A man's ethical behaviour should be based effectually on sympathy, education, and social ties and needs; no religious basis is necessary. Man would indeed be in a

*poor way if he had to be restrained by fear of punishment
and hope of reward after death.*[1]

Humanism is non-theistic. By this, we don't mean to say that
there is no God. Instead, we say that there is no proof for the
existence of God, any gods, the supernatural or an afterlife;
therefore, we take very seriously the idea that 'no deity will save
us; we must save ourselves'. We are living the only life we'll ever
have – in the only world we know about. The responsibility for
the choices we make is ours and ours alone. Humanism is not an
organised system of thought or belief – rather, humanists tend
to debate and tease out the ethics of an issue to try to decide
on the most beneficial, or least harmful, solution for humanity
and the rest of this world. This can be simply expressed as, 'A
humanist is someone who does the right thing even though she
knows that no one is watching.'[2]

Humanism, Spirituality and Theism

It is possible to actively practise a religion and still be a humanist;
however, in the twenty-first century, humanism is generally used
as a shorthand term for secular humanism. Those identifying as
humanists usually do not believe in the existence of a higher
power or divine being and feel that it is up to each of us during
this lifetime to try to live our lives in the best possible manner as
we do not know what comes after death.

Belief or non-belief in a higher power or the supernatural
can be viewed as a spectrum or continuum. Theism (belief in the
existence of God with or without a belief in a special revelation)
lies on one extreme. Atheism (disbelief in the existence of a
God) lies on the opposite extreme. A range of belief systems
inhabit the middle ground, including agnosticism, rationalism,
free-thought, and humanism.

Generally, individuals self-identify as humanists depending on
how they see their personal beliefs fitting on this spectrum. Many
rational thinkers are prone to changing their minds and opinions

based on new evidence. There are as many routes to becoming a humanist as there are individual humanists and there are no entrance criteria. The Humanist Association of Ireland has a list of famous humanists on its website and personal stories of how people came to humanism are available all over the internet.[3] The British Humanist Association has a quick online quiz that you can take to see how humanist you are.[4] So what kind of people are humanists? Questions asked include: Are you concerned for the welfare of your fellow humans? Do you use a combination of reason and compassion to make decisions in your life? If so, you may already be a humanist.

Origins and History of Humanism

Humanism is a human-centred philosophy that rejects the supernatural. From a humanist perspective, it appears that humanism flourishes in civilisations that are relatively advanced, especially during times of peace and plenty. When peoples are beset by troubles – war, famine, pestilence, disease – they tend to revert in fear to belief in the supernatural. So, a cycle of civilisation and enlightenment followed by collapse of civilisation and reversion to superstition seems to be the nature of humankind. It is the hope of humanists and freethinkers that over time, the education and progress of humankind will help move towards longer periods of civilisation in more parts of the world and fewer episodes of trouble.

The oldest writings passed down to us today that express a humanistic philosophy that rejects the supernatural come from the Indus Valley around three thousand five hundred years ago, in the *Lokayata* or 'philosophy of the people'. The Hindu sacred text, the *Rig Veda* of the ninth century BCE, and the Buddha's words from the sixth century BCE[5] also express sceptical attitudes to the supernatural.[6]

Humanism flourished during the Greek enlightenment in the sixth century BCE. Thales of Miletus and Xenophanes of Colophon attempted to explain the world in terms of human reason rather than myth and tradition. These Ionian Greeks were the first thinkers to assert that nature is available to be studied separately from the supernatural realm. In Western Europe and the Middle East an atmosphere of free and open discussion about the meaning of life and death, about science, philosophy and religion continued for about eight hundred years. During this period in history a magnificent library was founded in Alexandria, Egypt, by the ruling Macedonian Greek Ptolemaic dynasty. It became the repository of all the recorded knowledge the intelligentsia at that time could gather. During the period 48 BCE to 650 CE, this library and its contents were destroyed by a series of fires, probably instigated by new rulers or invaders. The loss of the Library of Alexandria has become a symbol of cultural and knowledge destruction. Thus, began the era we have come to refer to as the Dark Ages. For nearly a thousand years the Christian religion in the form of the Holy Roman Empire controlled the major sources of knowledge in Europe and the Middle East. Consequently, it also controlled the political climate.

Meanwhile, a flourishing of philosophy was taking place across the Muslim world. Many medieval Muslim thinkers pursued humanistic, rational and scientific discourses in their search for knowledge, meaning and values. A wide range of Islamic writings on love, poetry, history and philosophical theology shows that medieval Islamic thought was open to the humanistic ideas of individualism, occasional secularism, scepticism and liberalism.

The humanist philosophy was revived in Christian Europe during the Renaissance of the fourteenth to seventeenth centuries CE. This was a cultural rebirth based on the rediscovery of the classical literature of Greece and Rome. The Renaissance emphasised human dignity, beauty and potential, and affected every aspect of culture in Europe, including philosophy, music, and the arts. This humanist emphasis on the value and importance of the individual influenced the Protestant

Reformation, and brought about social and political change in Europe.[7]

The printing press was developed about the same time and the thoughts of those rebelling against authoritarian controls were widely distributed. Once again knowledge became public property and increasing numbers of people began to think about human relationships, the purpose of life and the meaning of death. The French philosopher Pierre Charron (1541–1603) is hailed as one of the founders of modern secularism. He summarised a dominant theme of the Renaissance when he wrote: 'The proper science and subject for man's contemplation is man himself.'[8]

There was another revival of humanism in the Age of Enlightenment in the seventeenth and eighteenth centuries as a reaction against the newly prevalent dogmatic authoritarianism of Lutheranism, Calvinism, Anglicanism, and the Counter-Reformation or Catholic Revival. Freethinkers continued to challenge secular and religious authority. The English philosopher John Locke (1632–1704) wrote his essays on human nature and the right to think freely and express one's views without public censorship or fear of repression. The English poet and philosopher Alexander Pope (1688–1744) in his famous *An Essay on Man* wrote: 'Know then thyself, presume not God to scan; the proper study of mankind is man.'[9]

Locke's writings were a major influence on Thomas Jefferson, who put humanist principles into the revolutionary document, *The Declaration of Independence* (1776) of the United States, and later an orderly public document establishing a humanistic form of popular government, the *Constitution of the United States*. During the nineteenth and twentieth centuries, various elements of Enlightenment humanism have been manifested in philosophical trends such as existentialism, utilitarianism, pragmatism, and Marxism. Today, secular humanism, which denies God and attributes the universe entirely to material forces, has replaced religion for many people.

Contemporary Humanist Community in Ireland

The predecessor of the HAI, the Association of Irish Humanists, was founded in 1993, and initially consisted of a group of like-minded individuals who met monthly to discuss topics of mutual interest. Over time the association grew to a membership of several hundred people in all parts of Ireland and represents non-religious people at a national level. There is a healthy sense of community amongst humanists in Ireland and in recent years several local humanist groups have sprung up in many parts of the country. Local groups hold meetings, lectures, seminars, workshops, meals, nights out, coffee mornings, information stands in public spaces, as well as an annual summer school. Humanist meetings can become heated and groups can fracture as opinions differ, but that is all part of people taking responsibility for their own beliefs and actions, rather than following dogma.

Humanists are represented on the world stage by the International Humanist and Ethical Union (IHEU), to which the HAI is affiliated. The IHEU is an international non-governmental organisation with representation on various United Nations committees and other international bodies. It seeks to influence international policy through representation and information, to build the humanist network, and let the world know about the world view of humanism.

Demographics

In the 2016 census, 10 per cent of the population, just over four hundred and sixty-eight thousand people, stated that they had 'no religion'. This represented a major increase of over one hundred and ninety-eight thousand additional people who stated that they had no religion over the five years since the 2011 census. In the 2011 census, 6 per cent of the population of the Republic of Ireland identified as non-religious.[10] The 'no religion' group were the second largest group in the state after Roman Catholics in the 2016 census. Prior to the 2016 census the HAI ran a public campaign urging those who do not practise a religion to tick the 'no religion' box on the census form. In Western Europe, 37 per cent of citizens say they are not religious, and worldwide one in five or 20 per cent of people are not religious.[11]

Ceremonies and Celebrations

Humanists, like most humans, like to celebrate significant life events, but want to do so without any reference to a god or higher power. We hold naming ceremonies to welcome children into our families and guide parents promise to be there as mentors for the child. We celebrate weddings with informal readings and vows and our own choice of music. In Ireland there are many registered humanist solemnisers who can legally solemnise the marriage without the need for a civil registrar to be present. The most common and moving ceremonies we take part in are funerals and celebrations of a life for persons of no religion who have expressed a desire not to have a religious funeral. All these ceremonies are dignified but relaxed and welcoming and very personal, with personal statements and readings of appropriate prose or verse by family and friends, often coordinated by a trained humanist celebrant. As a humanist celebrant, I am especially proud when I am approached after a ceremony by a guest who says, 'I didn't know what to expect, but the ceremony was really lovely – so personal. Thank you.'

Accusation of Hypocrisy

The majority of secular humanists in Ireland have been raised with a Christian cultural background and celebrate the local holidays and traditions in their own fashion, without attending a church; for example, by giving and receiving eggs at Easter or singing carols and exchanging gifts at Christmas. This may be considered hypocritical by others. Professor Richard Dawkins, the ethologist, evolutionary biologist and author, has defended the position of such 'Cultural Christian' non-believers thus:

I'm not one of those who wants to stop Christian traditions. [The UK] is historically a Christian country. I'm a cultural Christian in the same way that many of my friends call themselves cultural Jews or cultural Muslims. So, yes, I like singing carols along with everybody else. I'm not one of those who wants to purge our society of our Christian history. If there's any threat [from] these sorts of things, I think you will find it comes from rival religions and not from atheists.[12]

False Perceptions of Amorality

Religious believers are often taught values and morals entwined with the teachings of their religion, and many find it difficult to understand how one could have a moral compass if one rejects or has been raised from childhood without a religion. On the contrary, humanism subscribes to the golden rule, common to many belief systems, that you should treat others as you would like them to treat you, with tolerance, consideration and compassion. Humanists like the golden rule because of its universality and because it is derived from human feelings and experience. It requires people to think about others and try to imagine how they might think and feel. It is a simple and clear default position for moral decision-making.

Perceived Threat to Religion from Non-Believers

One concern held by religious believers is that humanists are trying to destroy religion and replace it with secularism.[13] This is not true. There is no conspiracy by humanists to force people to reject religion. We do take philosophical issue with the beliefs of religious followers; however, what concerns us even more is when religious believers attempt to use the power of the government to force their beliefs upon the rest of society. As has been shown throughout history, no one benefits when religious belief and government power mix. We strongly support Thomas Jefferson's call for a 'wall of separation between church and state'.[14] This ideal can best be reached through a secular government. This would mean a government that neither favours religion nor discriminates against it. For any government to best serve the diverse needs of its people it must remain neutral in matters as personal as religion.

Campaigns for Equal Rights

As humanists believe in equality of rights and opportunity, they fight for the rights of those who are oppressed. Gloria Steinem, author, feminist, founder of *Ms.* magazine, and 2012 Humanist Pioneer Award winner, said: 'When we speak of equality, of women and men, of blacks and whites, of all the world's people, we are talking about humanism.'[15]

Recent campaigns run by the HAI include:

- The promotion of a Yes vote in the 2015 Marriage Equality Referendum.
- Lobbying over a ten-year period to have secular humanist wedding ceremonies recognised legally, in parity with religious wedding ceremonies. The Civil Registration (Amendment) Act 2012 amended the Civil Registration Acts 2004 to 2008 and since then humanist weddings have grown in popularity year on year. In 2015, humanist celebrants conducted 1,264 marriages (5.7 per cent of the total).[16]
- The removal of religious barriers to school enrolment.[17]
- Lobbying for the removal of the obligation on judges and presidents of Ireland to take a religious oath.
- Taking part in the movement to repeal of the Eighth Amendment of the Constitution.[18]
- A call for a reduction of the age barrier for the president of Ireland.[19]

Failures of the Irish Educational System – Teach, Don't Preach

Once a child is enrolled in a school with a religious patron, the child may be forced to take part in religious education during the school day – usually thirty minutes per day in the primary school or three classes per week in post-primary school. School management teams are often unaware of the student's constitutional right to withdraw from religious education or any subject which goes against their or their parents' beliefs. Interestingly in 2018 a circular issued by the DES on religious instruction and worship in Education and Training Board (ETB) and community post-primary schools mandates that schools must consult parents and provide alternative subjects to students not taking religious education.[20] This was subsequently changed by a new circular issued in October 2018 to clarify the opt-out requirements. In effect, children who are opted out of religious education may still have to remain in the classroom and many parents suggest that their human rights are not respected as they are physically present during faith formation in the religion of the patron.[21]

Meaningful Dialogue between Teachers and Humanist Students

After a fruitful dialogue involving expert research, educational collaboration and resource building, in 2017 Educate Together and the Humanist Association of Ireland produced a groundbreaking series of lesson plans designed for primary schools in Ireland. The lessons were designed, piloted and evaluated with primary school children from first to fourth class in mind. These lessons are widely available and ensure that educators have high-quality, creative, Irish-generated resources around philosophical world views such as humanism, atheism and agnosticism drawing on child-friendly, age-appropriate, educationally sound methodologies.[22]

For a teacher to have a meaningful dialogue with a humanist student, they need to be aware of the differences between humanist philosophy and religious belief systems. The British Humanist Association provides excellent teaching resources about humanism and ethics on its website.[23] Here are some points to consider:

- The student has probably not been baptised and will not have a baptismal certificate but will have been registered at birth on the register of births, marriages and deaths, as would any child, and will have a birth certificate.

- The student will probably not believe in the existence of a god or gods and should not be expected to accept as fact any claims to the existence of such. Students may have no reservation in expressing their views in this regard. Educators need to be informed and sensitive as this can cause friction with other students who hold religious beliefs.

- Humanist students should not be forced to participate in prayers during the school day and educators need to ensure that they do not feel excluded from the class group by their non-participation.

- Non-religious students may wish to forego religion classes and alternative educational or supervision arrangements may be required.

- Humanists are highly ethical and believe in doing good and humanist students should never be made to feel that their lack of religion makes them immoral, evil or destined for eternal damnation.

CHAPTER FOURTEEN

What's Wrong with the Cookstown Sizzlers?

Ken McCue

From 2012–14, teams from the social enterprise *Sport Against Racism Ireland* (SARI) were regular visitors to Belfast as guests of our partners Charter Northern Ireland (NI). On one occasion, I was the manager of a SARI team of Muslim boys drawn from our Soccernites programme playing in an interfaith football tournament. The other teams were drawn from Roman Catholic and Protestant communities. As a responsible official, it was my job to check if a room for prayer was available and if the menu included a halal option.

At the outset, I figured we had a problem when one of the organisers said, 'What's wrong with the Cookstown Sizzlers?' I am old enough to remember the famous TV advert featuring Northern Ireland goalkeeper, Pat Jennings, so I knew that we would have to make do with chips and mushy peas. As an atheist, I often find myself fighting the corner of our Muslim youngsters in terms of provision of prayer rooms and appropriate food. When I hear terms like 'Islamic Radicalism', I think of all the times I observe the young hijabis and boys keeping their heads down when they encounter Islamophobia. At that tournament in Belfast, I ended up trying to stop a referee blowing his whistle at the boys while they prayed in the open field.

196 CONNECTING LIVES: INTERBELIEF DIALOGUE IN CONTEMPORARY IRELAND

During one of the games, I noticed one of our young female Muslim supporters juggling with a ball. Fadhila Hajji was there to support her brother, Abdul, who was one of our players. She was a street footballer who was banned by the Football Association of Ireland from playing organised games while wearing her head covering. Although she had a great passion for the game and the skill to boot, she was frustrated by the fact that she was denied the right to play on a team. It was this young woman who was to become the inspiration for the SARI operational programme, Hijabs and Hat Tricks (H & H).

The Goals

Back in 2010, I was also the manager of the SARI youth football team playing in a tournament at the Islamic Cultural Centre, Clonskeagh, Dublin. This was a male-only event and the girls were occupied in an arts and crafts workshop in a classroom adjacent to the pitch. On the sideline, I informed an imam that it was SARI policy to have a gender balance in any sports activity whether on the playing area or on the sidelines. He told me that the hijabi girls had no interest in sports but were keen on indoor activity. When a fire alarm was activated by a wayward ball hitting a window, the girls mustered in the vicinity of the football pitch. Suddenly, the boys lost interest. When I told a group of the girls about the opinion of the imam, they told me that they were avid supporters of Barcelona and Arsenal but could only play indoors out of the sight of their religious teachers.

This discovery motivated me to carry out some research in schools where there was a high percentage of Muslim girls. I was facilitated by the Muslim school in Cabra, Dublin, and select ethnically and religiously mixed schools in the inner city and suburbs. Up to four hundred Muslim girls were surveyed at junior and senior levels. In carrying out the evaluation, I was surprised to discover that the most popular games the girls desired to play were association football, followed by basketball, with camogie and Gaelic football most popular in terms of participation. All of the respondents were aware of the head-cover bans in football. The national governing body of the game in the Irish Republic was particularly strict in observing the FIFA ban on religious head covering and vigilant in policing the rule. Despite the fact that all referees had received state-funded intercultural training, they refused to allow players wearing hijabs, kippahs and turbans from playing the game. Previously, the FAI had imposed a ban on the young Sikh footballer, Karpreet Singh, who refused to remove his head covering during a game. SARI took this case to the European governing body of football at UEFA and made the World Sikh Council aware of this discriminatory practice. By the time the ban was lifted by FIFA in 2014, the young footballer had switched to cricket.

Growing the H & H/Diverse City Organisation
The lifting of the ban encouraged SARI to take the Hijabs and Hat Tricks operational programme down from the shelf and onto the playing field. The H & H plan was an integral part of the SARI strategic programme 'Living Together Through Football' that was designed as an anti-sectarian through-sport initiative, and piloted with SARI partners, Glentoran FC in East Belfast.

Through our membership of the Berlin-based streetfootballworld, Abdul Hajji, SARI youth leader and coach, won an award in the form of a stipend that provided capital for his winning H & H project and a practical training stint in the San Antonio favela in Rio de Janeiro, Brazil. Abdul was a qualified youth development worker with coaching and playing experience. He was a graduate of the British Council's Sporting Diversity course in Yorkshire and had considerable networking experience among Muslim youth in the Irish Republic. These credentials made him an ideal candidate to shift Hijabs and Hat Tricks from theory into practice.

On his return, with his head full of ideas, he convened a meeting of young hijabis to progress the project. Within a few weeks the SARI resource centre was full of young Muslim girls who formed a committee. While I provided technical assistance in a cultural planning context, I adopted a hands-off approach. From the outset they agreed on a number of ground rules including adopting the UN-recognised charity Islamic Relief as their shirt livery, raising funds for their projects and designing their own bespoke playing kit and badge. Along with these initiatives, they decided to establish a football team called Diverse City FC that would be open to members of all faiths and none.

With an anti-sectarian philosophy, the collective was now transformed into a sanctuary for Sunni, Shia, Sufi, Roman Catholic, other Christians and non-religious alike. With up to forty young women registered, the group morphed into a movement where the members engaged with civil society organisations and campaigns to ensure their voices were heard outside of SARI. This strategy had the dual purpose of providing a grounding for the young women in democratic structures and also positioning them, hijabs included, in the public arena.

In order to build their self-confidence, a number of bespoke workshops were designed and delivered on the topics of identity, diversity, human rights and the history of Islam. Bonding and teamwork-building sessions using bubble football, bowling and intercultural food events were organised with interfaith sessions at the Chester Beatty Library, Dublin. Alongside this came site visits to Croke Park and games at Aviva Stadium. On the sports front, workshops in nutrition, coaching and a visit to the sports department at RTÉ were very popular with the members.

To forge resilience and ability to tackle Islamophobia, racism and sexism, external training courses were employed using EU Erasmus+ programmes along with training provided by the National Youth Council of Ireland and Léargas. H & H and Diverse City FC members became very active in campaigns including Black Lives Matter, the Council of Europe No Hate Speech movement and organisations like the Islamic Students' Association and the Society of African Students in Ireland. In 2016, youth leader, Lesha Moustafa was elected to represent Europe on the youth forum of streetfootballworld.

Playing Together Leads to Staying Together

Within a short period of time, members were invited to speak at conferences and seminars at home and abroad, including the Mary Immaculate College, Limerick, seminar on the topic of interbelief dialogue in contemporary Ireland. This seminar included a football game as part of the interbelief dialogue with players from Diverse City FC and students from Mary Immaculate College. Other events that the group participated in include: the European Network Against Racism; Hate and Hostility Research Group at the University of Limerick; Women in Sport Conference at Dublin Castle; Institute for Strategic Dialogue at the Commonwealth of Nations, Youth Forum, Malta; United Nations Alliance of Civilisations Conference in Baku, Azerbaijan; and the Anna Lindh Foundation Conference in Tarragona, Spain. National and international recognition began to pour in with Fadhila Hajji, Diverse City FC captain, receiving the 2014 RTÉ/REHAB Person of the Year award. In 2014, H & H won the prestigious Global Beyond Sport Award. The UEFA Foundation for Children provided funding to help establish an underage academy along with a Thank You award from Coca-Cola followed by media profiles in the *Irish Times, She Kicks* (UK women's football journal), RTÉ's *Morning Ireland,* RTÉ's *Six One News* and a feature broadcast on Canadian national television to over eight million viewers.

Interfaith Strategy

Inspired by FC Barcelona's *Més que un Club* (More than a Club) philosophy, Diverse City FC adopted an action plan that placed them on the front line of the religious interface with civil and official society at home and abroad. At all times Diverse City FC presented an anti-sectarian perspective in all its dealings. In 2016 it participated in an exhibition football game with the support of the Irish School of Ecumenics in Trinity College, Dublin. Playing under the banner 'Believe in Football', this unique 'priests versus imams' encounter fell flat when senior clerics in the mosques refused to play with each other. My grand plan to unite Protestant, Catholic and dissenter in a peaceful joust with Islamic passers and tacklers was scuppered by the consequence of an ancient squabble. Coming to my rescue, a team of young hijabis, baffled by the intransigence of the clerics, offered to give the imams a lesson in the mediation potential of football. The adult males have yet to reply to the offer. Thankfully, this type of sectarian division has not manifested in the ranks of the hijabis and the young ones are an example of how playing together can lead to staying together.

Football as an Ecumenical Tool

Football as an ecumenical tool is an important player in tackling sectarianism. Recently, Yitzhak Eldan, President of the Ambassadors' Club of Israel, brought over thirty of his students to a Hijabs and Hat Tricks/Diverse City FC training session. There, his young charges met the 'three wise men' (male coaches, Azeez and two Abduls) who gave the young students the background to this unique project. The Moroccan-born elder statesman, who still possesses a North African body swerve, was impressed by the potential for the transfer of the concept to Tel Aviv. On their return, the Ambassadors' Club officials contacted Mifalot, our streetfootballworld partners in Tel Aviv, who introduced them to their interfaith and international football programmes.

Closer to home, SARI partners in Belfast, the Glentoran Football Academy, is planning an exchange with the members of the Belfast Mosque. SARI youth leader, Amina Moustafa has been invited to facilitate a workshop and talk about her short film *Never Judge a Woman by Her Cover*, which she developed at a No Hate movement workshop in the Methodist Hall in Belfast in 2016.

Solidarity and Global Development Programmes

The solidarity and global development programmes, again influenced by the work of FC Barcelona, is an integral part of the set-up developed and managed by the members themselves and includes raising funds, through the running of football tournaments, the Eid World Cups for Islamic Relief projects in Nepal (earthquake recovery), Gaza (medical supplies) and Lebanon (school scholarships for Syrian orphans in a refugee camp). Bilateral focus is on supporting girls' football in Gaza. The 3G Campaign – 'Goals, Girls, Gaza' – is dedicated to raising funds to build a MUGA (multiple-use green area) for the sole use of young school girls who will manage the facility. Continuation of the 'Scoring Sustainable Development Goals' education campaign will culminate in an exhibition that will demonstrate how sport can contribute to the promotion and the achievement of the UN Sustainable Development Goals.

Employability Programme

The SARI employability programme is part of a pan-European consortium coordinated by streetfootballworld in Berlin. Funded by the EU, this 'Team Up' for NEETS (Not in Education, Employment or Training) programme caters for sixteen participants from the SARI firm (six from Hijabs and Hat Tricks and six from Soccernites for boys). The participants are offered a series of training modules covering 'soft skills', including CV construction, mock interviews, literacy and numeracy top-ups. A mentor will be allocated to each trainee who will support the boys and girls to move onto the second phase of the programme that covers areas including social entrepreneurship, labour law and enterprise development. The programme includes work experience mobility exchanges through EU Erasmus+ with our partners in Portugal, Spain, Germany, France and England.

This innovative scheme, which is guided by a job training toolkit, carries universal certification and is particularly relevant for young hijabis as there is anecdotal and scientific evidence that discrimination exists in the hiring of young Muslim women into the world of work.

Threats to Progress and the Response

From the outset, H & H/Diverse City took great care to stay in line with Islamic religious requirements but from time to time some objections are made, usually from adult male Muslims who object to women playing sport. As the cultural planner, the complaints are sent in my direction. A couple of fathers, who were veterans of the SARI Soccerfest flagship, contacted me with concerns. I was able to field them by quoting from the annals of the 'beautiful game' and references to sport in the Quran. On the theological front, I was confident that we were on safe ground as we had consulted a prominent Quranic lawyer from the kick off. Given that the strength of a team lies in the supporters, the SARI network and media coverage were able to build up a solid foundation of advocates. To the fore were a group of mothers of the players and high-profile clerics like the Islamic scholar, Shaykh Dr Umar Al-Qadri, chair of the Irish Muslim Peace and Integration Centre.

Unfortunately, official Ireland ignores the progress of these brave young women. Unlike our supporters and partners abroad, who admire our achievements and have copied our template, in Ireland government departments and local authorities have no interest in the impact that is being made on the lives of these young women, on their families, their peers and their communities. Despite the fact that we have built up a skills bank of coaches and educators, we have never been approached by agencies attempting to integrate 'refugees in waiting' and more recently refugees coming from Syria. This seems ironic given people's concern about ISIS brides. With funding coming from UEFA and Football Against Racism Europe, we send our Muslim coaches into schools in every county in the Irish Republic to carry out workshops on racism, sexism, homophobia and Islamophobia. The feedback from the schools is very positive but evaluation reports sent into the Department of Education and Skills are ignored. The negative attitudes of the mandarins in Leinster House have been in contrast to the views of the EU Radicalisation Awareness Network, who see our programme as a good-practice model that can be transferred across the continent. In academia, Dr James Carr from the Department of Sociology at University of Limerick, who carried out the first-year evaluation on the programme, has presented papers on Hijabs and Hat Tricks at conferences in Glasgow and Manchester while SARI youth leader, Abdul Abdallah facilitated a workshop with FIFA Master students at De Montfort University, Leicester, UK. Along with this exposure, SARI delegates have consistently highlighted our work to the Organisation for Security and Cooperation in Europe and the Anna Lindh Foundation.

Developing the Movement

Having established a strong foundation in the first two years of operation, a movement will develop through the creation of a number of working groups that will grow the programme and the team into a stand-alone entity with technical support from SARI. In recent years, the movement continued to build up a solidarity portfolio including further support for projects in Palestine including 3G pitch construction and the development of a coaching programme with Al Helal Football Academy as an extension of the work carried out by SARI head coach, Azeez Yussuf with young footballers from Al Helal during their visit to Ireland in summer 2016.

Six female players, having completed their coaching badges, were invited to work on the development of a female football academy in Kosovo. Closer to home, the novice coaches are working with the Glentoran FC Academy, our partners in East Belfast, as they cement their relationship with the Belfast Mosque. With the emergence of the underage youth academy, the organisation introduced other sports including hockey, cricket, athletics and basketball along with the Gaelic games, Camogie and rounders during the multisport summer academy.

The connections with streetfootballworld will be strengthened with players participating in their Football3 projects and trainees graduating from the 'Team Up' for NEETS course.

The strategy is straightforward: build capacity and the skill base of the players, make sure they are resilient to stand up to Islamophobia, racism and sexism and maximise integration and participation in football league clubs and into the international teams. The introduction of a cultural and arts programme will include singer-songwriter and dance workshops along with the establishment of a reader's circle and a film club.

The second phase of the Socrates 'Football for Democracy' campaign was initiated by SARI in 2016. Inspired by the Brazilian footballers' campaign for democracy in Brazil, this phase targets Muslim men and women and invites them to join the register of electors. This will result in this cohort's further participation in democratic structures. In 2019, a major conference, where SARI Soccerfest is a flagship project, takes place as part of the European Week of Sport. Keynote speakers from Germany and the UK will focus on the topic of 'Muslim Women in Sport in Ireland'.

Football and Dialogue

This conference represents SARI's contribution to opening up channels of dialogue around the FIFA Human Rights Policy (2017) in order to encourage other national governing bodies of sport to follow suit and insert equity, integration, inclusion and equality clauses in their constitutions. The young women in the SARI programmes will be to the forefront in driving the dialogue that will emphasise the social responsibility of sport in line with the *European Commission White Paper on Sport* (2007), thus proving that sport is the great universal language that can contribute in no small way to the promotion of human rights.

CHAPTER FIFTEEN

The Dialogue of Life: Hope for the Future

Nadia Moussad

As I look back and remember details of my life so far, there are so many happy memories which come crawling back to me effortlessly. I guess being the youngest of seven children has its advantages as they all care for you. My family was characterised by a strong unity, and despite financial constraints we were happy. Back then we lived in Casablanca. My family spoke a common language, Arabic, and shared the same Muslim faith and culture. This was certainly a time of stability for me.

A change came as the family moved to France. Marseille became my adopted city and a part of me will always be there. My memories of the first years growing up in France are mixed with complex feelings. On the one hand, there was the excitement of making new friends and the drive to learn a new language and settle into a new culture. On the other, there was a confusing incomprehension of aspects of this new culture. Most of my focus was on learning a new language because at the time, for me, integration was all about the ability to speak the language. I was not interested in sophisticated dialogue, but rather I sought pure, basic communication. Furthermore, as a young child I was unaware of problems that could emanate from being perceived as 'different' in a society. Little by little

I felt more at ease in France as I progressed linguistically and discovered the rich diversity of thinkers such as Camus and Zola. I became estranged from my Muslim faith and at times the sense of being 'the other' in French society overwhelmed me.

Naturally, I compared my family's lifestyle with that of the other ethnic groups I encountered in France in an effort to comprehend what made us different. Sometimes a feeling of being part of the one human race overcame my young heart and it was obvious to me that people are paradoxically united in their difference. I found this idea of unity in difference comforting. At that time, it helped me to deal with the curiosity others sometimes exhibited toward me as part of a different culture in France. I am not sure I was too familiar with this difference myself.

Well-meaning Show-and-Tell in School

At school an approach was taken where all of the 'foreign' children were asked to make presentations about their religions and cultures. This involved a kind of show-and-tell process where children from different faiths and cultures were invited to stand up at the front of the class, and speak to the whole class about their traditions. This process often led me to feel alienated. Somehow it singled me and other 'foreign' kids out and reinforced the notion that we were different. An unwelcome spotlight was often placed on us. We had to respond to the need of the teacher and of other children to understand who we were. It made us vulnerable. In a sense, it was almost as if *we* needed *them* to understand, accept and humanise us. I never perceived this sharing of my clan and culture with other children in the classroom as a form of dialogue. It was experienced more as a monological form of public exposure. After the show-and-tell, to conclude the lesson, the well-meaning teacher would summarise by saying that we all had similar festivities. However, this homogenising acceptance of the other because of some perceived similarity always appeared to diminish participants' distinct complex identities. I desired to learn about people's differences and to come to understand and simply accept them on their own terms.

One consequence of these 'exposure' classroom-based exercises was that I got to know myself better. As I exhibited my culture and faith in school, I became more informed and knowledgeable. I thought deeply about my beliefs and searched to discover more about the faith I was born into. In effect, the show-and-tell exercises led me to a greater understanding of my own religion and culture while enhancing my sense of identity. In the process, I defined my own sense of who I was as a human being. Although this was a welcome space for self-discovery, I began to realise that remaining within my own community was insufficient to understand who I was. I needed to cross bridges in order to experience 'the other'. This was a watershed for me, driving me to attempt to engage in dialogue.

Dialogue

I can honestly say that my search for real dialogue was very often met with cruel and negative attitudes. Often in the initial stages of attempted dialogue I had to retract and defend a part of my identity that I was certainly not knowledgeable about. Maybe because of that I seemed to constantly question my own beliefs, and subsequently those of my relatives and finally those of the entire world itself. In retrospect, I now realise that in school when we were asked to do whole-class presentations, mine were always about Islam. It was as if there was an understanding that this was the only thing that I could talk about and that it entirely represented me and my community. I was never invited to make a presentation on other festivals from diverse cultures or to explore literature, music or art. I think it would have been beneficial if it were understood that religion was not my only identity marker. Other children in my class also presented on their culture but when they presented, it did not necessarily include their religion or conviction. I came to realise that the religion I was born into seemed to define me exhaustively in the eyes of others with no consideration for alternative diverse aspects of my culture. I grasped that nothing else seemed to matter. My voice as a unique, dynamic, multifaceted human being was silenced. My concern was that I was defined exclusively by a religious affiliation that was personally restricting and engendered misunderstanding in the dialogue process. I longed to speak about other things such as the musicality of Arabic as my spoken language, its richness, as well as the traditions of literature, art and history I was embedded in.

What Dialogue is Not

Looking back on all of this as an adult, I now know that dialogue is not a recruitment process for public acceptance or a space to advertise and market personal beliefs as if they were a great underappreciated product. Rather it is an occasion to celebrate with others the different ways we embark upon life and find peace within ourselves as human beings. Despite the blurring of boundaries between culture and faith or the notion that these boundaries are non-existent, a reciprocal telling of the stories of our distinctive lives, with respectful consideration for our own particular circumstances, can help us all to achieve growth as human beings.

During my final year in secondary school in France, I would often have lunch with my brother and his friends at the university, which was next door to my school. These vibrant lunches were usually accompanied by intense yet playful philosophical discussions about life in general and often focused on faith and beliefs. Listening to others share the love they had for their own well-being increases one's own sense of well-being. I liked the way this group of friends managed to speak about their faiths and beliefs and the interest each one of them expressed in understanding the other better. It was during one of those lunches that I realised that we didn't need to have the same dish to enjoy a nice dinner together. That's how I perceive dialogue now. Dialogue somehow implies an equilibrium of power. Dialogue involves listening to the other and taking their distinct ideas seriously while simultaneously discovering yourself in the process.

My Own Beliefs

As an adult, I ask myself if I became an atheist to inhabit what I believe to be a neutral zone. This said, I always find that religions offer a great comfort and strength to those who embrace them. I certainly believe that faith is based on love and understanding. I still remember the day I woke up with an ice-cold feeling travelling through my body with a certainty I couldn't shake out of me: 'There is no god.' God was gone and a feeling of emptiness was there instead. Atheism was never a choice for me. It just happened.

So, when I listen to someone sharing the love of their faith, I understand the importance of that tale and the great strength that emanates from it. Engaging in dialogue requires trust, and sharing the same love of opening up to welcome the other and express yourself is difficult.

Often I encounter people blinded by the fear of losing their beliefs. They seem to be challenged by the idea of engaging in dialogue, maybe for fear of diluting the very essence of their own being or of losing their anchor. Yet this disengagement, no matter how understandable, jeopardises the chance of harmony and mutual respect. We need to be generous, courageous and reflective in our dialogue, so that human kind has the prospect of peace. Dialogue is not easy, but what is?

SECTION THREE

Challenges and Opportunities of Interbelief Dialogue

CHAPTER SIXTEEN
Are We Just Going to Stand By?
Tomi Reichental

The fifteenth day of April is a very significant day for me. On 15 April 1945, at around 2 p.m., we heard the loud rumbling of heavy vehicles driving through the central road of the Bergen-Belsen camp. This noise was different to the sound of occasional cars driving on the road that split the camp into two parts. On the other side of the road was the men's camp and we were in the women's camp. I recall this day very clearly. Everybody was running to see what was happening: 'Who is entering the camp?'

We immediately realised that it was not Germans in the jeeps, lorries and armoured vehicles that were slowly moving through the camp. Loudspeakers were blaring in different languages, in Polish, German and English, telling us, 'This is the British Army, you are being liberated.' There was no jubilation. Ninety per cent of the Bergen-Belsen inmates were very sick. Most inmates were only skeletons. They had no strength to cheer or dance. I recall that some of the women who were well enough were throwing small branches from trees to the soldiers as a welcoming gesture. Most just stared through their sunken lifeless eyes. They smiled in delight as they had managed to survive.

At this stage, I was in a very bad way from starvation. I was just a little skeleton. If we were not liberated at the time, I wouldn't have survived much longer. Maybe a couple of weeks.

I was put into the hospital after the liberation to recuperate. Indeed, it is estimated that over twelve hundred inmates died after the liberation of Bergen-Belsen as their health had deteriorated to such an extent that it was too late to save them. At this time, we didn't know if my father had survived. He was arrested before us and taken away. My mother thought she would never see him again, but by a miracle we were reunited. Years earlier he had jumped from a moving cattle cart that was taking him to Auschwitz and to a certain death. One of the people in the cart managed to smuggle a saw blade hidden in the handle of a suitcase. While the train was speeding towards its destination during the night, the man pulled the blade from the suitcase handle and cut a hole in the door which allowed him to open the sliding door from the outside. He called in a loud voice, 'Anybody that wants to save himself should jump after me.' My father jumped out. When we returned to Slovakia from Bergen-Belsen, we discovered that tragically thirty-five members of my family perished in the Holocaust.

It took me fifty-five years before I had the courage and the strength to speak about my experiences in Bergen-Belsen Concentration Camp. Thankfully, I never suffered any trauma as a result of my incarceration. I achieved much happiness in my life, by embracing the motto, 'Make peace with the past so it won't spoil the present.'

It Starts with Whispers

We must remember that the Holocaust did not start with gas chambers but with whispers, taunts and abuse. The Holocaust was about many things: racism; loss of freedom; loss of dignity; humiliation; loss of education; confiscation of property; enslavement; starvation; torture; execution; and finally, as the 'Final Solution to the Jewish Question', it was about mass murder.

Kristallnacht

On 9 and 10 November 1938, there was a series of pogroms in Germany and Austria. These were coordinated attacks on the Jews. They earned the name Kristallnacht, meaning 'night of the broken glass'. Many historians view this as the beginning of the Holocaust. It was the beginning of Nazi Germany's broader racial policy and the beginning of the Final Solution. During this period, many Jews were murdered. Up to thirty thousand were arrested and sent to concentration camps. Over one thousand synagogues were burnt. Seven thousand Jewish businesses were destroyed. On 20 January 1942, fifteen high ranking officials of Nazi Germany held the Wannsee Conference, which was called by the Reich's security officer, Reinhard Heydrich. The purpose of this conference was to ensure cooperation in implementing the Final Solution to the Jewish Question, whereby most of the Jews of German-occupied Europe would be murdered. The Jews were trapped and consequently were nearly wiped out in central Europe. I was marked amongst them. Four thousand Irish Jews were too.

The Reichental Family

I was born in Slovakia in 1935. My family had lived and thrived in Slovakia for generations. My father served in the Slovak army. The Reichentals were people to be reckoned with. Our family homestead was the address in the village where people went to if they needed advice and help. My father was a farmer and my grandfather owned the village shop.

In 1939 the fascist government came to power in Slovakia. They soon introduced the first racial laws called the 'Jewish Codex'. This document contained two hundred and seventy paragraphs restricting the life of Slovak Jewry. From the age of five we had to wear a yellow star. We were not allowed to go to public places like cinemas, parks, swimming pools, theatres and national schools. Most Jewish businesses were closed or confiscated.

I started my education in the village, but I was kicked out of the national school once the Jewish Codex was introduced, simply because I was a Jew. I had to move to the nearest city, Nitra, to attend a Jewish school. As a six-year-old, I had to wear a yellow star. On the way to the school I experienced abuse and humiliation for the first time when gentile (non-Jewish) children on the street would call to me 'you dirty Jew, smelly Jew' and other insults that I can't even mention. Later they became more aggressive. They would spit at me and a couple of times they caught me, kicked me in my backside and let me go. It was a very frightening time for a six-year-old boy.

Deportation of Jews to Concentration Camps

The Jews were trapped in Slovakia, and in March 1942 the first deportation of Slovak Jewry began to the extermination camps. At the time, the Jewish population in Slovakia was about eighty-five to ninety thousand. Within six months, 70 per cent of Slovak Jewry was murdered, amongst them thirty-five members of my family. This first phase of deportation lasted for six months. During this time fifty-two convoys left Slovakia. Each one contained between one thousand and fifteen hundred Jews. In total, fifty-eight thousand Jews were deported. According to the statistics, less than five hundred survived the war.

When our teachers where taken away, the school closed and so my education ended. I returned to the village. The next time I returned to school was at the end of 1945. I completely lost my basic education, and when I returned to school as a ten-year-old, I had to sit in classes with six- to seven-year-old children, because I couldn't read or write. It was very humiliating for me. In the evenings, I had to learn for hours after attending school and it took eighteen months for me to catch up with my own age cohort. Despite this setback, I am happy to say that I attended college, qualified as an engineer and eventually became self-employed.

I was nine years old in November 1944 when we were betrayed and thirteen members of our family were captured by the Gestapo.[1] We were taken to the Sered detention camp, where we experienced the brutal selection. Our family group of thirteen was split up. Seven went to the right and six of us – my mother, grandmother, aunt, cousin, my brother and me – to the left. It all happened very quickly. When we waved goodbye to our aunts, uncles and cousins, we did not realise that we would never see six of them again. Only my cousin survived. He was fifteen years old. We were herded into a cattle cart and the door was closed behind us. I will never forget this moment. Our civilised life ended. It is indescribable. One moment you are still a human being and the next moment you are worse off than the animals routinely transported in these carriages. There was no privacy or hygiene. The stench and conditions were unbearable. There was very little food or water.

Bergen-Belsen

Eventually, after seven nights the cattle train stopped. The doors were opened and we were greeted with shouts '*Heraus! Heraus! Schnell! Schnell!*' from the SS guards, with guns at the ready, and the barking of their Alsatian dogs. We had arrived at our destination! This was Bergen-Belsen concentration camp. We were there from November 1944 until the liberation of the camp by the British Army in April 1945.

What I witnessed and experienced as a nine-year-old boy is impossible to describe. The starvation, the cruelty of the camp guards, the cold and disease. People, who were just skin and bone and looked like living skeletons, were walking around very slowly. Some of them dropped to the ground, never to get up again. The starvation was unbearable. We didn't starve for a day or a week. We starved for months. The daily intake of food was equivalent to six water crackers. By February 1945 the inmates were dying in their hundreds. Their emaciated bodies were left where they fell or they were thrown onto heaps. In front of our barracks there were piles of rotting and decomposing corpses. As children, we used to play amongst the corpses. The smell was unbearable, but after a while we got used to it. For many prisoners in Bergen-Belsen the conditions were too much to bear and at night they would throw themselves onto the camp perimeter, to be shot, in order to put an end to their misery. We heard the shots during the night and saw the corpses of the victims in the morning.

Despite the fact that there were no gas chambers in Bergen-Belsen and it was not described as an extermination camp, fifty thousand inmates, mostly Jews, are buried there in mass graves. When I consider what I went through and experienced as a nine-year-old boy, my survival is a miracle. When we were liberated by the British troops on 15 April 1945, there were many Irish soldiers among the ranks. Did I ever dream that I would be an Irish citizen, and one day I would be able to meet some of these brave soldiers and thank them for saving our lives?

Some years ago, I finished a documentary film called *Close to Evil*.[2] This documentary was based on my attempted encounter and reconciliation with an SS guard and convicted war criminal, Hilde Lisiewicz, who served in Bergen-Belsen at the same time that I was there. In the course of filming this documentary I met two veterans who liberated Bergen-Belsen and helped to save our lives. One of the men was John Stout from Cork, and the other was Albert Sutton from Dublin. This was the first opportunity I had to thank these brave veterans for their sacrifices to liberate us. John Stout responded with these words, 'It was the best thing I ever did in my life and I would do it again if I could.' Unfortunately, John passed away in 2015.

Life in Ireland
I came to Dublin in late 1959 to set up a factory to manufacture zips and zip fasteners. I married a Jewish girl from Dublin in

1961 and became an Irish citizen in 1977. I had been living in Ireland for ten years when the disturbances in Northern Ireland began. I watched the Troubles unfold from my home in Dublin. As a father and Holocaust survivor, I was deeply saddened by the constant bloodshed and human suffering on all sides. It is a great tribute to the Irish people and to individuals who worked tirelessly with perseverance and patience to achieve a reconciliation, that there is finally peace on the island of Ireland. For the past thirteen years since my retirement I have devoted my life to travelling all over Ireland and abroad, speaking about the Holocaust and my experiences, in schools, colleges, universities and private events.[3] I have spoken to over one hundred thousand students so far. I owe it to the Holocaust victims that their memory is not forgotten.[4] The Holocaust must never be forgotten and must never be compared to anything that has happened since.

My message is to reject racism, hate and bigotry and to embrace tolerance and reconciliation. I call this work my mission of remembrance and understanding amongst people of different backgrounds. In November 2012, the President of the Federal Republic of Germany, Joachim Gauck awarded me the Order of Merit for my untiring commitment to furthering mutual understanding, reconciliation and German–Irish friendship. The awarding of the Order of Merit of the Federal Republic of Germany is a prestigious recognition and the highest honour that the Federal Republic of Germany bestows for services to the nation. Since then I have received many other accolades for combatting racism and bigotry, and advancing reconciliation and tolerance. My devotion to this work is not motivated by receiving these awards, but they are a recognition and a great honour for me.

Dialogue

In my film *Close to Evil*, I reached out to be reconciled with one of my jailers in Bergen-Belsen. This happened in January 2012 when I discovered that one of the SS women guards in Bergen-Belsen was still alive and living in Hamburg, Germany. After I established contact with her, she agreed to meet me. She was ninety-two years old at the time. I started out on this journey open to the idea that this SS guard, Hilde Lisiewicz, could be a different person today than the young woman that was convicted of war crimes in 1945. I was prepared to meet Hilde Michnia (as she is called today), who had been convicted as a war criminal for killing two inmates and mistreating prisoners. I thought she would have seen the light and changed her values by now. I was prepared to reconcile with her and shake her hand, because in my naive thinking she was also a victim of her own time. I reasoned that she was brainwashed and indoctrinated from a very young age. In the end Hilde refused to meet me. The fact that I did not meet Hilde was not the let-down; rather, the fact that Hilde is still stuck in the 1940s world view and mentality is what disappointed me. In retrospect, I have come to realise that if meeting Hilde and shaking her hand had taken place, without Hilde showing any regret, compassion or sorrow for what happened during the Holocaust, I would have regretted the encounter with her for the rest of my life.

Atonement

As Jews, we have a tradition of atonement, which is a rich and noble concept. I am not a Rabbi, nor am I a very observant Jew, but I am a product of my background. I understand atonement as a person's effort to acquire a new heart and a new spirit. Atonement, as I see it, is about repentance and reparation. Hilde had no interest in any of this. By her refusal to meet me, she chose to deny the murders of the inmates in Bergen-Belsen, and to justify and distort her own role during the Third Reich.[5]

Dialogue and Hope

My involvement in documentary film-making did not end there. Later, I met Alexandra Senfft, the granddaughter of

Hanns Ludin, the Nazi war criminal who was directly implicated and had a part in sending thirty-five members of my family to death in the gas chambers. The encounter with and embrace of Alexandra were not acts of forgiveness; they were the embrace of a 'kindred spirit'. Alexandra sought me out, to demonstrate our common humanity. She wants to proclaim the truth and urge people not to forget. My mission is the same. We must remember. She has also met my brother and she is now a good friend and a new member of our large family.

In the late thirties, Jews wanted to escape central Europe due to the threat of Nazi tyranny, but the world stood by, most people stood by, and the Jews were not welcome. The Jews were nearly wiped out in central Europe. Today, we are again witnessing the plight of refugees who are escaping persecution, torture, rape and murder. They are looking for sanctuary in Europe. Are we going to stand by and witness another tragedy?

CHAPTER SEVENTEEN

Islamophobia in Ireland

James Carr

Illuminating the Darkness: Initiating Dialogue

Recent decades have witnessed an amplification of anti-Muslim rhetoric and discourse. As Edward Said has so famously demonstrated, constructions of Muslim as 'other' are by no means new;[1] however, the so-called 'War on Terror' and associated securitisation policies and practices *inter alia* have certainly increased the discursive volume. I have spent over a decade endeavouring to understand and evidence what impact these discourses are having on Muslim men, women and children in the Irish context. On this basis, in 2009, I undertook an evaluation of what we know at the level of the Irish State about anti-Muslim hostility and discrimination in Ireland.[2] I quickly discovered that we knew next to nothing about Islamophobia, or as I prefer to call it anti-Muslim racism in Ireland.[3] Whatever limited, yet valuable, insights we did have on anti-Muslim hostility and discrimination were soon lost with the onset of 'austerity'.[4]

The research that this chapter is focused on has a very simple goal, even though it is complex to realise. It aims to shed a heretofore absent light on the experiences of anti-Muslim hostility and discrimination in the Irish context in order to inform societal dialogue and effect change at the level of official anti-racism policies and practices. To do so, this study utilised a range of research methods that, together, could provide a deep understanding of the phenomenon at hand. The first phase of this research utilised a survey to get some statistical insight on levels of anti-Muslim racism in Ireland. The second phase involved interviews and group discussions with Muslim men and women. The use of qualitative methods in the second phase added depth to the statistics, providing an understanding of the subjective experiences of anti-Muslim racism in Ireland. In total, three hundred and forty-five Muslim men and women participated in this research from fourteen towns and cities in Ireland; incorporating multifarious ethno-national backgrounds, ages, genders (47 per cent female, 53 per cent male) and aspects of Islam. All participants were aged eighteen or over. In what follows, I will elaborate briefly some of the realities of anti-Muslim hostility and discrimination in Ireland, while emphasising important nuances of this phenomenon as appropriate.

Anti-Muslim Racism in Ireland
The research findings presented here break new ground in our understanding of anti-Muslim racism in Ireland. In the first phase of this study, involving a survey of Muslim men and women, just over half of the participants indicated that they did experience some form of hostility.[5] Given that this study centred specifically on anti-Muslim racism, it was necessary to ask a question that validated the centrality of participants' Muslimness in their experiences. The data that emerged revealed that over one-third (36 per cent) of survey participants felt they had been targeted on the basis of their being identified as Muslim. The manner in which this hostility manifested varied, with participants reporting physical assaults (22 per cent) ranging from being struck, having hijabs forcibly removed, to being pushed and/or spat at, while some reported being threatened or harassed (20 per cent). A white Irish male con/re-vert to Islam recalled his

experiences of physical abuse, 'I have been pushed and have had people spit in my face, for being Muslim.' The predominating form of hostility reported was verbal assault (81 per cent). The manner in which this verbal abuse manifested, as will be demonstrated below, frequently made direct reference to the contemporary Muslimness identity, indicative of contemporary racialised images of Muslims and Islam.

Participants were also asked about their experiences of discrimination.[6] One third of all participants indicated that they had experienced anti-Muslim discrimination. As with anti-Muslim hostility, experiences of discrimination which are elaborated further below are heavily gendered. In terms of context, in/accessing work, education and using public transport were the key domains for experiences of discrimination. It is worth noting at this point that there are striking similarities between the experiences of participants here in Ireland and those present in international evidence of anti-Muslim racism.[7] Given the focus of this collection on interfaith dialogue, the next section will focus on the experience of those who con/re-verted to Islam.[8]

Irish Con/Re-verts to Islam

'[I've been] told by a lot of people on the street I'm Irish... [I] don't need to follow Islam and betray Ireland.' This comment, shared by an Irish female Muslim survey participant, chimes with studies across Europe that also document how Muslim citizens are perceived as 'traitors' to their nation or 'race' after they accept Islam.[9] The following quotes are provided by white Irish con/re-verts to Islam and evidence how they come to be perceived by some in Irish society as 'other' upon con/re-version. Here they elucidate experiences of hostility on the basis of a perceived 'betrayal', their frustrations are palpable:

> *When they find out you're Irish they feel like you're a traitor ... Because you've put a scarf on your head? Or*

because you changed your religion? ... then [you] are no more an Irish person, you have then lost your identity of who you are, you are ... classed as non-Irish. (Aalia, Irish female Muslim)[10]

Confronted with this perception of being a 'traitor', participants underscore their Irishness and emphasise their belonging in Ireland. The comments of a white Irish male Muslim con/re-vert who participated in the survey are indicative of such sentiments: 'My family have been traced back to the 1700s in Ireland on both sides.' During one group discussion, Jada, a white Irish female con/re-vert to Islam shared her experience as a medical professional. Here a male patient confronted Jada, saying, 'Take that rag off your head; you're too good looking for that ... you're betraying Ireland.' Zaheen, a female Irish con/re-vert to Islam describes her experience with a male assailant:

I just told him look, I'm not a terrorist and I'm not a foreigner, I'm Irish and he just kept going and going, just getting more and more [aggressive] then we crossed the road and he turned around to me and he spat in my face and I was just really shocked because that was the first ... I've had comments before, just about terrorism and Bin Laden's wife and all these things, like whatever, but that was the first kind of like physical abuse.

Religious Identifiability

Muslim communities in Ireland are rich in their diversity. In this study alone, over fifty different countries of origin and multifarious ethnic groups are represented. This diversity means that a Muslim person may be exposed to exclusionary practices on the basis of any one of their identity characteristics including, but not restricted to, gender and skin colour, in isolation or at intersection. Survey participants were asked to indicate which aspects of their identity they felt played a role in their experiences of anti-Muslim racism. While skin colour (47 per cent), cultural identity (45 per cent) and real or perceived immigrant status (37 per cent) featured strongly, the overriding characteristic in participants' experiences was their religious identity. In experiences of hostility, the vast majority of participants (81 per cent) stated that their religious identity played a role in their being targeted for abuse. Similar numbers of participants (87 per cent) felt their religious identity factored in experiences of discrimination. Fahima details the experience a female Muslim friend who wears the niqab[11] had when out shopping with her young child:

> *[A Muslim] lady [at] one of the kiosk sweet sections in the centre of the shopping centres [was with] her young son; he ... wanted a packet of crisps ... this lady wears the niqab ... she stood there [at the counter] ... the [staff member] was engrossed in a conversation with a friend across the counter ... she [Muslim woman] said, 'Excuse me!' She was ignored. She said [that] four times and she was ignored, completely dismissed ... another lady came up to purchase something and was served immediately.*

The findings of this study demonstrate that both Muslim men and women experience discrimination when they are identified as Muslim. When we think of a person being recognisably Muslim we may first think of the hijab, the burqa or the long beard. However, revealing one's name in a job application also potentially reveals one's Muslimness. The following male participant found his job interview focused inappropriately on his faith even though he was devoid of overt markers of Muslimness but for his name.

> *During job interviews, questions are more focused on religion, although I do not practise. It is like hiring an Irish [person] for a management position and ask[ing]*

him/her about being Catholic. For every single interview I attended, it is exclusively about Islam and Muslims, the fact of being secular doesn't mean anything, then and during the interviews. I know it very well that I was asked to come for questioning and having a job, after an interview focused on what type is my religion rather than my educational background or previous multinational experience, [the interview] was ending as it always used to end. I became intimidated by attending further interviews because of the religious or ethnic prejudice [that] has already formed in the mentality of the interviewer and I became guilty until proven innocent. (Arabic male)

Jeehan, a Black African Muslim woman, who wears a 'full long hijab', provides a female perspective on discrimination while looking for work:

I went to a clothes shop and a restaurant/coffee shop. The girl in the coffee shop actually she smiled, 'I don't think you'll get work here', meaning because of the way I was dressed. I left a CV for the manager who was out. I left a CV in a sports clothes shop. The guy working there, not the manager, said, 'I don't think you will get a job because of the way you are dressed.' He didn't even hide it. When I left him, I thought maybe he said that because he compared my clothes to the uniform of the shop. At this point I was wearing a full long hijab. I was new here.

'Suspect' Communities

Experiences of hostility and discrimination are not restricted to interactions in the private sector. Aatif, a male Muslim participant, explicitly presents the core of the concept of 'suspect community'. This term, originally coined in reference to Irish communities in the UK during the Troubles, refers to the treatment of a person as a suspect on the basis of an association with a group identity.[12] Ehan (South-Asian Irish Muslim male) describes his experience and that of his friends as they were leaving an anti-war protest. Although attended by a large and diverse group, Ehan noted that they were 'singled out [because they] just happened to look different'. When the time came to leave:

> *We went to the car park to sit down and turn on the car ... we were just reversing to come out of the car park and head back ... with the rest of the crowd and then guards came.[13] Two guards in plain clothes and then two others in uniforms were standing in the near distance ... they came to us and I could see most of our colleagues ... going; it was just our car left in the car park near Shannon airport ... I was sitting in the back, so two guys [Gardaí] came in the car ... inside the car and we just took it easy ... they're [asking] what's your name? Do you have an ID on you? You know, whose car is this? Where did you get it? Where do you live? When did you come to Ireland? What do you think of Saudi Arabia? What do you think of Hezbollah?*

The impact of pathologising practices such as these that collate Muslimness with a 'suspect' identity permeates beyond the immediate context. Indeed, the repercussion of such profiling can inform and 'legitimise' broader experiences of hostility and discrimination lived by Muslim men and women. Repeatedly throughout this study, survey participants recalled how they have been subjected to taunts of 'Muslims are terrorists', 'Suicide bombers', and 'Taliban'. Consistent across these lived experiences is the continuing theme of Muslims as a 'suspect community':

> *In June 2011, at the Luas station, an older man said to me and shouted, 'She has a bomb in her bag! She has*

a bomb in her bag!' because I was wearing a burqa.
(Arabic Muslim female)

Gender and Anti-Muslim Racism

I now want to turn specifically to the role of gender, and in particular the experiences of female Muslims in Ireland. In terms of gender and religious identifiability, the vast majority of Muslim women (86 per cent) that took part in the survey stated that they were 'identifiably Muslim' compared to less than half of Muslim men (46 per cent). Furthermore, the overwhelming majority of Muslim women (96 per cent) who experienced hostility also reported that they were religiously identifiable compared to less than half of Muslim men. A similar pattern emerged in relation to discrimination, where again the vast majority of Muslim women (98 per cent) who experienced discriminatory practices stated they were identifiably Muslim compared to a smaller number of Muslim men (45 per cent). Survey findings are clear on this point, with Muslim women (44 per cent) reporting higher levels of anti-Muslim hostility than Muslim men (28 per cent). As noted already, female Muslims (40 per cent) reported higher levels of discrimination than their male co-religionists (22 per cent). Discourses of Muslim women in the West construct them as 'passive victims of oppressive cultures ... the embodiment of a repressive and "fundamentalist" religion'.[14] The repercussions of these discourses are made clear by Ghadir, a female Irish con/re-vert to Islam: 'They think that, like, everyone that wears a scarf is oppressed.'

The racialised symbolism of Muslim women being oppressed is a powerful theme in this study, evident in manifest and latent hostility. 'You get the same questions, you know, the women are put down ... is your husband domineering?' (Jada, female Irish con/re-vert to Islam) This perception of being oppressed is met with frustration and what I refer to as 'oppression fatigue' as succinctly put by Samira: 'It's really tiring.' And sarcastically by Sara: 'You no longer care; you are like: yeah, I'm oppressed!'

Not only do the women express their tedium at being typecast as oppressed, they are also keen to demonstrate their agency. In spite of the stereotypes, they are keen to show that they are intelligent, engaging people. In the case of Irish reverts to Islam, a common perception they are greeted with is one whereby they are deemed lacking in agency and must have been coerced into taking the *Shahadah*. This marks a further point of frustration for female Muslim con/re-verts who underscore that it was *their* decision alone to choose Islam:

> *I chose to be this religion. It's not because I'm married to a Muslim, because everyone meets me [says], 'Oh you must be married to a Muslim then and that's why you're a Muslim.' Hello! I have my own brain! I can think for myself!*
> (Ghadir, Irish female con/re-vert to Islam)

The discourse of oppressed Muslim women also serves to 'legitimise' the deployment of 'liberation tactics' by those would-be liberators of the oppressed. The impact these 'tactics' have on the Muslim female participants in this study includes shock, depression, feelings of fear and vulnerability. It is ironic that Muslim women, assumed to be oppressed and repressed, and alleged 'property' of Muslim men, are being 'liberated' through acts of coercion; becoming manifestly oppressed at the hands of their assailants. In addition to the above, participants also recalled, with notable similarity, the manner in which their items of dress, such as the hijab or niqab, had been forcibly removed. Indeed, it is almost expected. As one survey participant put it, 'Since I am a female Muslim, I got to experience that my scarf got pulled down off my head in school' (Arabic Muslim female).

Conclusion

The findings discussed in this chapter illustrate the complex and multifaceted character of anti-Muslim racism in Ireland. Thankfully, the experiences detailed in this study may not be those of every Muslim in Ireland. Nonetheless, it is striking and disheartening to hear repeated in so many narratives, the implicit resignation to the normality of this reality on the part of some participants. My ongoing research with Muslim communities continues to detail experiences of hostility and discrimination towards Muslim communities, as well as increased activity by far-right political groups. This underscores the urgency with which the fight against this phenomenon in Ireland must be treated.[15] Positive soundings have come from An Garda Síochána. They now have the facility to record anti-Muslim hostility on their crime database. It is too early to ascertain if this new facility is being implemented on the ground. What is for certain though is that effective action must be taken to change the normality of racism in the lives of Ireland's Muslim communities. The time is ripe for dialogue; we must work together to ensure that diversity is respected and protected and that our shared humanity is cherished.

CHAPTER EIGHTEEN

The Transformative Power of Dialogue

Eamon Rafter

'What we must fight is fear and silence and with them the spiritual isolation they involve. What we must defend is dialogue and the universal connection of men.'

Albert Camus[1]

I have been involved in dialogue-based work with Glencree Centre for Peace and Reconciliation for more than ten years and have experienced the challenges, impediments and inspiration that can be part of the process; however, I am never ready to call myself an expert or authority on the subject of dialogue. Every situation is different and every group is different, with its own specific needs and difficulties, each made up of individuals who cannot and should not be manipulated but rather helped to find a way forward, however hard that may be. It can be both daunting and liberating to be in the midst of such complexity and to be part of a positive dialogue process where people commit, movement is made and participants are energised to keep going. In this chapter, I want to reflect on the meaning of dialogue, how the dialogue process works and why it is one of the only genuine options for transforming conflict. These are my personal reflections rather than any official Glencree perspective, but they are based on practical experience and understandings which have developed through this work.

The Challenge of Dialogue

As human beings, listening and talking to each other should be the most straightforward things in the world; however, there are many reasons and circumstances that make it difficult or even impossible. This is even more evident when temperatures are raised and emotions engaged. I recall a day in a room in Jerusalem where a group of young Irish people were working together in a dialogue with young Palestinians. People were asking, 'Where are the Israelis?' They had been withdrawn from the project because there was an attack on Gaza and the Palestinians could not agree to dialogue under such conditions. The mood in the room was quite tense as participants were deeply worried about what was happening and perhaps feeling that this was not the right time for dialogue. As the facilitator with the responsibility of hearing their views and engaging the wider group, I was in the hot seat. There was a woman present who came from an Israeli organisation and she had been involved in the development of the project. She wanted to address the group, but I was concerned about what she might say. My concern was heightened because she had not been present when we created a group agreement on how we would work in a way that respected everyone in the room. When she did speak, considerable offence was taken. I don't need to outline here precisely what was said. The response of the group, with the exception of one person who challenged her, was to get up and walk out. I was left as a facilitator without a group and the dialogue was now about how to get them back into the room. I will return to what happened next at the end of this chapter.

What is Dialogue?

This is by way of setting out the challenges of dialogue and the need to deal with whatever is in the room and to be clear about what is involved if we are to undertake the adventure involved. However, I want to make the case for the potential of dialogue and the places it can take us to, while acknowledging also that they are not always what we might have hoped for. Though I propose to speak from personal experience, it is important to start by defining what I mean by dialogue as there are many interpretations and misunderstandings about this term. The IDEA/UNDP practitioners understanding is a good place to start as it reflects a certain practicality that comes from engagement in actual dialogue encounters:

> *Dialogue is a process of genuine interaction through which human beings listen to each other deeply enough to be changed by what they learn. Each makes a serious effort to take others' concerns into her or his own picture, even when disagreement persists. No participant gives up her or his identity, but each recognises enough of the other's valid human claims that he or she will act differently toward the other.*[2]

There is a realistic emphasis here on bringing about a real exchange, an acknowledgement of the difficulties involved and the need for change to happen. However, I would also look for a more essential understanding, which David Bohm offers in defining dialogue as a 'stream of meaning, flowing among, through and between us', a kind of 'thinking together' which ultimately is the only way that conflict gets worked through and resolved.[3]

The way I approach dialogue is very much from the sense that it is a process rather than an instrument or an event. The nature of this process is that it has a kind of complexity that can be off-putting, but as J.P. Lederach suggests, there is a great simplicity and directness on the far side of this complexity, if we are able to embrace it. People are invited rather than compelled to participate, so its voluntary nature is essential.[4]

The process itself is best characterised as one that requires participants to question and reflect on their own assumptions and positions and those of others while they examine carefully the needs that underpin them. They are then more able to develop understanding and identify shared needs and perhaps those which they do not feel they hold in common. This search for understanding is always challenging when it is done with honesty and depth, and it may or may not offer a basis for developing trust and building relationships. At the very least, the engagement of real dialogue allows for the possibilities of such things to emerge. We may hear something that contradicts our assumptions and this can change our attitude to the other allowing us to see them in a different and more human light. If they are not quite like us, they are at least not all that different and there is therefore hope for some positive change. There is also the hope that dialogue then allows us to see difference as non-threatening and value or re-imagine the areas where we are not alike.

Dialogue is Not Debate

Before I came to work with dialogue processes I confused dialogue with other narrative and discursive practices like 'debate', so I think it's important to say something about this. Like many people in Ireland I recall how school involved learning the skills of debate, which I would characterise as 'developing an argument to score points and find flaws', 'listening for ammunition', 'defending a position' and 'the insistence that one person is right and the other therefore wrong'. These may be useful life skills but are less helpful in situations of conflict. Rather than arguing and trying to convince the other, we need to try and discover the truth that can emerge from hearing different sides. It is the meaning of the disagreement that is really important and we can only really get this when we understand the underlying interests. In earlier attempts at facilitation, I began to see how easily people go into debate mode when difficulties arise and how defensive positions makes progress unlikely or even impossible. When people feel themselves under threat, they frequently resort to typical behaviours which include an extremely defensive mode of communication. These reactions then create major impediments to progress as people cling to their positions for fear of losing something or being forced into an agreement they don't want. I began to understand how important the facilitation process was in turning debate into dialogue to help reverse this defensiveness and encourage more positive interpersonal communication.

This brings us closer to understanding what the dialogue process is all about and how important the role of facilitator is in fostering it. A key to this for me has been the question of whether dialogue should have an intended outcome or rather be characterised by the absence of an agenda and therefore be in and of itself. If I am asked what is the purpose of any particular dialogue, I may answer that I do not yet know because that cannot actually be created in advance. I could, of course, add that we hope it will lead to better understanding, more positive relationships and even the opening of some element of trust, but essentially, I cannot be the one to say what might be achieved by a group of people coming together in this kind of engagement. The purpose has to emerge from the group and that for me is what characterises real dialogue process. Logically, this also implies that no specific outcomes will emerge, though if people find reason to meet again and continue the conversations, this suggests that they are getting something useful, even if it is hard to be precise about where that will take them. If I require a group, in advance of meeting, to conform to a particular purpose because I think that is what they need to address, then it is about my agenda rather than theirs. I am attracted to David Bohm's ideas of 'impersonal fellowship', 'participatory consciousness' and 'shared meanings' as essentials of the process, but that does not require a defined objective that I want the group to work towards.[5] If a purpose emerges from the dialogue, then there may be a possibility to work towards that, but it is not the reason for entering into the process. The transformational aspect of dialogue is not about getting what you want so much as the place where new understandings may take us. If a moment emerges when we can see things differently and our assumptions have been challenged sufficiently, there is potential for this transformation to happen. This is not predefined in any sense and frequently it may not occur, but when it does take place it renews our belief that dialogue has the potential to be transformative. For people who cannot trust each other, there is a need to have some trust in the process and this is where the responsibility of the facilitator rests.

Glencree

The work of Glencree has mostly been in relation to the legacy of the conflict in Ireland, north and south, and aims to address the question of how to transform political violence. Dialogue is one of the approaches that contributes to this, but we always have to be careful not to let our priorities as an organisation take precedence over the people who we are working with and how they define their needs. Our role, therefore, is to invite people in and to 'hold the space' so they can begin to engage from the place they are in. This can be hugely different for individuals and groups and some may characterise themselves as victims, others as survivors and others may say they were not particularly affected or defined by the conflict at all. However, when people come into dialogue in relation to particular themes, they are there on a voluntary basis and, therefore, presumably have something to gain by either listening to or contributing to the process. This would also apply to interbelief or intercultural dialogue as nobody can be forced into such a setting.

A dedicated or at least an appropriate place for dialogue is important so that it is acceptable and accommodating to people coming from different political, cultural or religious backgrounds. Glencree has sought to provide this over a number of years. This has allowed the organisation to work with quite diverse individuals and groups and develop some guidelines and good practices around doing this work. Creating safety is an essential prerequisite, and this involves respecting the dignity of all present and developing a group agreement for each group that helps them to achieve that sense of safety and trust in the process. The space that needs to be held is a physical one, usually a circle in a room where there are no disturbances, but it also has non-physical dimensions. I would question the notion that people who come from different or even conflictual backgrounds do not want to engage with each other. People frequently have a deep need to come together, and find the separation and awkwardness that goes with conflict deeply uncomfortable. Many times, in Glencree, I have seen this play out. At first, it feels necessary to keep up the appearance of separation but there is a sense of relief and release when there is a shift and something happens to put people into the natural state of being together. This is the 'universal connection' that Camus refers to, though of course it needs to be a possibility for everyone.

So, 'holding the space' needs to take a lot of things into consideration and it is the art of peace-building that allows us to imagine a way to bring it into being. It is not about following a formula or a series of defined stages, but more about listening carefully and easing the process forward. Forcing it may be tempting but it is always the wrong option and will not support people to move forward. If we are to view conflict as an aberration, we are likely to look on dialogue as a way of fixing or restoring something. I am more inclined to view conflict as part of the natural state, and dialogue is then a process that allows us to work with this creatively. Of course, it is an unpredictable journey that may not always work or may not work for everybody. It is an exploratory and open-ended process and not an end result in itself. It may help relationships to develop, but this is a matter for those who are involved. Even if it does not provide a change at this level, if the process has been well guided, it should help toward new understandings of ourselves and others. If the participants have been able to take on responsibility for what is happening, that will lead to a new basis and a blurring of the boundaries of separation. This in itself is transformative and can empower people to take positive action to build on this.

The Transformative Potential of Dialogue

The story from Jerusalem provides an epilogue to this piece. In the days following the group walkout, I went through a learning process as we worked with the support of a great team to have an honest discussion about what had taken place and how best to help people to deal with the challenges in other ways. The conversations were not easy, but a supportive and even transformative environment was created, which helped people to deal with what they were seeing on the news and the senseless slaughter that they were powerless to respond to. Nothing was sorted or fixed, but the engagement of those who came back into the room showed what could be achieved through a supportive process.

The group had only come back into the room on the understanding that what happened would not be allowed to happen again. They took ownership of the process and agreed that leaving the room was not the best thing that could have happened. Their deeper exploration of what had happened helped them to see it in a different light. Blaming others was not a solution for them. They felt they needed to become more resilient and though dialogue could not solve their problems, it could help them along the way. Some of them asked to meet with the Israeli woman and they told her why they had reacted in the way they did. There was no happy ending, but the week had been worthwhile. The Palestinian participants said they hoped that there could still be an opportunity to meet with the Israeli group. The Irish members of the group went away enriched by the experience and, hopefully, with an insight into the transformative potential of dialogue. I do not want to suggest here that dialogue is the solution to the problems of the world. There are limitations to what can be achieved through this process and there are frequently huge difficulties that make it impossible for people to even sit together. When bombs are falling, as in the instance above, the possibility is not really there for any openness or talk about trust and developing understanding. When the inequalities are too big to allow any approximation of people being treated as equals, then there will not be a real option for dialogue. When there is no respect for the voices of the disempowered, there will be no appetite for such engagement. Yet these are the very situations that require change and new ways to view the impasse and search for small shafts of light. If the people in the room are ably assisted by good facilitators and have the courage and determination to engage, there can be a softening and an opening up. Nobody has been defeated and nothing has been lost, but there has been a change, and now there are possibilities and a sharing of a common burden which can be faced together. Though we cannot predetermine where this might lead us, it is almost certain to be in the right direction.

CONCLUSION

Patricia Kieran

This book is just one tiny step on the journey to a much greater dialogue about religious and philosophical beliefs in contemporary Ireland. It suggests that meaningful dialogue is pluriform and is enriched by religious and non-religious participants coming together in trust and openness in what Gert Biesta describes as 'a way of being together that seeks to do justice to all partners involved'.[1] In this book, the term 'interbelief dialogue' is used to designate a broad, inclusive and multilayered dialogical activity. The chapters are written by people from a range of religious as well as humanist, agnostic and atheist traditions, and they give voice to some of the complex and challenging issues arising from the varieties of dialogue undertaken by belief-diverse communities. It would be impossible to represent all belief traditions in one volume and so the selection of religions and beliefs is partial and particular. The fact that there are absent voices is not a deliberate oversight. It simply reflects the context of the Limerick IBD seminar, which inspired this book.

Dialogue Matters

In essence, this book suggests that interbelief dialogue is not an exceptional activity of relevance to a few. In an age of global communications, more frequent international travel and multi-belief populations, people are increasingly coming into contact with a diverse array of religions and beliefs. This book hopes to dispel the myth that IBD is a specialised minority activity that, as one IBD participant at an interbelief event stated, 'involves talking to strange people who have unusual surnames, wear funny clothes and believe bizarre things'. It is impossible to quantify the number of religions or convictional stances in the world, but estimates suggest that there are over four thousand religions in a world of over 7.5 billion people. It is worth noting too that approximately 1.1 billion people in the world are secular, non-religious, agnostic and atheist.[2] Unless humans want to isolate themselves from others for fear of religious or non-religious contamination, they need to learn the skill of engaging with people of different belief commitments and world views. In so doing, they will begin to appreciate that religions and beliefs are significant and, in many instances, central to people's lives. Interbelief dialogue should be of concern to people in Ireland because it shapes who we are as a society and how we relate to each other. Moreover, in a multi-belief democratic society, many groups are genuinely curious about, excited about and interested in exploring their own and others' beliefs. Dialogue among people of diverse beliefs generates opportunities for mutual appreciation and understanding and for living harmoniously in respect and openness.

IBD in Ireland

It is sobering for people on the island of Ireland to remember the historic consequences of belief segregation and the lack of dialogue during the Troubles. Anyone familiar with the Craigavon Bridge in Derry city will know the Hands Across the Divide monument. This bronze sculpture of two men reaching out to each other was erected in 1992, twenty years after Bloody Sunday. It is a visual reminder that reaching out through dialogue has the potential to bridge divides. The opposite is also true. Non-engagement with others through monologue and silence can lead to divided, hostile and fractured societies. While it might seem easier to disengage from the other, to stay within one's tribe, the consequences of filling in the gaps about an unknown other with indifference, stereotypes and hatred are potentially toxic for society.

Increasing Diversity of Beliefs

In recent decades, the island of Ireland has gained recognition for its rich tradition of transforming violent conflict and building peace through dialogue. There is an appreciation that coming together in dialogue and weaving a web of positive relationship is central to the flourishing of society. Patrick Sullivan's chapter on the proposed ERB and ethics curriculum gave an overview of educational developments responding to the increased diversity of religions and beliefs in Ireland. Many curricula and programmes, such as the *Catholic Preschool and Primary Religious Education Curriculum* (2015), the *Grow in Love* programme (2015–19), the CNS *Goodness Me, Goodness You* curriculum (2018), and the HAI and Educate Together *Lessons on Humanism* (2017) were designed to support interbelief literacy and dialogue in schools. A number of chapters in this book identified key educational challenges relating to Ireland's growing diversity of belief. The book outlines a range of approaches, including dialogue in the form of email communication between young pupils in schools, and educational initiatives that encourage children's exploration of distinct religious and secular traditions and narratives.[3] Between 2011 and 2016, the number of people with 'no religion' rose by 73.6 per cent, while the fastest growing religions in that period were Islam (growth of 28.9 per cent), Hinduism (growth of 34.1 per cent) and Orthodox Christianity (37.5 per cent).[4] Though Ireland is becoming increasingly belief plural, this does not translate automatically into positive engagement with those of different beliefs.[5] As noted by Faas et al.:

Each year during the past decade, a minimum of three thousand new entrants from outside Ireland to mainstream primary schools have been recorded, with a peak of eight thousand per annum around the time of the start of the recession in 2008. As a multi-ethnic, multi-faith society, it is imperative that Ireland continues to strengthen a non-discriminatory perspective in education and promote religious pluralism.[6]

This book emphasises that belief diversity in Ireland is a positive resource to be realised rather than a problem to be solved. However, we live in a society that sometimes perceives belief difference as inherently binary, divisive and problematic. Trisha Rainsford observes that somewhere along the line, as a human race, we seem to have lost sight of the fact that it is possible to hold to our own truth while engaging with different perspectives. Interbelief dialogue offers humans the opportunity to engage in a powerful shift of gear, to move from seeing others as hostile competitors to seeing them as supportive collaborators. Viewed in this manner, our differences are not inhibitors to dialogue but rather motivating factors impelling us toward it.

John Paul II commented on the great fruits of dialogue when he noted that Christians no longer view those who hold beliefs different to their own as 'enemies or strangers'.[7] Many authors in this volume emphasise the transformative power of dialogue based on the golden rule (treating others as one would wish to be treated) to unite people of secular and religious world views in solidarity and respect. In order to engage in such dialogue, it is necessary to move out of our comfort zones, to meet others, listen attentively, represent voices accurately and work through multiple challenges respectfully. There will be difficulties and difficult conversations. Yet, since we do not all share identical beliefs, we must ask ourselves whether the way we practise our tradition has a negative impact on people of different beliefs.

Different Forms of Dialogue

This book set out to create a space to reflect on the nature and process of dialogue resulting from open engagement and respect involving people from a range of different religious traditions and philosophical world views. The chapters told the story of the variety of approaches to dialogue, moving from dialogue as verbal communication to dialogue as personal engagement and communal encounter with others. A core theme of this volume is that interbelief dialogue is not exclusively verbal and that its pluriform nature is manifest through art, music, sport, social engagement and many more creative forms of interaction. The chapters in this volume cover different forms of reflection on and participation in dialogue. These include dialogue through autobiographical narrative, dialogue resulting from religious experience, the dialogue of everyday life, theological dialogue, as well as dialogue focusing on education. The chapters illustrate the different types of dialogue, from grass-roots movements to structured theological dialogue involving official representatives of belief traditions and professional theologians. Dialogue is versatile and unpredictable. Dialogue is not a form of verbal debate or a contest of ideas. It results from a profound desire to engage with people and to explore collaboratively what it might mean to be human in a world that takes diversity seriously.

Chapters from members of the Dublin City Interfaith Forum and the Mid-West Interfaith Network point to the practical, experiential and vibrant ways that people of faith engage on the ground with traditions and beliefs that are different to their own. The book presents a glimpse of innovative programmes being designed by the Chester Beatty Library to use historical and cultural artefacts as stepping stones to engaging in a rich dialogue about historical beliefs and traditions as well as exciting contemporary and creative ways of viewing, thinking about and experiencing beliefs. For many, but not all, contributors, dialogue involved the four key players identified by Julia Ipgrave in chapter one: 'I', 'We', 'You' and 'God'. For these religious believers, dialogue with God is ultimately meaningful and is a defining feature of their lives. Siobhán Wheeler explains that trusting, loving and knowing God 'has been the bedrock of my life. God is the atmosphere in which I draw each breath and exhale again.' Sister Mary O'Sullivan, from the Centre for Dialogue and Prayer in Auschwitz, highlights the key role that listening to the voice of God plays in her work. She outlines four listening stages culminating in listening to the voice of God. However, atheist and humanist contributors believe passionately that reason is a more reliable approach to understanding reality and morality than faith and religion. In this one volume, what is seen as eminently reasonable by one is deemed unreliable by another. This diversity should not be an inhibitor to dialogue but rather an invitation to listen and learn from one another and to engage more deeply in it.

Keeping People Out

Three decades after the celebrated tearing down of the Berlin Wall (9 November 1989) and the end of the Cold War, the world has witnessed the rise of nationalism and nativism accompanied by the construction of border walls and security fences in response to the international migrant crisis. Much human energy has focused on segregating and isolating ourselves from the strange 'other'. In many countries, a swing to the right in politics revealed an angry, disillusioned electoral population in favour of military expansion, the deportation of illegal immigrants and economic protectionism. The building of walls has become an alarmingly common political strategy. Examples of border fences or walls include: the fence erected between Saudi Arabia and Yemen; the Israeli–West Bank Barrier; Hungary's 4-metre, 345-kilometre Croatian border fence; Macedonia's 3-metre razor-topped fence along the Greek border; Bulgaria's proposed 30-kilometre fence on the Turkish border; and Austria's proposed border barrier with

Slovenia.[8] President Trump's election pledge to build a wall along the US–Mexico border can be seen in this global context of keeping out the stranger.[9]

Despite this political turbulence, as well as the considerable challenges facing the global community, it is important to keep sight of the positive developments and opportunities for meaningful collaboration and effective interbelief dialogue in the world. There are many positive signs. In 2019, the United Arab Emirates hosted the Global Human Fraternity Conference in Abu Dhabi, which was attended by seven hundred religious leaders and scholars. This interreligious event provided an opportunity for encounter, dialogue and peace-building. It was the first time a pope visited the Arabian peninsula. Pope Francis addressed the conference and said that 'religious behaviour needs continually to be purified from the recurrent temptation to judge others as enemies and adversaries', while noting that the heavenly perspective 'embraces persons without privilege or discrimination'.[10] Such a coming together of the world's religious leaders is not unprecedented. In chapter seven, Brendan Leahy writes about the incredible momentum generated by the first interfaith peace gathering in Assisi in 1986 and its legacy in the founding of the Sant'Egidio movement and subsequent interfaith gatherings in Assisi. Indeed, members of the United Nations have included representatives of different faith traditions in an official high-level conversation on 'Religions for Peace' as an attempt to 'recall the significance of maintaining respectful tolerance across diverse cultures and religions'.[11]

Conditions for Dialogue

For dialogue to take place, a person must be in the presence of the other. Presence can occur in multiple forms. This volume has shown that dialogue can be mediated by technology, or supported by skilled facilitators as described in the work of Eamon Rafter at the Glencree Peace Centre. What is crucial in all dialogue is that the other is not a 'projected' but a 'genuine' other.[12] Martin Buber (1878–1965) held that all actual life is encounter, and dialogue is at the heart of what it is to be human as it represents the desire for communication with another. Dialogue understands that we are not all the same but we can disagree without being disagreeable. At the Limerick interbelief dialogue workshops, everyone was invited to speak about their personal experience but nobody was forced to talk. Dialogue is not a form of proselytism or conversion. Misunderstanding and confusion are part of dialogue since there is no assumed homogeneity. Imam Noonan describes his surprise at being invited to dialogue when he says, 'I thought to myself, "What? Atheists, Christians and Muslims coming together?"' His testimony tells how these groups have managed to develop a good friendship and deep respect for each other. Dialogue requires courage. Sometimes the unfamiliar belief system of the other seems so dissonant and disconnected from what is familiar that people shy away from encounter, or misconceive, stereotype or despise others. Without dialogue and collaboration, the end result can lead to sectarianism, bigotry, belief intolerance and conflict.[13]

A Messy Process

The book testifies to the fact that IBD is messy and there is no neat resolution to seemingly irreconcilable differences among belief groups. Often we have to continue to engage in dialogue knowing that we are seeing the world in radically different ways. What is crucial is that people are invited to engage in dialogue in a safe, open, respectful and mutually enriching manner. There are serious, and for some dialogue partners insurmountable, difficulties in dialogue as different religious and belief groups may arrive at a place where they have irreconcilable interpretations of language, belief and culture. The Limerick seminar was a very tentative initial step toward interbelief dialogue. It acknowledged that we are not the same; our beliefs are not identical. The process of dialogue is a long-term, continuous process and the resolution of difficulties is not immediate. Sometimes the act of appreciating the complexity and depth of very real differences between dialogue partners is the major advancement in the dialogue. Resolution may take generations. For some IBD groups, theological or formal dialogue about beliefs is not the main focus. Instead, participants might work together on areas of common concern and share a common goal. In this manner, AI, Ahmadi Muslims and HAI have bridged what may be seen as major differences to work together through dialogue to respect and support each other in an alliance to further secular schooling in Ireland. In this manner too, MWIN come together to support each other and celebrate members' sacred festivals.

Difference

Sometimes dialogue is difficult. It is frustrating. It involves participants in moments of misunderstanding, confusion and potential conflict. It challenges participants to re-evaluate their own world view. It is difficult to appreciate the other's perspective and to learn from their world view, especially when one is convinced that one's own is preferable. In *The Holocaust as Active Memory*, Seeberg, Levin and Lenz hold that, 'In many contexts the Holocaust has been, and to some extent still is such an invisible "elephant", shaping personal lives, relationships and processes by its very real, but unapproachable, presence.'[14] Tomi Reichental's chapter is a sign of hope that dialogue is possible after the Holocaust, even after the most violent and horrific experiences. Reichental testifies to the fact that it is imperative to engage in dialogue to ensure that such hatred and violence never reoccurs. Wherever dialogue about religions and beliefs takes place, the Holocaust acts as a constant reminder that the consequences of not listening to, engaging with and respecting the other can lead to unspeakable evil. Reichental speaks passionately about the need to cross the boundaries that separate us and to reach out in dialogue to the feared other. The other can take many forms. He warns us of the dangerous consequences of missing opportunities for dialogue. His chapter ends with an exhortation to us to act: 'Today we are again witnessing the plight of refugees who are escaping persecution, torture, rape and murder. They are looking for sanctuary in Europe. Are we going to stand by and witness another tragedy?'

Dialogue and Hope

In an environment where conservative far-right nativist parties are on the rise, where there is talk of building walls and keeping people out, the call to IBD might seem naively optimistic. A problematising of cultural and belief difference may speak of 'them' and 'us'. A polarising language, that talks of repatriating the unwanted other, can be used on behalf of 'the great silent majority who have seen the beginnings of "multi-culturalism" with growing dismay'.[15] Ignorance and fear of the other, whether it be in the form of asylum seekers, atheists, religious believers, Travellers or other minority groups, might encourage people to disengage and retreat to the safety of their own ethnic, belief or national group. However, the basic human instinct for dialogue cuts through and challenges this desire to stick with what you know and who you know. It is crucial to remember that there have been wonderful developments in Ireland that facilitate IBD and engagement. The proliferation of organisations that support culturally, educationally, ethnically and religiously diverse communities in Ireland is impressive.[16] The educational system in Ireland is attempting to address the real and complex needs of a belief-diverse society.

In a world marred by conflict, interbelief dialogue offers the opportunity for constructive engagement, cooperation and peace-building. It is not a panacea for all ills. It is sometimes profoundly challenging. It necessitates gathering together and moving beyond defensiveness. It involves an open-ended, respectful encounter with the other. Eamon Rafter reminds us that sometimes it can be profoundly difficult or indeed impossible to meet or sit with the other, especially if there are power imbalances or if there is no real openness or respect. However, through taking the other's differences seriously and through listening and engagement, little by little, dialogue offers profound opportunities for transformation. Dialogue roots us in our own context and tradition, yet it involves reciprocity, humility and generosity. It connects us as humans and startles us with the opportunities it provides to learn new ways from others and to see the world differently.

In contemporary Ireland, there are multiple vigorous and exciting opportunities for interbelief dialogue, connecting lives across a range of belief and religious traditions. The seeds of dialogue grow and flourish in communities that accept difference and work positively to promote each other's rights and well-being. Dialogue and collaboration with followers of other religions and traditions is not an optional extra. It is core to who we are as humans. When carried out with openness, respect, dignity and mutual love, it transforms our lives and our world.

AFTERWORD

Anna Lindh Foundation: Connecting Lives

Ann Luttrell

The Anna Lindh Foundation (ALF) is an international organisation working to promote intercultural and civil society dialogue in the face of growing mistrust and polarisation. This book about dialogue and connecting lives is a manifestation of what the foundation is all about. Dialogue between cultures is the roadmap of the ALF. The ALF works to restore trust in dialogue and bridge the gaps in mutual perceptions, as well as promoting diversity and coexistence.

Since its launch in Dublin in 2005, the ALF has supported global actions impacting mutual perceptions among people of different cultures and beliefs, including the 2016 interbelief dialogue seminar at Mary Immaculate College, Limerick, which has led to the publication of this book. These actions are dependent on the energy and enthusiasm of people in a whole range of communities and organisations.

Triskel Arts Centre's relationship with the ALF began in 2008, when we participated in an initiative titled '1001 Actions for Dialogue'. Up until then we had been involved in facilitating and coordinating creative activities locally and nationally, but partnering with ALF meant that a new vista of forty-two countries and over three thousand ALF members lay wide open as a resource not only for us but also for Ireland.

Triskel was elected as head of network for ALF in 2010, at which time there were approximately twenty members of the Irish network. Today there are sixty-two members. My role as coordinator for the ALF Ireland Network involves the scheduling of a meeting of the network once a year, as well as a 'capacity building' event with the aim of promoting intercultural dialogue around a theme of interest to the national network. The role also involves encouraging and supporting network members to participate meaningfully in ALF activities both within and outside Ireland. In the current phase, five members participated in an ALF event in Tunisia, two members participated in an event in Italy, six participated in the ALF Forum in Malta, and a contingent of eleven members participated in a cross-network event in Tarragona, Spain. One member was successful in a very competitive bid for funding during that phase, and members were actively involved in compiling the ALF's *Handbook on Intercultural Citizenship Education*.

Dialogue is key to the work of ALF and this book has contributed significantly to that ongoing dialogue about religions and beliefs in contemporary Ireland and beyond.

CONTRIBUTORS

James Carr

Doctor James Carr teaches and researches at the Department of Sociology in the University of Limerick. In 2010 he was awarded a three-year scholarship from the Irish Research Council to engage in research into discrimination and racism directed towards Muslim communities in Ireland. He is a well-known speaker on the topic of discrimination and Islamophobia in Ireland. His latest publication is entitled *Experiences of Islamophobia: Living with Racism in the Neoliberal Era* (2016).

Adrian Cristea

Adrian Cristea has a background in sociology and social work. He is currently the executive officer of Dublin City Interfaith Forum. He led the process of devising the Irish Churches' Affirmations on Migration, Diversity and Interculturalism. Adrian holds a master's degree from Trinity College Dublin. He helped to establish the first official interfaith forum in Ireland launched in January 2012. He lives in Dublin where he works in interfaith and integration in a multicultural city context. He has also organised the first Interfaith Walk of Peace in Dublin city and in Ireland. He is passionately committed to the achievement of racial justice and interfaith dialogue. His interests include human rights, interculturalism, interreligious dialogue and activity, and the role of religion in Integration and social cohesion.

Jane Donnelly

Jane Donnelly is human rights officer of Atheist Ireland, which promotes atheism, reason and ethical secularism in Ireland and around the world. She runs the website TeachDontPreach. ie, and assists parents who are discriminated against in Irish schools. She has spoken at human rights meetings of the United Nations, the OSCE and the Council of Europe. In 2013, she organised an international conference in Dublin on empowering women through secularism.

Julia Ipgrave

Doctor Julia Ipgrave is senior research fellow in the Department of Humanities at the University of Roehampton and supervises PhD students at the Centre for Education Studies, University of Warwick. She taught for sixteen years in Leicester as class teacher, assistant head and head teacher and has been involved in teacher formation for many years. Julia's research interests focus on young people's attitudes towards religion and interreligious dialogue and community engagement. Previous research includes an EC-funded study of young people's perspectives on religion in school and society in Europe REDCo (2007–9) and the AHRC/ESRC-funded *Young People's Attitudes towards Religious Diversity* (2009–12). She has undertaken evaluation studies of a number of interfaith dialogue programmes for schools. She was responsible for the East London strand of *Religion and Dialogue in Modern Societies* (2013–18), a comparative study of interreligious engagement in six north European metropolitan areas. She is an education specialist on the national Christian–Muslim Forum and member of the Intercultural Encounter Working Group (part of the Language Policy Division of the Council of Europe) where she is involved in producing resources for intercultural dialogue. She is a distinguished scholar with an international reputation. She has written extensively and her research has pioneered the development of pedagogies for dialogical religious education.

Patricia Kieran

Patricia Kieran is a British Foreign and Commonwealth Chevening Scholar who teaches religious education at Mary Immaculate College, Limerick. She is director of the Irish Institute for Catholic Studies. She previously lectured in theology and religious education at Newman University, Birmingham. She is keenly interested in interbelief dialogue and is a member of the Mid-West Interfaith Network. She has written a number of books: With Anne Hession she co-authored and co-edited books on Catholicism, theology in an intercultural context and children and religious education. She has published chapters and articles on the subject of Catholic education, Roman Catholic modernism, inclusive religious education and gender and interreligious education. She has edited, with Thomas Grenham, *New Educational Horizons in Contemporary Ireland: Trends and Challenges* (2012) and co-edited with Gareth Byrne, *Toward Mutual Ground: Religious Pluralism in Educational Practice in Ireland* (2013).

Brendan Leahy

Bishop Brendan Leahy was appointed the forty-ninth Catholic bishop of Limerick by Pope Benedict in April 2013. Brendan did a law degree in UCD (1977–80) and was treasurer of UCD Law Society. He entered formation to be a priest at Clonliffe College (1980–3) and qualified as a barrister in King's Inns. He did a doctorate in theology at the Pontifical Gregorian University, Rome (1983–6). He was professor of systematic theology in the National Seminary in St Patrick's College in Maynooth and is chair of the Catechetics Council of the Irish Episcopal Commission. He is committed to the promotion of Christian unity and interreligious dialogue. He has worked with Trevor Williams (former archbishop of Canterbury) among others and co-founded, with Rev. Dennis Cooke, a programme of studies in theology for Catholics and Protestants entitled 'Exploring Theology Together'. From 2007–12 Brendan was a member of a team from the Vatican's Pontifical Council for Promoting Christian Unity in conversation with the Salvation Army. In recent years, Brendan has engaged in interreligious dialogue, becoming a member of the Three Faiths Forum of Ireland. This forum creates a space for religious dialogue, promotes education and the provision of accurate information about the three Abrahamic faiths – Jewish, Christian and Muslim.

Ann Luttrell
Ann Luttrell is national coordinator for the Anna Lindh Foundation (ALF) network in Ireland and is a member of the ALF Advisory Council. She is also head of education and outreach programmes at Triskel Arts Centre, Cork. Ann is also programmer of literature events and is co-director of the Cork World Book Fest. She was educated at UCD and UCC and is a former secondary school teacher of English and French. She worked for over ten years in the USA and was a former aide to the mayor of Cincinnati, Ohio. Her passions are literature and politics.

Nadia Moussed
Nadia was born in Casablanca to a Yemenite father and a Moroccan mother. When she was six, the family moved to Marseille, France where she lived for seventeen years before moving to Germany in 1990 and then to Ireland. Nadia holds a degree in applied economics from the University of Aix-en-Provence, a diploma in international freight administration (Munich), a degree in German language and cultural studies from the University of Aix-Marseille and a degree in community and youth work from UCC. She is a polyglot, fluent in English, French, German, Arabic and Italian. In April 2014, she was co-coordinator at an ALF cross-network activity involving seven countries that took place in Taroudant, Morocco, entitled 'ART as an Instrument and Expression of Social Change'. In June 2014, she was chosen to represent the Irish ALF Network at the third

Alexandria Education Convention under the framework of the Education Programme for Intercultural Citizenship in the Euro Mediterranean region at the Swedish Institute in Alexandria, Egypt.

Ibrahim M. Noonan

Imam Ibrahim M. Noonan is the imam of Galway Mosque, Masjid Maryam. He is also the missionary in charge of Ireland and the vice national president of the Ahmadiyya Muslim Association Ireland. He has served in other countries as a missionary and imam. He is a graduate of a number of universities, including the University of Wales (degree in theology), the Dominican Institution of Theology and Philosophy, the London Islamic Institution of Theology and Languages, and the Islamic University of Rabwah in Pakistan.

Michael Nugent

Michael Nugent is chairperson of Atheist Ireland, which promotes atheism, reason and ethical secularism in Ireland and around the world. He also campaigns for the right to assisted dying for terminally or seriously ill people. He previously campaigned against terrorism in Northern Ireland, including founding and chairing the peace group New Consensus. He has written and co-written a number of books and the hit comedy musical play *I, Keano*. His website is: michaelnugent.com

Mary O'Sullivan

Sister Mary O'Sullivan is a Mercy Sister from Dublin. In the 1970s, she lived in California, where she taught in parish schools. She studied theology and history at the University of San Francisco and included as part of her study a course on the history of the Jewish people. Returning to Ireland in 1980, she taught religious education in a Mercy secondary school in Dublin and completed further studies in theology and education at Maynooth and at the University of Swansea.

In 1980, she brought her first group of Irish students to the synagogue. Visits to the mosque followed later. From 2001–4, she attended the summer programme for Christian educators at Bat Kol Institute Jerusalem, where Christian teachers learned how to teach Torah using Jewish sources. From 2004–8, she was registrar of this institute and taught the weekly Torah portions. In Jerusalem she attended meetings at a grass-roots level with groups engaged in Christian–Jewish dialogue and also Christian–Jewish–Muslim dialogue. During these years, she developed contact with Yad Vashem Holocaust Memorial Museum. Since January 2009, she has lived in Poland at the Catholic Centre for Dialogue and Prayer in Auschwitz, where she is part of the education department. In March 2015, Mary was awarded the honorary title, Person of Reconciliation, by the Polish Council of Christians and Jews.

Nick Park

Pastor Nick Park has been senior pastor of Solid Rock, a multicultural Pentecostal church in Drogheda, for twenty-two years. He also serves as the national bishop of the Church of God denomination and as executive director of Evangelical Alliance Ireland. Nick has been married to Janice for thirty years, and they live in Dromin village in Co. Louth.

Eamon Rafter

Eamon Rafter is learning coordinator at Glencree Centre for Peace and Reconciliation in Co. Wicklow, where he has worked since 2005. He is a peace educator and facilitator with responsibility for education and training programmes with schools, youth, universities, adult and community groups. He has managed and worked on peace-building projects in Ireland, north and south, Israel and Palestine, South Africa, Afghanistan and in several European countries. His role also involves documenting and sharing the learning of Glencree Peace Centre's programme of work.

Trisha Rainsford

Trish Rainsford is a Bahá'í and has been a member of the Mid-West Interfaith Network (MWIN) since it began in May 2010. The Mid-West Interfaith Network is a grass-roots group comprised of friends from diverse faiths and cultures who meet regularly in Limerick. Over the years, members in the MWIN have come from the Anglican, Bahá'í, Buddhist, Catholic, Hindu, Islamic, Jewish, Quaker, Sikh, Zoroastrian – and other – traditions. The motto of the Mid-West Interfaith Network – 'Living our tomorrows together' – describes the primary aim of the group, which is to help to promote understanding, learning, tolerance and sharing.

Tomi Reichental

Tomi Reichental was born in 1935 in Piestany, Slovakia. In 1944, he was captured and deported to Bergen-Belsen concentration camp with his mother, grandmother, brother, aunt and cousin. When he was liberated in April 1945, he discovered that thirty-five members of his extended family were murdered in the Holocaust. Tomi is one of only two Holocaust survivors left in Ireland. Thousands of pupils in schools all over Ireland have heard the Tomi Reichental story, and he has spoken to the European Parliament. A teacher's guide and DVD (*Till the Tenth Generation*) based on Tomi's story was developed for schools to teach children about the Holocaust. Two documentary films based on his life have been made. *I Was a Boy in Belsen* and *Close to Evil* were both directed by the Emmy-award-winning producer Gerry Gregg. In 2011, Tomi wrote an acclaimed autobiography entitled *I Was a Boy in Belsen* and he was awarded the Order of Merit by the President of the Federal Republic of Germany. In 2014, the people of Ireland named him International Person of the Year, and in the same year, the Irish Diplomatic Core awarded him the Global Achievement Award. Trinity College Dublin conferred Tomi with an honorary doctorate in law in 2015. In 2016, Dublin City University awarded him an honorary doctorate of philosophy.

Keith Scott

Doctor Keith Scott is a Church of Ireland priest, married to Lyn. They have two adult children, who now live in England. Keith has always been involved in some kind of local community reconciliation work. His academic interests developed out of and followed alongside this work. Keith's master's dissertation for the Irish School of Ecumenics was on religion and community conflict in Northern Ireland. In 2002, supported by CMS Ireland, Keith and Lyn moved to Zambia where Keith researched and wrote his PhD thesis on conflict and identity in Zambia for Queens University Belfast, graduating in 2010. They moved back to Ireland in 2008, and worked in the Rathkeale and Kilnaughtin group of parishes, where Keith was a member of a group who founded a project to build reconciliation amongst the Settled and Travelling communities in Rathkeale. Keith also became involved in intercultural and interfaith dialogue as part of the Mid-West Interfaith Network. Keith and Lyn moved back to Zambia in 2017, with support from CMS Ireland, where they both teach at St John's Anglican Seminary in Kitwe, Northern Zambia.

Jennifer Siung

Jennifer Siung is head of education in the Chester Beatty Library, Dublin. She is an educator/facilitator specialising in cultural diversity and interfaith dialogue as well as creativity and innovation. Jennifer commenced her post in 2000 and has developed the first multi- and inter-cultural learning programmes in an Irish museum, *Ways of Seeing I* and *II*. Her work involves engaging with the Islamic, Asian, North African, East Asian and European collections of the library, devising numerous programmes including intercultural projects for schools, cultural festivals, and creating links with local multi-ethnic communities. Jennifer has studied art history, arts administration and adult and community education. She holds an MLitt degree exploring Japanese influence on twentieth-century Irish art. She has intermediate level in Mandarin and participated in the Getty NextGen for museum leaders in 2012 and Learning in Museums, International Council of Museums (ICOM) China in 2014.

Patrick Sullivan

Doctor Patrick Sullivan is director of curriculum and assessment at the National Council for Curriculum and Assessment (NCCA) with responsibility for overseeing curriculum developments at primary level. In this role he is responsible for the development of the new curriculum in education about religions and beliefs (ERB) and ethics for primary schools in Ireland. He is no stranger to the classroom. Patrick worked as a teacher in a variety of school contexts, urban and rural, large multifaith and denominational schools, in the UK and Ireland. He is a former principal teacher and has worked in teacher education programmes as a member of the Global Schoolroom in North-East India. He has completed his master's in education leadership in Maynooth University and a doctorate in religious education in Dublin City University, where he researched children's beliefs and values.

Tina Storey

Doctor Tina Storey was born in the USA of an American mother and a Northern Irish father. She was raised and educated in the countryside of Co. Clare as a Roman Catholic, with some instruction in the Church of Jesus Christ and Latter-Day Saints. She has a bachelor's degree in chemistry and biochemistry from University College Galway (now NUIG) and is a chartered chemist. She holds a PhD in organic chemistry from Trinity College Dublin, where she met her husband, a Methodist whose mother belonged to the Church of Ireland. With the birth of their first child, the couple realised that they did not want to raise their child in a single belief system. Humanism seemed to be the most suitable ethical concept for the family, and they joined the Humanist Association of Ireland in 2004. From 2013 to 2016, Tina conducted non-religious ceremonies for fellow humanists: naming ceremonies, weddings and funerals. She currently works as an environmental specialist and sits on the board of the local mental health association.

Siobhán Wheeler

Siobhán Wheeler is a local preacher in the Methodist Church, joining regularly with congregations in Adare and Ballingrane, Limerick, in worship and Bible study. She also shares in *Lectio Divina*, weekly, with a group in Corpus Christi parish, Moyross. She is blessed with many friends, including among those newly arrived in Limerick as asylum seekers. She coordinates the Free Dinner Trust, its ecumenical team of volunteers, and service in Limerick city. Recently, through membership of a diocesan support group of those working in similar ministries, she has been delighted, encouraged and challenged. Siobhán is currently studying for a MA in applied theology through the Irish Bible Institute in Dublin. She has five beloved children, Daniel, William, Christian, Isobel and Reuben.

BIBLIOGRAPHY

Abbott, W.M. (ed.), *The Documents of Vatican II*, New York: Guild Press, 1966.

Adorno, T.W., *Can One Live After Auschwitz: A Philosophical Reader,* Stanford, CA: Stanford University Press, 2003.

Ahlstrom, D., 'Leafing through Leonardo's library', *The Irish Times*, 7 June 2007.

Altman, L.J., *Adolf Hitler: Evil Mastermind of the Holocaust,* Berkeley Heights, NJ: Enslow, 2005.

Baab, L.M., *The Power of Listening*, Lanham, ML: Rowman and Littlefield, 2014.

Barnes, L.P. (ed.), *Debates in Religious Education*, London: Routledge, 2012.

Berler, W., *Journey through Darkness: Monowitz, Auschwitz, Gross-Rosen, Buchenwald,* Vallentine Mitchell & Co Ltd., 2004.

Biesta, G., *The Rediscovery of Teaching*, London: Routledge, 2017.

Boal, A., *Theatre of the Oppressed*, New York: Urizon Books, 1979.

Bohm, D., *On Dialogue*, London: Routledge, 1996.

Bosch, D.J., *Transforming Mission: Paradigm Shifts in Theology of Mission*, Maryknoll, NY: Orbis Books, 1991.

Brueggemann, W., *Inscribing the Text: Sermons and Prayers of Walter Brueggemann*, Fortress Press, 2004.

Buber, M., *Pointing the Way: Collected Essays*, New York: Harper Brothers, 1957.

Byrne, G. and Kieran, P. (eds), *Toward Mutual Ground: Pluralism, Religious Education and Diversity in Irish Schools*, Dublin: Columba Press, 2013.

Carr, J., 'Regulating Islamophobia: The Need for Collecting Disaggregated Data on Racism in Ireland', *Journal of Muslim Minority Affairs*, 3:4, 2011, pp. 574–93.

Carr, J., *Experiences of Islamophobia: Living with Racism in the Neoliberal Era*, London: Routledge, 2016.

Cassidy, E., *Ecumenism and Interreligious Dialogue*, New York: Paulist Press, 2005.

Chilcote, P.W., *Recapturing the Wesleys' Vision: An Introduction to the Faith of John and Charles Wesley*, Downers Grove: Inter-Varsity Press, 2004.

Church of Ireland and Committee for Christian Unity, *Guidelines for Interfaith Events and Dialogue*, Dublin: Church of Ireland Publishing, 2007.

Cloke, K., *Mediating Dangerously: The Frontiers of Conflict Resolution*, San Francisco: Jossey-Bass, 2001.

Comer, L., 'Museum Education: Adapting to Change' in M. Lynskey (ed.), *Irish Museums Association, Museum Ireland*, Vol. 25, Newtownabbey, Co. Antrim: Nicholson and Bass, 2015.

Congregation for Catholic Education, *Educating to Intercultural Dialogue in Catholic Schools: Living in Harmony for a Civilization of Love*, Vatican City: 2013.

Congregation for Catholic Education, 'Circular Letter to the Presidents of Bishops' Conferences on Religious Education in Schools', Vatican City, 2009.

Conlin, S. and Harbison, P., *Dublin: The Story of a City*, Dublin: The O'Brien Press, 2017.

Cosgrove, O., Cox, L., Kuhling, C., and Mulholand, P. (eds), *Ireland's New Religious Movements*, Newcastle: Cambridge Scholars Publishing, 2011.

Council of Europe, *White Paper on Intercultural Dialogue: Living Together as Equals in Dignity,* Strasbourg: Council of Europe, 2008.

Council of Europe, *The Religious Dimension of Intercultural Education,* Strasbourg: Council of Europe Publishing, 2004.

Cristea, A., *Integration and Interfaith: Faith/City Engagement in a Multicultural Context,* Dublin: Dublin City Interfaith Forum.

Croke, F., et al., *Chester Beatty's A-Z: From Amulet to Zodiac,* Galway: Castle Print, 2014.

D'Costa, G., *Christianity and the World Religions: Disputed Questions in the Theology of Religions,* Chichester: Wiley-Blackwell, 2009.

D'Costa, G., *The Catholic Church and the World Religions,* London: Continuum, 2010.

Dard, A.R., *Life of Ahmad as Founder of the Ahmadiyya Movement,* UK: Islam International Publications, 2008.

Davie, G., 'A European Perspective on Religion and Welfare: Contrasts and Commonalities', *Social Policy and Society,* 11:4, 2012, pp. 989–99.

De Souza, M., L. Francis, J. O'Higgins-Norman and D. Scott (eds), *International Handbook of Education for Spirituality, Care and Wellbeing,* Dordrecht: Springer, 2009.

Department of Education, *Primary School Curriculum,* Dublin: Government Publications, 1999.

Deselaers, M., 'The Significance of Two Papal Visits to Auschwitz' in M. Deselaers, L. Lysien and J. Nowak (eds), *God and Auschwitz: On Edith Stein, Pope Benedict XVI's Visit, and God in the Twilight of History,* Krakow: UNUM Publishing, 2008.

Dillen, A., 'Religious Participation of Children as Active Subjects: Toward a Hermeneutical-communicative Model of Religious Education in Families with Young Children', *International Journal of Children's Spirituality,* 12, 2007, pp. 37–49.

Donovan, V., *Christianity Rediscovered,* New York: Orbis Books, 2003.

Dwyer, C., 'Veiled Meanings: Young British Muslim Women and the Negotiation of Differences', *Gender, Place and Culture: A Journal of Feminist Geography,* 6:1, pp. 5–26., p. 7.

Eck, D., 'On Common Ground: World Religions in America', Harvard University Pluralism Project, 2006.

Einstein, A., 'Religion and Science', *New York Times Magazine*, 9 November 1930.

Everson, F.H., *This is Methodism*, London: The Epworth Press, 1959.

Faas, D., Darmody, M. and Sokolowska, B. 'Religious Diversity in Primary Schools: Reflections from the Republic of Ireland', *British Journal of Religious Education*, 38:1, 2015, pp. 83–98.

Fischer, K., *Schools and the Politics of Religion and Diversity in the Republic of Ireland: Separate but Equal?*, Manchester: Manchester University Press, 2016.

Flannery, T., *From the Inside*, Cork: Mercier Press, 1999.

Ford, D.F., *The Shape of Living Spiritual Directions for Everyday Life*, Norwich: Canterbury Press, 2012.

Forde, G., *A Journey Together: A Resource for Christian Muslim Dialogue*, Cork: Cois Tine, 2013.

Gandini, L. and Kaminsky, J.A., 'Reflections on the Relationship Between Documentation and Assessment in the American Context: An Interview with Brenda Fyfe', *Innovations in Early Education: The International Reggio Exchange*, 11:11, 2004, pp. 5–17.

Hazrat Mirza Ghulam Ahmad, *The Ark of Noah*, Muslim Literary Trust of Trinidad and Tobago, 2003.

Hederman, M.P., *I Must be Talking to Myself*, Dublin: Veritas, 2004.

Hegarty, T. and Titley, A., *Intercultural Events in Schools and Colleges of Education*, Dublin: Dice Project, 2013.

Hervieu-Léger, D., *Religion as a Chain of Memory*, New Brunswick, NJ: Rutgers University Press, 2000.

Higgins, G., Blythman, M., Curran, C. and Parkinson, S., *The Hard Gospel: Dealing Positively with Difference in the Church of Ireland: A Scoping Study Report to the Sectarianism Education Project, The General Synod of the Church of Ireland, 2003*.

Hillyard, P., *Suspect Community: People's Experience of the Prevention of Terrorism Acts in Britain,* London: Pluto Press, 1993.

Hopkins, P., Olson, E., Pain, R. and Vincett, G., 'Mapping Intergenerationalities: The Formation of Youthful Religiosities', *Transactions of the Institute of British Geographers*, 36:2, 2010, pp. 314–27.

Howe, C. and Abedin, M., 'Classroom Dialogue: A Systematic Review Across Four Decades of Research', *Cambridge Journal of Education*, 43, 2013, pp. 325–56.

Hull, J., Utopian *Whispers: Moral, Religious and Spiritual Values in Schools*, Norwich: Religious and Moral Education Press, 1998.

Ipgrave, J., 'Including Pupil's Faith Background in Primary Religious Education', *British Journal of Support for Learning*, 19:3, 2004, pp. 114–8.

Irish Episcopal Conference, *Catholic Preschool and Primary Religious Education Curriculum for Ireland*, Dublin: Veritas, 2015.

Irwin, J., 'Interculturalism, Ethos and Ideology: Barriers to Freedom and Democracy in Irish Primary Education', *REA: A Journal of Religion, Education and the Arts*, 6, 2009, pp. 1–26.

Kazepides, T., *Education as Dialogue*, Montreal and Kingston: McGill-Queens University Press, 2010.

Keane, E. and Heinz, M., 'Diversity in Initial Teacher Education in Ireland: The Socio-Demographic Backgrounds of Postgraduate Post-Primary Entrants in 2013 and 2014', *Irish Educational Studies*, 34:3, 2015, pp. 281–301.

Kerman, S., Kimball, T. and Martin, M., *Teacher Expectation and Student Achievement,* Bloomingdale: Phi Delta Kappa, 1980.

Knauth, T., Josza, D.P., Bertram-Troost, G.D, Ipgrave, J. (eds), *Encountering Religious Pluralism in School and Society: A Qualitative Study of Teenage Perspectives in Europe*, Munster: Waxmann, 2008.

Kramer, K.P., *Martin Buber's I and Thou: Practicing Living Dialogue*, New Jersey: Paulist Press, 2003.

Kuhling, C. and Keohane, K., *Cosmopolitan Ireland: Globalisation and Quality of Life*, London: Pluto Press, 2007.

Lane, D., *Stepping Stones to Other Religions: A Christian Theology of Interreligious Dialogue*, Dublin: Veritas, 2012.

Leahy, B., *Who Leads the Church?*, Dublin: Veritas, 2015.

Lederach, J.P., *The Moral Imagination: The Art and Soul of Building Peace*, Oxford: Oxford University Press, 2005.

Lewis, P., *Islamic Britain: Religion, Politics, and Identity among British Muslims: Bradford in the 1990s*, London: I.B. Tauris, 1994.

Lochhead, D., *The Dialogical Imperative: A Christian Reflection on Interfaith Encounter,* Oregon: Wipf and Stock Publishers, 2012.

Luther King, M., *I Have A Dream: Writings and Speeches that Changed the World*, San Francisco: Harper, 1986.

Macquarrie, J., *God-Talk: An Examination of the Language and Logic of Theology*, London: SCM Press, 1967.

McCreery, E., Palmer, S. and Voiels, V.M., *Teaching Religious Education: Primary and Early Years*, Exeter: Learning Matters, 2008.

McGarry, P., 'Mansion House Hosts Inter-faith Forum Examining Religion's Role in Global Conflict', *The Irish Times*, 19 March 2015.

McKenna, U., Ipgrave, J. and Jackson, R., *Interfaith Dialogue by Email in Primary Schools*, Munster: Waxmann, 2008.

Meadows, P., *The Wesleyan DNA of Discipleship Fresh Expressions of Discipleship For the 21st-century Church*, Cambridge: Grove Books, 2013.

Mercer, N., *Words and Minds: How We Use Language to Think Together*, London: Routledge, 2000.

Miles, S., *Take This Bread: A Radical Conversion, New York: Ballantine Books*, 2008.

Mullally, A., '*We Are Inclusive but Are We being Equal?' Challenges to Community National Schools Regarding Religious Diversity*, DCU: EdD Thesis, 2018.

Mullally, W., 'Inaugural address of the Rev Bill Mullally, President of the Methodist Church in Ireland', *Methodist Newsletter*, Vol. 44, No. 477 (2016), p. 44.

Thomas, R.M., *Overcoming Inertia in School Reform: How to Successfully Implement Change*, California: Corwin Press, 2002.

Musser, D. and Sutherland, D.D., *War or Words? Interreligious Dialogue as an Instrument of Peace*, University of Michigan: Pilgrim Press, 2005.

New Revised Standard Version of the Bible.

Newbigin, L., *The Gospel in a Pluralist Society*, London: Society for Promoting Christian Knowledge, 1989.

Newbigin, L., *The Open Secret*, London: Society for Promoting Christian Knowledge, 1995.

Newman, J.H., *The Idea of a University*, New Haven, CT: Yale University Press, 1996.

Nic Craith, M., *Culture and Identity Politics in Northern Ireland*, Hampshire: Palgrave MacMillan, 2003.

NIFCON, *Generous Love: The Truth of the Gospel and the Call of Dialogue*, London: Anglican Consultative Council, 2008.

O'Donovan, J., *Understanding Differently: Christianity and the World Religions*, Dublin: Veritas, 2013.

O'Sullivan, O., *One God Three Faiths*, Dublin: Columba Press, 2002.

O'Beirne Ranelagh, J., *A Short History of Ireland*, Cambridge: Cambridge University Press, 2001.

Ofsted, *Making Sense of Religion: A Report on Religious Education in Schools and the Impact of Locally Agreed Syllabuses*, London: HMI, 2007.

Pohlmann, H.R., *Encounters with Hinduism: A Contribution to Interreligious Dialogue*, London: SCM Press, 1996.

Pontifical Council for Interreligious Dialogue, *Dialogue and Proclamation*, Vatican City, 1991.

Pontifical Council for Interreligious Dialogue, *Letter to Presidents of Bishops' Conferences on the Spirituality of Dialogue*, Vatican City, 1999.

Pope Francis, Apostolic Exhortation on the Joy of the Gospel, *Evangelii Gaudium*, Vatican City, 2013.

Pruitt, B. and Thomas, P., *Democratic Dialogue: A Handbook for Practitioners,* USA: International IDEA, 2007.

Reichental, T., *I Was a Boy in Belsen*, Dublin: O'Brien Press, 2011.

Royal aal Al-Bayt Institute for Islamic Thought, *A Common Word Between Us and You*, Jordan: The Royal aal Al-Bayt Institute for Islamic Thought, 2009.

Rudduck, J. and Fielding, M., 'Student Voice and the Perils of Popularity', *Educational Review,* 58:2, 2006, pp. 219–31.

Ryan, M., 'Displaying Sacred Manuscripts: The Experience of the Chester Beatty Library' in *Cathedral Workshops on Religious Arts and Crafts, Proceedings, Pontifical Commission for the Cultural Heritage of the Church*, Rome: Edindustria, pp. 317–21.

Ryan, M., *Another Ireland: An Introduction to Ireland's Ethnic-Religious Minority Communities*, Belfast: Stranmillis College, 1996.

Said, E., *Orientalism*, London: Penguin, 2003.

Saint Augustine, *Confessions*, Oxford: Oxford University Press, 2008.

Sato, K.T., *Great Living: In the Pure Encounter Between Master and Disciple: A Volume of Essays ad Commentaries on the Shin Buddhist Text Tannishō in a New Translaton*, New York: Buddhist Center Press, 2010.

Seeberg, M.L., Levin, I. and Lenz, C., *The Holocaust as Active Memory: The Past in the Present*, Ashgate, 2013.

Shafiq, M. and Abu-Nimer, M., *Interfaith Dialogue: A Guide for Muslims*, Herndon, VA: The International Institute of Islamic Thought, 2007.

Sheridan, K., 'We, as a Human Race, have to Find Ways to Reconcile', *The Irish Times*, 8 January 2016.

Siung, J., 'Museums as Places for Intercultural Dialogue and Learning: Making Museums Relevant to Diverse Communities' in Maura Lynskey (ed.), *Irish Museums Association, Museum Ireland*, Vol. 25, Newtownabbey, Co. Antrim: Nicholson and Bass, 2015, p. 55–64.

Smith, D.W., *The Kindness of God*, Nottingham: Inter-Varsity Press, 2013.

Solzhenitsyn, A., *The Gulag Archipelago*, London: Vintage Publishing, 2003.

Sullivan, J. and Lloyd, S., 'The Forum theatre of Augusto Boal: A Dramatic Model for Dialogue and Community-Based Environmental Science', *Local Environment*, 11:6, 2006.

Swedish Schools' Inspectorate, *School's Work with Democracy and Fundamental Values: Quality Assessment Report*, Sweden: Skolinspektionen, 2012.

Thangaraj, M.T., 'Evangelism *Sans* Proselytism: A Possibility?' in J. Witte and R.C. Martin (eds), *Sharing the Book: Religious Perspectives on the Rights and Wrongs of Proselytism,* Oregon: WIPF and Stock, 2008.

Tracy, D., *Dialogue with the Other: The Interreligious Dialogue*, Louvain: Peters Press, 1990.

Ugba, A., *Shades of Belonging: African Pentecostals in Twenty-First Century Ireland*, Trenton, N.J., and Asmara: Africa World Press, 2009.

Valsiner, J., 'Culture and Human Development: A Co-constructivist Perspective' in P. van Geert and L. Moss (eds), *Annals of Theoretical Psychology*, 10, New York: Plenum, 1993, pp. 247–98.

Walls, A.F., *The Missionary Movement in Christian History: Studies in the Transmission of Faith*, New York: Orbis Books, 1996.

Walsh, J.R., *Religion: The Irish Experience*, Dublin: Veritas, 2003.

Watkins, C., 'Learners in the Driving Seat', *Leading Learning Pedagogy*, 1:2, 2009, pp. 28–31.

Watkins, C., Carnell, E. and Lodge, C., *Effective Learning in Classrooms*, Thousand Oaks, CA: Sage Publications, 2007.

Wells, G. (ed.), *Action Talk and Text: Learning and Teaching through Inquiry*, New York: Teachers College Press, 2001.

Wesley, J., *A Collection of Hymns for the use of the people called Methodists,* London: Wesleyan Conference Office, 1779.

White, J. (ed.), *Rethinking the School Curriculum: Values, Aims and Purposes*, London: Routledge, 2004.

Williams, K., *Faith and the Nation,* Dublin: Dominican Publications, 2005.

Woolverton, J.F., 'The Chicago–Lambeth Quadrilateral and the Lambeth Conferences' in *Historical Magazine of the Protestant Episcopal Church*, 53:2, 1984, pp. 100–1.

NOTES

INTRODUCTION

Patricia Kieran

1. H.G. Pöhlmann, *Encounters with Hinduism: A Contribution to Inter-religious Dialogue*, London: SCM Press, 1996, p. 6.

2. J. O'Donovan, *Understanding Differently: Christianity and the World Religions*, Dublin: Veritas, 2003.

3. The Seminar on Interbelief Dialogue in Contemporary Ireland took place on 17 February 2016 in Mary Immaculate College (MIC) Limerick. It was funded by the Anna Lindh Foundation (ALF) and organised in collaboration with ALF, the Chester Beatty Library, Mary Immaculate College, the Dublin City Interfaith Forum with support from the NCCA.

4. Participants came from a variety of faith groups and belief traditions including members of the Mid-West Interfaith Network, Kilkenny Interfaith Friendship Group, the Glencree Peace and Reconciliation Centre, Doras Luimní and community members from direct provision centres and cultural and educational groups.

5. O. Cosgrove, L. Cox, C. Kuhling, and P. Mulholland, *Ireland's New Religious Movements*, Newcastle: Cambridge Scholars Publishing, 2011.

6. J.R. Walsh, *Religion: The Irish Experience*, Dublin: Veritas, 2003, p. 114.

7. A. Mullally, *'We Are Inclusive but Are We being Equal?' Challenges to Community National Schools Regarding Religious Diversity*, DCU: EdD Thesis, 2018, p. 81.

8. T. Hegarty and A. Titley, *Intercultural Events in Schools and Colleges of Education*, Dublin: Dice Project, 2013.

9. E. Keane and M. Heinz, 'Diversity in Initial Teacher Education in Ireland: The Socio-Demographic Backgrounds of Postgraduate Post-Primary Entrants in 2013 and 2014', *Irish Educational Studies*, 34:3, 2015, pp. 281–301.

10. J. Ipgrave, 'Including Pupil's Faith Background in Primary Religious Education', *British Journal of Support for Learning*, 19:3, 2004, pp. 114–8.

11. The Swedish Schools' Inspectorate, *School's Work with Democracy and Fundamental Values: Quality Assessment Report*, Sweden: Skolinspektionen, 2012, p. 43. The report states, 'Teachers who have said that they find this difficult and that they feel insecure when it comes to dealing with critical and ethical discussions in the teaching and the school's everyday life.'

12. M. Ryan, *Another Ireland: An Introduction to Ireland's Ethnic-Religious Minority Communities*, Belfast: Stranmillis College, 1996. O. O'Sullivan, *One God Three Faiths*, Dublin: The Columba Press, 2002. G. Forde, *A Journey Together: A Resource for Christian Muslim Dialogue*, Cork: Cois Tine, 2013. In UCC's Honan Public Lectures Series on 'The Encounter of Religions' (2003–4), the relationship between Buddhism, Christianity, Paganism and Primal religions was explored.

13. D. Bohm, *On Dialogue*, London: Routledge, 1996, p. vii.

14. J. Sullivan and S. Lloyd, 'The Forum theatre of Augusto Boal: A Dramatic Model for Dialogue and Community-Based Environmental Science', *Local Environment*, 11:6, 2006.

15. A. Boal, *Theatre of the Oppressed*, New York: Urizon Books, 1979.

16. C. Howe and M. Abedin, 'Classroom Dialogue: A Systematic Review Across Four Decades of Research', *Cambridge Journal of Education*, 43, 2013, pp. 325–56.

17. Cambridge Dialogue Education Research Group, educ.cam.ac.uk/centres/networks/cedir/; accessed 6 October 2017.

18. G. Byrne and P. Kieran, *Toward Mutual Ground: Pluralism, Religious Education and Diversity in Irish Schools*, Dublin: The Columba Press, 2013, p. 24 ff.

19. For instance, the Irish Muslim Peace and Integration Council, Mid-West Interfaith Network, Dublin City Interfaith Forum, Three Faiths Forum, Northern Ireland Interfaith Forum, Cois Tine in Cork, the UCC Irish Society for the Academic Study of Religions, DCU's Centre for Interreligious Dialogue, the Irish School of Ecumenics' Intercultural Theology and Interreligious Studies (IT and IS) Course and the work of Pobal, pobal.ie/Publications/Documents/A%20Journey%20Together%20-%20Cois%20Tine%20-%202013.pdf; accessed 10 May 2017. There are many intercultural groups engaging in dialogue work including Afra-Eorpach intercultural group in Dublin and Kerry One World Centre (KOWC).

20. Parliament of the World's Religions, parliamentofreligions.org/articles; accessed on 10 May 2017.

21. The Pluralism Project at Harvard University, pluralism.org/; European Commission Platform for Intercultural Dialogue, ec.europa.eu/culture/policy/strategic-framework/intercultural-dialogue_en; Lifelong Learning Platform, lllplatform.eu/events/education-for-intercultural-dialogue/; John Paul II Center for Interreligious Dialogue in the Angelicum University in Rome, facebook.com/JP2center/; World Council of Churches' Programme on Interreligious Dialogue and Cooperation (WCC-IRDC), vatican.va/roman_curia/pontifical_councils/interelg/documents/rc_pc_interelg_doc_20111110_testimonianza-cristiana_en.html; accessed on 4 October 2017.

22. D. Lane, *Stepping Stones to Other Religions: A Christian Theology of Interreligious Dialogue*, Dublin: Veritas, 2012, p. 19. He cites as evidence that Orbis Books alone had published over sixty-five volumes on this theme by 2011.

23. Quoted in D. Musser and D.D. Sutherland, *War or Words? Interreligious Dialogue as an Instrument of Peace*, University of Michigan: Pilgrim Press, 2005.

24. The Cambridge Inter-faith Programme, interfaith.cam.ac.uk/; accessed on 4 October 2017.

25. Archdiocese of Chicago, Office for Ecumenical and Interreligious Affairs, archchicago.org/departments/ecumenical/Relations.htm; accessed on 5 November 2016.

26. See the Pontifical Council for Interreligious Dialogue, vatican. va/roman_curia/pontifical_councils/interelg/documents/rc_pc_ interelg_pro_20051996_en.html; accessed on 14 November 2016.

27. See WCC, 'My Neighbour's Faith and Mine: Theological Discoveries through Interfaith Dialogue', 1992, oikoumene.org/en/resources/ documents/wcc-programmes/interreligious-dialogue-and-cooperation/christian-identity-in-pluralistic-societies; accessed on 14 November 2016.

28. Byrne and Kieran, *Toward Mutual Ground*, p. 23.

29. D. Faas, M. Darmody and B. Sokolowska, 'Religious Diversity in Primary Schools: Reflections from the Republic of Ireland', *British Journal of Religious Education*, 38:1, 2016, pp. 83–98. They state, 'At a time of increased migration and diversity Religious education in state-funded primary schools should include the study of humanism and faiths outside of Christianity.'

30. UCD Confucius Institute was founded in 2006. A Chinese language pack in Mandarin has been developed for Junior Certificate to further understanding of Chinese culture, performing arts, games, beliefs, literature, etc. UCC also has a Confucius Institute.

31. Bahá'í Faith Ireland, bahai.ie/; accessed on 4 October 2017.

32. K.P. Kramer, *Martin Buber's I and Thou: Practicing Living Dialogue*, New Jersey: Paulist Press, 2003.

33. M. Friedman (trans. and ed.), *Pointing the Way: Collected Essays by Martin Buber*, New York: Harper Borthers, 1957.

34. 'Dialogue, starting from an awareness of one's own faith identity, can help people to enter into contact with other religions. Dialogue means not just talking, but includes all beneficial and constructive interreligious relationships, with both individuals

and communities of other beliefs, thus arriving at mutual understanding ... [I]t is fundamental that the Catholic religion, for its part, be an inspiring sign of dialogue.' Congregation for Catholic Education, *Educating to Intercultural Dialogue in Catholic Schools Living in Harmony for a Civilization of Love*, Vatican City, 2013, 13, 70.

35. D. Eck, 'On Common Ground: World Religions in America', Harvard University Pluralism Project, 2006, pluralism.org/ocg/; accessed on 14 November 2016.

36. H.G. Pöhlmann, *Encounters with Hinduism*, p. 18.

37. For example: Leviticus 19:18; Matthew 7:12; *Mahābhārata Shānti-Parva* 167:9; *Guru Arjan Dev Ji* 259, Guru Granth Sahib.

38. 'Quotes on Religious Tolerance Hinduism', hinduwebsite.com/hinduism/saivismtolerance.asp; accessed on 14 November 2016.

39. A homily on Micah 4:1–5 preached by Walter Brueggemann at Grace and Holy Trinity Cathedral, Kansas City, Missouri on 4 May 2003. W. Brueggemann, *Inscribing the Text: Sermons and Prayers of Walter Brueggemann*, Fortress Press, 2004, pp. 211–13.

40. M. Shafiq and M. Abu-Nimer, *Interfaith Dialogue: A Guide for Muslims*, Herndon, VA: The International Institute of Islamic Thought, 2007, p. 2.

41. M. Shafiq and M. Abu-Nimer, 'The Qur'anic Perspective on Interfaith Dialogue', messageinternational.org/the-quranic-perspective-on-interfaith-dialogue/; accessed 9 October 2017. This article suggests that the Quran supports interfaith engagement and encourages Jews, Christians and Muslims to come to a common understanding: '"Say [O Mohammad]: O people of the book, come to a common understanding between us and you, that we shall worship no one except One God that we shall take no partners with Him and none of us shall take others for Lord beside One God" (Quran 3:64).' It is noteworthy that on 31 March 2016, the Irish Peace and Integration Council signed an anti-extremism declaration.

42. From the *Bishárát (Glad-Tidings)*, reference.bahai.org/en/t/b/TB/tb-4.html; accessed 6 October 2017.

43. Congregation for Catholic Education, *Education to Intercultural Dialogue in Catholic Schools Living in Harmony for a Civilization of Love*, Vatican City, 2013.

44. Joanne Hunt, 'Higgins sets out his vision of multicultural Ireland', *The Irish Times*, 29 November 2012.

45. The Pew Forum on Religion and Public Life, *Rising Tide of Restrictions on Religion*, pewforum.org/2012/09/20/rising-tide-of-restrictions-on-religion-findings/; accessed on 10 November 2016.

46. 'Young People Worldwide Facing "Daunting" Challenges', Office of the Secretary-General's Envoy on Youth, un.org/youthenvoy/2015/06/young-people-worldwide-face-daunting-challenges/; accessed on 10 November 2016.

47. '244 Million International Migrants Living Abroad Worldwide, New UN Statistics Reveal', Sustainable Development Goals, un.org/sustainabledevelopment/blog/2016/01/244-million-international-migrants-living-abroad-worldwide-new-un-statistics-reveal/; accessed 6 October 2017.

48. M.T. Thangaraj, 'Evangelism *Sans* Proselytism: A Possibility?' in J. Witte and R.C. Martin (eds), *Sharing the Book: Religious Perspectives on the Rights and Wrongs of Proselytism*, Oregon: WIPF and Stock, 2008, p. 351. G. Biesta, *The Rediscovery of Teaching*, London: Routledge, 2017.

49. J. O'Donovan, *Understanding Differently*, p. 328.

50. Congregation for Catholic Education, *Educating to Intercultural Dialogue*.

CHAPTER ONE
Interreligious Encounter and Dialogue in Schools
Julia Ipgrave

1. Council of Europe, *White Paper on Intercultural Dialogue: Living Together as Equals in Dignity*, Strasbourg: Council of Europe, 2008, p. 3.

2. Council of Europe, *White Paper*, p. 42.

3. U. McKenna, Julia Ipgrave and Robert Jackson, *Inter Faith Dialogue by Email in Primary* Schools, Münster: Waxmann, 2008.

4. D. Hervieu-Léger, *Religion as a Chain of Memory*, New Brunswick, NJ: Rutgers University Press, 2000.

5. G. Davie, 'The Religious Life of Modern Europe: Understanding Relevant Factors', patheos.com/resources/additional-resources/2010/09/religious-life-of-modern-europe-understanding-relevant-factors; accessed 10 February 2016.

6. N. Mercer, *Words and Minds: How We Use Language to Think Together*, London: Routledge, 2000.

7. 'Chapter Five: Developing Thinking Skills in RE' in E. McCreery, S. Palmer and V. Voiels, *Teaching Religious Education: Primary and Early* Years, Exeter: Learning Matters, 2008, pp. 54–68.

8. Ofsted, *Making Sense of Religion: A Report on Religious Education in Schools and the Impact of Locally Agreed Syllabuses,* London: HMI, 2007, p. 40.

9. IPPR, *What is Religious Education For? Getting the National Framework Right,* London: Institute for Public Policy Research, 2004, p. 8.

10. Ofsted, *Making Sense of Religion,* p. 41.

11. M. Shafiq and M. Abu-Nimer, *Interfaith Dialogue: A Guide for Muslims,* Herndon, VA: The International Institute of Islamic Thought, 2007, p. 2.

12. Mercer, *Words and Minds,* pp. 102–3.

13. M. Hand, 'Religious Education' in John White (ed.), *Rethinking the School Curriculum: Values, Aims and Purposes,* London: Routledge, 2004, p. 162.

14. Inter Faith Network UK, 2014, interfaith.org.uk; accessed 18 January 2016.

15. John Hull, *Utopian Whispers: Moral, Religious and Spiritual Values in Schools,* Norwich: Religious and Moral Education Press, 1998, p. 115.

16. Shafiq and Abu-Nimer, *Interfaith Dialogue*, p. 7.

17. NIFCON, *Generous Love: The Truth of the Gospel and the Call of Dialogue*, London: Anglican Consultative Council, 2008, p. 6.

18. K.T. Sato, *Great Living: In the Pure Encounter Between Master and Disciple: A Volume of Essays ad Commentaries on the Shin Buddhist Text Tannishō in a New Translaton*, New York: Buddhist Center Press, 2010. This last example from a Buddhist tradition raises an important question about 'God' language. While I shall be using the term 'God' to make my argument in what follows I do acknowledge that this word is not used for the transcendent in all religions.

19. J. Macquarrie, *God-Talk: An Examination of the Language and Logic of Theology*, London: SCM Press, 1967, p. 19.

20. Among these, Richard Dawkins and the late Christopher Hitchens.

CHAPTER TWO
Interbelief Learning and Dialogue in the Proposed Curriculum on Education about Religions and Beliefs (ERB) and Ethics
Patirck Sullivan

1. J. Coolahan, C. Hussey and F. Kilfeather, *The Forum on Patronage and Pluralism in the Primary Sector: Report of the Forum's Advisory Group*, education.ie/en/Press-Events/Events/Patronage-and-Pluralism-in-the-Primary-Sector/The-Forum-on-Patronage-and-Pluralism-in-the-Primary-Sector-Report-of-the-Forums-Advisory-Group.pdf; accessed 10 October 2017.

2. Department of Education and Science, *Primary School Curriculum: Introduction*, Dublin: Government Publications, 1999.

3. A. Looney, *What Will We Tell the Children? Address to the Irish National Teachers' Organisation, 2011*, into.ie/ROI/NewsEvents/Conferences/AnnualCongress/AnnualCongress2011/Congress2011AddressesandSpeeches/AnneLooney_Congress2011.pdf; accessed 10 October 2017.

4. W. Pinar, *Race, Religion, and a Curriculum of Reparation: Teacher Education for a Multicultural Society*, New York: Palgrave Macmillan, 2006.

5. W. Pinar, W. Reynolds, P. Slattery and P. Taubman, *Understanding Curriculum*, New York: Peter Lang, 1995.

6. A. O'Donnell, 'Securitisation, Counterterrorism and the Silencing of Dissent: The Educational Implications of *Prevent*', *British Journal of Educational Studies*, 64:1, 2016.

7. Central Statistics Office (CSO), *Statistical tables at a glance: Persons usually resident and present in the state on census night, classified by place of birth and age group*, 2011, cso.ie/multiquicktables/ quickTables.aspx?id=cdd22; accessed 7 June 2016. Census 2016 Religion, cso.ie/en/media/csoie/releasespublications/documents/ population/2017/Chapter_8_Religion.pdf; accessed 10 October 2017.

8. R.M. Thomas, *Overcoming Inertia in School Reform: How to Successfully Implement Change*, California: Corwin Press, 2002.

9. J. Macmurray, *Learning to be Human*, Moray House Annual Public Lecture, 5 May, Unpublished, 1958.

10. P. Sahlberg, *Finnish Lessons: What Can the World Learn from Educational Change in Finland?* New York: Teachers College Press, 2011.

11. S. Kerman, T. Kimball and M. Martin, *Teacher Expectation and Student Achievement*, Bloomingdale: Phi Delta Kappa, 1980.

12. N. Hayes, *Perspectives on the Relationship Between Education and Care in Early Childhood*, Research Paper, Dublin: National Council for Curriculum and Assessment, 2007.

13. G. Wells, 'The Case for Dialogic Inquiry' in G. Wells (ed.) *Action Talk and Text: Learning and Teaching through Inquiry*, New York: Teachers College Press, 2001, pp. 171–94.

14. Department of Education and Science, *Primary School Curriculum: Introduction*, Dublin: Government Publications, 1999.

15. J. Valsiner, 'Culture and Human Development: A Co-constructivist Perspective' in P. van Geert and L. Moss (eds), *Annals of Theoretical Psychology*, 10, New York: Plenum, 1993, pp. 247–98.

16. J. Rudduck and M. Fielding, 'Student Voice and the Perils of Popularity', *Educational Review*, 58:2, 2006, pp. 219–31.

17. M. Fielding, 'Transformative Approaches to Student Voice: Theoretical Underpinnings, Recalcitrant Realities', *British Educational Research Journal*, 30:2, 2004, pp. 295–311.

18. C. Watkins, 'Learners in the Driving Seat', *Leading Learning Pedagogy*, 1:2, 2009, pp. 28–31.

19. L. Gandini and J.A. Kaminsky, 'Reflections on the Relationship Between Documentation and Assessment in the American Context: An Interview with Brenda Fyfe', *Innovations in Early Education: The International Reggio Exchange*, 11:11, 2004, pp. 5–17.

20. Department of Education and Science, *Primary School Curriculum: Introduction*, Dublin: Government Publications, 1999. National Council for Curriculum and Assessment, *Aistear: The Early Childhood Curriculum Framework and the Primary School Curriculum. Audit: Similarities and Differences*, Dublin: NCCA, 2009.

21. R. Karr-Morse and M. Wiley, *Ghosts from the Nursery: Tracing the Roots of Violence*, New York: The Atlantic Press, 1997.

22. J.S. Bruner, *The Process of Education*, Cambridge: Harvard University Press, 1960.

23. A. Dillen, 'Religious Participation of Children as Active Subjects: Toward a Hermeneutical-communicative Model of Religious Education in Families with Young Children', *International Journal of Children's Spirituality*, 12, 2007, pp. 37–49. P. Hopkins, E. Olson, R. Pain and G. Vincett, 'Mapping Intergenerationalities: The Formation of Youthful Religiosities', *Transactions of the Institute of British Geographers*, 36:2, 2010, pp. 314–27. C.J. Boyatzis, 'Examining Religious and Spiritual Development during Childhood and Adolescence' in M. De Souza, L. Francis, J. O'Higgins-Norman and D. Scott (eds), *International Handbook of Education for Spirituality, Care and Wellbeing*, Dordrecht: Springer, 2009, pp. 51–67.

24. B. Rogoff, *Apprenticeship in Thinking: Cognitive Development in Social Context*, New York: Oxford University Press, 1990.

25. J. Coolahan, C. Hussey and F. Kilfeather, *The Forum on Patronage and Pluralism in the Primary Sector: Report of the Forum's Advisory Group*, education.ie/en/Press-Events/Events/Patronage-and-Pluralism-in

-the-Primary-Sector/The-Forum-on-Patronage-and-Pluralism-in-the-Primary-Sector-Report-of-the-Forums-Advisory-Group.pdf; accessed on 10 October 2017.

26. Government of Ireland, Education Act, 1998.

27. Education Secretariat of the Dublin Diocese, written submission to NCCA.

28. Department of Education and Science, *Primary School Curriculum: Introduction,* Dublin: Government Publications, 1999.

29. Third Level Educators, written submission to NCCA.

30. Catholic Primary Schools Management Association (CPSMA), written submission to NCCA.

31. Government of Ireland, Education Act, Section 15(2)(b), 1998.

32. P. Sullivan, *Consensus Making, Brokerage and Compromise: The Process of Curriculum Design in Ireland as Evidenced in the Development of a Curriculum in Education about Religions and Beliefs (ERB) and Ethics,* Dublin: Dublin City University, 2018.

CHAPTER THREE
Museums as Public Spaces for Intercultural Dialogue and Learning
Jenny Siung

1. For details of the seminar, including presentations by speakers, see: S. Bodo, K. Gibbs and M. Sani (eds), *Museums as Places for Intercultural Dialogue: Selected Practices from Europe,* MAP for ID, 2009, ne-mo.org/fileadmin/Dateien/public/service/Handbook_MAPforID_EN.pdf

2. For the conference held in 2014, see, 'Intercultural Dialogue and Creativity', *Chester Beatty Library,* chesterbeatty.ie/learning/intercultural-dialogue/

3. 'Chester Beatty Library Ireland 2016 Vox Pop', youtu.be/Z_e76YhcB58; accessed 10 October 2017.

4. Chester Beatty Library Mission Statement, cbl.ie/About-Us/The-Chester-Beatty-Library.aspx; accessed 10 October 2017.

5. Interview, Dr Michael Ryan, Director of the Chester Beatty Library, 1993–2010, Dublin, 26 May 2016. M. Ryan, 'Displaying Sacred Manuscripts: The Experience of the Chester Beatty Library' in *Cathedral Workshops on Religious Arts and Crafts, Proceedings, Pontifical Commission for the Cultural Heritage of the Church*, Rome: Edindustria, pp. 317–21.

6. This figure does not include paintings, prints, print series, drawings or decorative arts which contain religious themes.

7. M. Ryan, 'Displaying Sacred Manuscripts'.

8. Dick Ahlstrom, Science Editor, 'Leafing through Leonardo's library', *The Irish Times*, 7 June 2007.

9. F. Croke, et al., *Chester Beatty's A–Z: From Amulet to Zodiac*, Galway: Castle Print, 2014.

10. See, 'Learning', *Chester Beatty Library*: chesterbeatty.ie/learning/

11. L. Comer, 'Museum Education: Adapting to Change' in Maura Lynskey (ed.), *Irish Museums Association, Museum Ireland*, Vol. 25, Newtownabbey, Co. Antrim: Nicholson and Bass, 2015, p. 112.

12. The Celtic Tiger was a period of rapid economic growth from 1995–2007 in Ireland.

13. J. Siung, 'Thoughtful and respectful engagement: intercultural dialogue and the Chester Beatty Library, Ireland' in Simona Bodo, Kirsten Gibbs, Margherita Sani (eds), *Museums as places for intercultural dialogue: selected practices from Europe*, Map for ID, A Lifelong Learning Project published for the European Union, (2009) p.19.

14. J. Siung, 'Museums as Places for Intercultural Dialogue and Learning: Making Museums Relevant to Diverse Communities' in Maura Lynskey (ed.), *Irish Museums Association, Museum Ireland*, Vol. 25, Newtownabbey, Co. Antrim: Nicholson and Bass, 2015, p. 55–64.

15. See, 'Intercultural Dialogue and Creativity', *Chester Beatty Library*, chesterbeatty.ie/learning/intercultural-dialogue/

16. Ibid.

17. See, 'Intercultural Dialogue and Creativity', *Chester Beatty Library*, chesterbeatty.ie/learning/intercultural-dialogue/

18. See, 'Teachers and Educators Resources', Chester Beatty Library, chesterbeatty.ie/learning/resources-for-educators/

19. For details of Sacred Texts interactive website, British Library, UK, see: bl.uk/learning/citizenship/sacred/sacredintro.html; accessed 10 October 2017.

20. The handling kit is based on the Brent Museum and Archive Islamic loan box, brent.gov.uk/services-for-residents/brent-museum-and-archives/; accessed 10 October 2017.

21. Feedback gathered from the workshop participants by the Chester Beatty Library.

22. C. Kuhling and K. Keohane, *Cosmopolitan Ireland: Globalisation and Quality of Life*, London: Pluto Press, 2007, p. 67.

23. The Migrant Integration Strategy – A Blueprint for the Future, justice.ie/en/JELR/Pages/SP17000040; accessed 10 October 2017.

24. See 'Integration Policy', *Office for the Promotion of Migrant Integration, Department of Justice and Equality*, integration.ie/en/isec/pages/integrationpolicy

25. M. Nic Craith, *Culture and Identity Politics in Northern Ireland*, Hampshire: Palgrave MacMillan, 2003, p. 18.

CHAPTER FOUR

Dialogue About Belief: Voices from the Centre for Dialogue and Prayer in Oświęcim/Auschwitz, Poland

Sr Mary O'Sullivan

1. 'Address of John Paul II to the Representatives of the Jewish Municipality', Vienna, 24 June 1988, w2.vatican.va/content/john-paul-ii/de/speeches/1988/june/documents/hf_jp-ii_spe_19880624_comunita-ebraica.html; accessed on 8 May 2016. There have been a number of papal visits to Auschwitz. See Manfred Deselaers, 'The Significance of Two Papal Visits to Auschwitz' in M. Deselaers, L. Lysien and J. Nowak (eds), *God and Auschwitz: On Edith Stein, Pope Benedict XVI's Visit, and God in the Twilight of History*, Krakow: UNUM Publishing, 2008.

2.   'History', Auschwitz-Birkenau Memorial and Museum, auschwitz. org/en/history/; accessed 5 May 2016.

3.   W. Berler, *Journey through Darkness: Monowitz, Auschwitz, Gross-Rosen, Buchenwald*, Vallentine Mitchell and Co Ltd., 2004.

4.   M. Deselaers, et al., *God and Auschwitz*.

5.   See Jan Andrzej Kloczowski, 'Did God suffer in Auschwitz? Where was He? Why Was He Silent?' in M. Deselaers, et al., *God and Auschwitz*. L.J. Altman, *Adolf Hitler: Evil Mastermind of the Holocaust*, Berkeley Heights, NJ: Enslow, 2005.

6.   T.W. Adorno, *Can One Live After Auschwitz? A Philosophical Reader*, Stanford, CA: Stanford University Press, 2003.

7.   'Final Declaration of the Colloquium in Rome of the Pontifical Council for Interreligious Dialogue and the Royal Institute for Inter-Faith Studies (R.I.I.F.S.)', 7 May 2016, press.vatican.va/content/ salastampa/it/bollettino/pubblico/2016/05/07/0322/00753.html; accessed on 4 May 2016.

CHAPTER FIVE
Dialogue in Dublin City Interfaith Forum
Adrian Cristea

1.   'Census 2016 Results Profile 2 – Population Distribution and Movements', CSO, cso.ie/en/csolatestnews/ pressreleases/2017pressreleases/pressstatementcensus2016resu ltsprofile2-populationdistributionandmovements/; accessed 17 October 2017.

2.   J. O'Beirne Ranelagh, *A Short History of Ireland*, Cambridge: Cambridge University Press, 2001.

3.   S. Conlin and P. Harbison, *Dublin: The Story of a City*, Dublin: O'Brien Press, 2017.

4.   'Census 2016 Profile 7 – Migration and Diversity', CSO, cso.ie/en/ csolatestnews/pressreleases/2017pressreleases/pressstatementcens us2016resultsprofile7-migrationanddiversity/; accessed 15 October 2017.

5. Dublin City Interfaith Forum, dublincityinterfaithforum.org/; accessed 5 September 2017.

6. Corrymella, corrymeela.org/about/who-we-are; accessed 10 October 2017.

7. See Adrian Cristea's report in Irish Council of Churches, *Churches in Ireland: Connecting in Christ: 2011 Annual Report*, p. 13, irishchurches.org/cmsfiles/resources/Reports/2011Annualtweb.pdf; accessed 10 October 2017.

8. For an account of the establishment of the DCIF and a reflection on its principles, see Adrian Cristea, *Integration and Interfaith: Faith/City Engagement in a Multicultural Context*, Dublin: Dublin City Interfaith Forum.

9. Adrian Cristea, *Integration and Interfaith*.

10. P. McGarry, 'Interfaith Group in Urgent Call for State Funding to be Doubled', *The Irish Times*, 10 December 2018, irishtimes.com/news/social-affairs/religion-and-beliefs/interfaith-group-in-urgent-call-for-state-funding-to-be-doubled-1.3726634

11. C. McGrail, 'Come and See How I Live', *The Irish Catholic*, 17 March 2016, irishcatholic.com/come-and-see-how-i-live/

12. Martin Luther King, Jr, *I Have A Dream: Writings and Speeches that Changed the World*, San Francisco: Harper, 1986, pp. 102–6.

13. Martin Luther King, Jr, *I Have A Dream*.

CHAPTER SIX
Learning from Diverse Beliefs in the Mid-West Interfaith Network
Trisha Rainsford

1. Aleksandr Solzhenitsyn, *The Gulag Archipelago*, London: Vintage Publishing, 2003, pp. 77–8.

2. 'David Bohm on Perception', youtu.be/Mst3fOl5vH0; accessed October 10, 2017.

CHAPTER SEVEN
Catholic Perspectives on Interreligious Dialogue
Bishop Brendan Leahy

1. The World Day of Prayer for Peace in Assisi, 27 October 1986, was a remarkable event. There were over sixty religious leaders who fasted and prayed, representing thirty-two Christian religious organisations and eleven non-Christian world religions.

2. Pontifical Council for Inter-Religious Dialogue, *Reflection and Orientations on Interreligious Dialogue and The Proclamation of the Gospel of Jesus Christ*, 19 May 1991, 9.

3. Focolare Movement, focolare.org; Sant'Egidio, santegidio.org/; accessed on 6 September 2016.

4. An open letter entitled 'A Common Word Between Us and You' in 2007 was a major landmark in this relationship. It was a statement of peace and friendship from one hundred and thirty Muslim scholars to Christian leaders around the world.

5. See the opening paragraph of the Second Vatican Council document on the nature of the Church, *Lumen Gentium*, 21 November 1964.

6. See the Second Vatican Council document on the Church in the Modern World, *Gaudium et Spes*, 7 December 1965, 22.

7. Gavin D'Costa, *Christianity and the World Religions: Disputed Questions in the Theology of Religions*, Chichester: Wiley-Blackwell, 2009.

8. Pope Francis, Apostolic Exhortation on the Joy of the Gospel, *Evangelii Gaudium*, 24 November 2013, 254.

9. 'Vision and Mission', Religions for Peace, rfp.org/learn/vision-mission/; accessed on 6 September 2016.

10. Patsy McGarry, 'Mansion House Hosts Inter-faith Forum Examining Religion's Role in Global Conflict', *The Irish Times*, 19 March 2015.

11. Pope Francis, *Evangelii Gaudium*, 251.

12. Introduction to Congregation for Catholic Education, *Educating to Intercultural Dialogue in Catholic Schools: Living in Harmony for a Civilization of Love*, Vatican City: 2013.

13. Conclusion to Congregation for Catholic Education, *Educating to Intercultural Dialogue in Catholic Schools: Living in Harmony for a Civilization of Love*, Vatican City: 2013.

14. Irish Episcopal Conference, *Catholic Preschool and Primary Religious Education Curriculum for Ireland*, Dublin: Veritas, 2015.

15. Irish Episcopal Conference, *Catholic Preschool and Primary Religious Education Curriculum*, p. 21.

CHAPTER EIGHT
Interbelief Dialogue and the Church of Ireland
Keith Scott

1. Anglican Communion, anglicancommunion.org/identity/about. aspx; accessed 28 May 2016.

2. Statement of Anglican essentials for a reunited Christian Church adopted by the House of Bishops Chicago, 1886 and Lambeth Conference in 1888, 'The Chicago–Lambeth Quadrilateral 1886, 1888', Anglicans Online, anglicansonline.org/basics/Chicago_ Lambeth.html; accessed on 16 November 2016.

3. J.F. Woolverton, 'The Chicago–Lambeth Quadrilateral and the Lambeth Conferences' in *Historical Magazine of the Protestant Episcopal Church*, 53:2, 1984, pp. 100–1.

4. 'In Full Communion', Anglicans Online, anglicansonline.org/ communion/infull.html; accessed 6 June 2016.

5. 'The Chicago–Lambeth Quadrilateral 1886, 1888', Anglicans Online, anglicansonline.org/basics/Chicago_Lambeth.html; accessed 6 June 2016.

6. David Lochhead, *The Dialogical Imperative: A Christian Reflection on Interfaith Encounter*, Oregon: Wipf and Stock Publishers, 2012, pp. 49–53.

7. Lochhead, *The Dialogical Imperative*, p. 96.

8. Lochhead, *The Dialogical Imperative*, pp. 41–5.

9. Philip Lewis, *Islamic Britain: Religion, Politics, and Identity among British Muslims: Bradford in the 1990s*, London: I.B. Tauris, 1994, p. 16.

10. 'The Porvoo Communion is a fellowship of Anglican and Lutheran churches who celebrate their unity as churches and who share a common sacramental life and ministry through the Porvoo Common Statement (agreed in 1992). ... The Church of Ireland signed this statement in 1995.' 'The Provoo Communion', Church of Ireland, ireland.anglican.org/about/general-synod-its-committees/commission-for-christian-unity-and-dialogue/the-porvoo-communion; accessed on 9 November 2016.

11. 'The Methodist Covenant', Church of Ireland, ireland.anglican. org/about/general-synod-its-committees/covenant-council/the-methodist-covenant; accessed 2 June 2016; 'General Synod 2014: interchangeability of Ministry between Church of Ireland and Methodist Church in Ireland', Church of Ireland, ireland.anglican. org/news/5119/general-synod-2014-interchangeability-of; accessed 2 June 2016.

12. G. Higgins, M. Blythman, C. Curran and S. Parkinson, *The Hard Gospel: Dealing Positively with Difference in the Church of Ireland: A Scoping Study Report to the Sectarianism Education Project*, The General Synod of the Church of Ireland, 2003, ireland.anglican. org/cmsfiles/files/information/issues/scstudy1.pdf; accessed on 10 November 2016.

13. Higgins et al., *The Hard Gospel*, p. 14.

14. Hard Gospel: Central Church Structures, ireland.anglican.org/archive/hardgospel/index.php?id=18?id=18; accessed 7 May 2016.

15. M. Jackson, 'The Hard Gospel and Interfaith Encounter: Why Would You Bother?' ireland.anglican.org/news/3155/the-hard-gospel-and-inter; accessed 7 May 2016.

16. Church of Ireland and Committee for Christian Unity, *Guidelines for Interfaith Events and Dialogue*, Dublin: Church of Ireland Publishing, 2007.

17. Jackson, 'The Hard Gospel and Interfaith Encounter'.

18. J. Liechty, *Roots of Sectarianism in Ireland*, Irish Inter-Church Meeting, Belfast, 1993.

19. A.F. Walls, *The Missionary Movement in Christian History: Studies in the Transmission of Faith* New York: Orbis Books, 1996, p. 20.

20. J. Liechty, 'Remembering 1641: The October 23 Thanksgiving Sermons 1685–1770', Draft text of a public lecture, October 1991.

21. Ibid.

22. T. Macaulay, *Hard Gospel Project Evaluation Report*, Church of Ireland, ireland.anglican.org/cmsfiles/pdf/Information/Resources/HG/final_eval.pdf; accessed 2 June 2016.

23. Ibid., pp. 40–1.

24. Ibid., p. 41.

25. 'Some Images of the Inter Faith Seminar Held in Limerick', Church of Ireland, ireland.anglican.org/news/4785/some-images-from-the-inter; accessed 7 June 2016.

26. Lochhead, *The Dialogical Imperative*, p. 1.

27. D.J. Bosch, *Transforming Mission: Paradigm Shifts in Theology of Mission*, Maryknoll, NY: Orbis Books, 1991, p. 11.

CHAPTER NINE
A Perspective on Dialogue from a Member of the Methodist Faith
Siobhán Wheeler

1. Saint Augustine, *Confessions*, Oxford: Oxford University Press, 2008, p. 230.

2. D.F. Ford, *The Shape of Living Spiritual Directions for Everyday Life*, Norwich: Canterbury Press, 2012, p. 70.

3. D.J. Bosch, *Transforming Mission*, New York: Orbis Books, 1991, p. 128.

4. V. Donovan, *Christianity Rediscovered*, New York: Orbis Books, 2003, p. 37.

5. F.H. Everson, *This is Methodism*, London: The Epworth Press, 1959, p. 21.

6. W. Mullally, 'Inaugaral Address of the Rev. Bill Mullally, President of the Methodist Church in Ireland', *Methodist Newsletter*, 44:77, August 2016, p. 44.

7. F.H. Everson, *This is Methodism*.

8. J. Wesley, A. Russie (ed.), *The Essential Works of John Wesley*, Ohio: Barbour, 2011.

9. P.W. Chilcote, *Recapturing the Wesleys' Vision: An Introduction to the Faith of John and Charles Wesley*, Downers Grove: Inter-Varsity Press, 2004, p. 99.

10. Everson, *This is Methodism*, p. 22.

11. P. Meadows, *The Wesleyan DNA of Discipleship Fresh Expressions of Discipleship For the 21st-century Church*, Cambridge: Grove Books, 2013, p. 23.

12. J. Wesley, *A Collection of Hymns for the Use of the People called Methodists,* London: Wesleyan Conference Office, 1779, p. 485.

13. Everson, *This is Methodism*, p. 51.

14. 'Sermon 63: General Spread of the Gospel', godonthe.net/wesley/ jws_063.html; accessed 12 September 2017.

15. Chilcote, *Recapturing the Wesleys' Vision*, p. 102.

16. T. Flannery, *From the Inside*, Cork: Mercier Press, 1999, p. 135.

17. J.H. Newman, *The Idea of a University*, New Haven, CT: Yale University Press, 1996, p. 45.

18. B. Leahy, *Who Leads the Church?* Ireland: Veritas, 2015, p. 11.

19. D.W. Smith, *The Kindness of God: Christian Witness in Our Troubled World*, Nottingham: Inter-Varsity Press, 2013, p.11.

20. P. Meadows, *The Wesleyan*, p. 14.

21. Pope Francis, 'Meeting with the Participants in the Fifth Convention of the Italian Church: Address of the Holy Father', Florence, 10 Nvember 2015, w2.vatican.va/content/francesco/en/ speeches/2015/november/documents/papa-francesco_20151110_

firenze-convegno-chiesa-italiana.html; accessed 17 December 2017.

22. S. Miles, *Take This Bread: A Radical Conversion*, New York: Ballantine Books, 2008, p. xi.

23. L. Newbigin, *The Gospel in a Pluralist Society,* London: Society for Promoting Christian Knowledge, 1989, p. 243–4.

24. L. Newbigin, *The Open Secret*, London: Society for Promoting Christian Knowledge, 1995, pp. 182–3.

25. Everson, *This is Methodism*, p. 21.

CHAPTER TEN

Atheists and Theists in Dialogue Jointly Promoting Mutual Respect and Ethical Secularism

Michael Nugent and Jane Donnelly

1. Atheist Ireland, atheist.ie/; accessed 19 October 2017.

2. Teach Don't Preach, teachdontpreach.ie/; accessed 19 October 2017.

3. 'Report: World's Happiest Countries Are Also Least Religious', Patheos, patheos.com/blogs/progressivesecularhumanist/2016/03/report-worlds-happiest-countries-are-also-least-religious/; accessed 19 October 2017.

4. Congregation for Catholic Education, 'Circular Letter to the Presidents of Bishops' Conferences on Religious Education in Schools', vatican.va/roman_curia/congregations/ccatheduc/documents/rc_con_ccatheduc_doc_20090505_circ-insegn-relig_en.html; accessed 19 October 2017.

5. 'It is the responsibility of the school to provide a religious education that is consonant with its ethos and at the same time to be flexible in making alternative organisational arrangements for those who do not wish to avail of the particular religious education it offers. It is equally important that the beliefs and sensibilities of every child are respected. Since the Department of Education and Science, in the context of the Education Act (1998), recognises

the rights of the different church authorities to design curricula in religious education at primary level and to supervise their teaching and implementation, a religious education curriculum is not included in these curriculum documents.' Department of Education and Science, *Primary School Curriculum: Introduction*, Dublin: Government Publications, 1999 p. 58.

CHAPTER ELEVEN
The Importance of Beliefs, Respect, Secularism, Dialogue and Equal Treatment
Imam Ibrahim Ahmad Noonan

1. Ahmadiyya: Muslim Association Ireland, islamahmadiyya.ie/; accessed 10 May 2018.

2. Al Islam, alislam.org; accessed 3 February 2017.

3. *Sa* is an abbreviation of the Arabic phrase *sallallahu alayhi wa salaam*, which means 'may God's prayers and peace be with him'.

4. The use of the words *swt* after the name of Allah is an abbreviation of the Arabic phrase *Subhanahu wa ta'ala which* translates as 'Glory to Him, the Exalted'. It is used as a term of reverence and devotion to God.

5. For an account of his life, see A.R. Dard, *Life of Ahmad as Founder of the Ahmadiyya Movement*, UK: Islam International Publications, 2008.

6. Quran 3:56; New Testament Hebrews 5:7.

7. Hazrat Mirza Ghulam Ahmad, *The Ark of Noah*, Muslim Literary Trust of Trinidad and Tobago, 2003. Kashti-e-Nuh, *Noah's Ark*, p. viii.

8. The entire speech can be found at: 'Jalsa Salana Germany 2011, Concluding Address by Hadhrat Mirza Masroor Ahmad, Islam Ahmadiyyat', youtu.be/w8uW9EhFBhU; accessed 18 October 2017.

9. 'Why Ahmadi Muslims are Doomed in Pakistan', Ahmadiyya, 18 March 2018, islamahmadiyya.ie/why-ahmadi-muslims-are-doomed-in-pakistan/; accessed 17 October 2017.

10. S. Shams, 'The Persecution of Ahmadis in Pakistan and Beyond', DW, 13 December 2016, dw.com/en/the-persecution-of-ahmadis-in-pakistan-and-beyond/a-36748924; accessed 17 October 2017.

11. M. Tarar, 'Why Ahmadi Muslims are Doormed in Pakistan', Daily O, 11 March 2018, dailyo.in/voices/pakistan-ahmadi-muslim-islambad-high-court-islam/story/1/22768.html

12. 'Algeria: New Trials Shake Ahmadi Minority', Human Rights Watch, 22 January 2018, hrw.org/news/2018/01/22/algeria-new-trials-shake-ahmadi-minority

13. 'Church Leaders Support Muslims after Galway Mosque Attack', Ahmadiyya, 20 June 2017, http://islamahmadiyya.ie/church-leaders-support-muslims-after-galway-mosque-attack/; accessed 17 October 2017.

14. 'Church Leaders Support Muslims after Galway Mosque Attack', *The Irish Times*, 7 June 2017, irishtimes.com/news/social-affairs/religion-and-beliefs/church-leaders-support-muslims-after-galway-mosque-attack-1.3111078

CHAPTER TWELVE
Why Secular Education is Good for Children, Good for Religion, and Good for Society
Nick Park

1. 'Choosing Segregation? The Implications of School Choice', Oireachtas Library and Research Service, 2015, p. 1, data.oireachtas.ie/ie/oireachtas/libraryResearch/2015/2015-09-28_spotlight-choosing-segregation-the-implications-of-school-choice_en.pdf; accessed 20 May 2018.

2. K. Fischer, *Schools and the Politics of Religion and Diversity in the Republic of Ireland: Separate but Equal?* Manchester, UK: Manchester University Press, 2016.

3. T. Walsh, 'The National System of Education, 1831–2000' in B. Walsh (ed.), *Essays in the History of Irish Education*, London: Macmillan, 2016, p. 9.

4. M. Heinz, K. Davison and E. Keane, 'I will do it but religion is a very personal thing: teacher education applicants' attitudes towards teaching religion in Ireland', *European Journal of Teacher Education*, 2018, pp. 1–14.

5. G. Davie, *Religion in Britain Since 1945: Believing Without Belonging: Making Contemporary Britain*, Wiley-Blackwell, 1994; *Religion in Britain: A Persistent Paradox*, Wiley-Blackwell, 2015.

6. Census 2016: Religion, Dublin: ROI.

7. O. Cosgrove, L. Cox, C. Kuhling and P. Mulholland (eds), *Ireland's New Religious Movements*, Newcastle: Cambridge Scholars Publishing, 2011.

8. 'Dramatic Fall in Irish Religious Beliefs', BBC News, 6 April 2017, bbc.com/news/world-europe-39516154

9. In 2018 the Amendment to Education (Admission to Schools) Bill 2016 removed what was known as the 'the baptism barrier' as an entry requirement to 90 per cent of schools.

10. H. Bielefeldt, 'The Liberal Concept of Political Secularism' in R. Tinnevelt and G. Verschraegen (eds), *Between Cosmopolitan Ideals and State Sovereignty: Studies in Global Justice*, Basingstoke: Palgrove Macmillan, 2006, p. 103.

CHAPTER THIRTEEN
A Humanist Perspective on Dialogue about Religions and Beliefs
Tina Storey

1. A. Einstein, *'Religion and Science'*, *New York Times Magazine*, 9 November 1930.

2. D. McMahan, New York, Letter to the editor, Humanist Network News, American Humanist Association, 2004, paraphrasing C.S. Lewis.

3. 'Famous Humanists', Humanist Association of Ireland, humanism. ie/about-us/famous-humanists/; accessed 10 August 2016.

4. 'How Humanist Are You?', Humanists UK, humanism.org.uk/ humanism/how-humanist-are-you/; accessed 10 August 2016.

5. Common Era or Current Era, abbreviated CE, is a calendar era that is often used as an alternative naming of the Anno Domini system ('in the year of the Lord'), abbreviated AD. The system uses BCE as an abbreviation for 'before the Common (or Current) Era' and CE as an abbreviation for 'Common Era'. The CE/BCE designation uses the same numeric values as the traditional Anno Domini year-numbering system (AD/BC) more generally by authors and publishers wishing to emphasise secularism or sensitivity to non-Christians, because it does not explicitly make use of religious titles for Jesus, such as 'Christ' and Dominus ('Lord'), which are used in the AD/BC notation, nor does it give implicit expression to the Christian creed that Jesus is the Christ.

6. S. Stenudd, 'The Creation in Rig Veda 10:129: The Paradox of Origin', Creation Myths, creationmyths.org/rigveda-10-129-indian-creation/; accessed 10 August 2016; Nasadiya Sukta, *Rigveda (10:129)*, translated from the Sanskrit by A.L. Basham in *The Wonder that was India*, London, 1953. Transliterated by Avinash Sathaye, sanskritdocuments.org, http://sanskritdocuments.org/doc_veda/naasadiiya.pdf, 25 July 2016; accessed 10 August 2016.

7. 'Humanism', New World Encyclopedia, newworldencyclopedia.org/entry/Humanism; accessed 20 September 2016.

8. P. Charron, *Trois Livres de la Sagesse*, Bordeaux, 1601.

9. A. Pope, *An Essay on Man: In Epistles to a Friend* (Epistle III), London: J. Wilford, 1733.

10. 'Census 2011: Profile 7: Religion, Ethnicity and Irish Travellers', CSO, cso.ie/en/media/csoie/census/documents/census2011profile7/Profile7EducationEthnicityandIrishTravellerEntiredoc.pdf; accessed 18 September 2016.

11. Source: Poll exploring the religious beliefs of 63,898 people from sixty-five countries across the globe, 13 April 2015, WIN/Gallup International, http://www.wingia.com/.

12. 'Dawkins: I'm a Cultural Christian', BBC News, 10 December 2007, news.bbc.co.uk/2/hi/uk_politics/7136682.stm; accessed 1 July 2016.

13. 'Frequently Asked Questions', American Humanist Association, americanhumanist.org/about/faq/; accessed 1 July 2016.

14. Thomas Jefferson, *Letter to the Danbury Baptists*, 1 January 1802.

15. J. Bardi, 'The Humanist Interview with Gloria Steinem', *The Humanist Magazine, 7 June 2012;* thehumanist.com/magazine/september-october-2012/features/the-humanist-interview-with-gloria-steinem; *accessed 9 August 2016.*

16. 'Marriages and Civil Partnerships 2015', CSO, 15 April 2016, cso.ie/en/releasesandpublications/er/mcp/marriagesandcivilpartnerships2015/; accessed 19 September 2016.

17. 2018 Amendment to Education (Admission to Schools) Bill 2016, education.ie/en/Press-Events/Press-Releases/2018-press-releases/PR18-05-09.html; accessed 25 May 2018.

18. Over two million people voted by 66.4 per cent to 33.6 per cent to repeal the Eight Amendment in May 2018.

19. During April and May 2009, the HAI ran a poster campaign on DART trains in Dublin to raise public awareness regarding the practice of judges and presidents of Ireland being obliged to take an oath. The poster, headed 'Unbelievable' asked: 'Did you know that you must take a religious oath in order to become a judge – or the president – in Ireland? In effect, this rule disbars up to 250,000 Irish citizens who are non-believers. It's discrimination. It's unfair. And it has to end.' P. McGarry, 'Humanists launch campaign against judicial religious oaths', *The Irish Times*, 4 April 2009, irishtimes.com/news/humanists-launch-campaign-against-judicial-religious-oaths-1.737423?via=mr; accessed 1 July 2016.

20. 'Religious Instruction and Worship in Certain Second Level Schools in Context of Article 44.2.4 of the Constitution of Ireland and Section 30 of the Education Act 1998', Department of Education and Skill, education.ie/en/Circulars-and-Forms/Active-Circulars/cl0013_2018.pdf; see also, 'How the State Religious Education Course Breaches Human and Constitutional Rights', Atheist Ireland Report, July 2016, atheist.ie/wordpress/wp-content/uploads/2016/07/AI_State_Religious_Education_Course_Report.pdf; accessed 10 August 2016.

21. 'Girl Can Opt Out of Religion Class but Must Stay in Room', RTÉ News, 24 November 2015, www.rte.ie/news/2015/1123/748507-schools-

religion/ and E. O'Kelly, 'Religious Education Opt-Out Highlights Parents' Rights', rte.ie/news/special-reports/2015/1124/748829-blog-limerick-school-religion/

22. 'Ireland's First Ever Humanism Lesson Plans for Primary Schools', Educate Together, educatetogether.ie/humanism-lessons; accessed 15 May 2018.

23. 'Teaching Resources for Schools', Understanding Humanism, understandinghumanism.org.uk/; accessed 10 August 2016.

CHAPTER SIXTEEN
Are We Just Going to Stand By?
Tomi Reichental

1. For an account of Tomi's life, see T. Reichental, *I Was a Boy in Belsen*, Dublin: O'Brien Press, 2011.

2. *Close to Evil* documents Tomi's attempts to meet with one of his former jailers from Bergen-Belson, Hilde (Lisiewicz) Michnia, who was alive and well and living in Hamburg. The film won the best single documentary award in 2015 from the Irish Film and Television Academy.

3. Some of Tomi's presentations have been recorded and are available online; for example, his lecture co-hosted by UCD Philosophy Society and UCD German Society on 31 March 2015, youtu.be/1GdVZ2mp7lg; accessed 17 October 2017.

4. Tomi's first documentary film telling the story of his experience in the Nazi death camps was made by RTÉ in 2009, *Till the Tenth Generation*, was directed by Gerry Gregg and produced by Praxis Pictures, screenireland.ie/directory/view/766/till-the-tenth-generation/archive; accessed 6 October 2017.

5. K. Sheridan, 'We, as a Human Race, have to Find Ways to Reconcile', *The Irish Times*, 8 January 2016, irishtimes.com/life-and-style/people/tomi-reichental-we-as-a-human-race-have-to-find-ways-to-reconcile-1.2489471; accessed 8 October 2017.

CHAPTER SEVENTEEN
Islamophobia in Ireland
James Carr

1. E. Said, *Orientalism*, London: Penguin, 2003.

2. J. Carr, 'Regulating Islamophobia: The Need for Collecting Disaggregated Data on Racism in Ireland', *Journal of Muslim Minority Affairs*, 3:4, 2011, pp. 574–93.

3. I use the term 'anti-Muslim racism' as it brings our attention to the manner in which society constructs different groups as holding particular, innate characteristics and tendencies. 'Races' of course do not exist; Muslims are not a 'race' but they are constructed as such through the process of racialisation. Racialised communities, whether based on faith identity, culture or skin colour etc., in isolation or intersection are frequently presented as, for example in the case of Muslims, holding proclivities towards terrorism, atavism, with all Muslim men as hyper-patriarchal males, and all Muslim women as passive, oppressed females. Constructions such as these elide the realities of the immensely vibrant diversity of Muslim communities in Ireland and across the globe. Instead we are presented with a narrow homogenising image of Muslims and Islam that is invoked to legitimise hostility and discrimination in Ireland and abroad. Interrogating these construction processes is a vital step in dialogue. For more see Carr, *Experiences of Islamophobia*, 2016; Runnymede Trust 1997.

4. J. Carr, *Experiences of Islamophobia: Living with Racism in the Neoliberal Era*, London: Routledge, 2016.

5. 'Hostility' was defined as: verbal abuse, physical assault, damage to property, graffiti, theft, threats/harassment.

6. 'Discrimination' was defined as: at/looking for work, in/accessing education, accessing health services, using public transport, restaurants, obtaining accommodation.

7. Enes Bayrakli and Farid Hafez (eds), *European Islamophobia Report 2015*, islamophobiaeurope.com/reports/2015/en/EIR_2015.pdf; accessed 1 June 2016.

8. Some, not all, Muslim people use the term 'revert' instead of 'convert'; I use the con/re-vert term to accommodate both of these opinions and also recognise the perspectives of non-Muslims in this regard.

9. Bayrakli and Hafez, *European Islamophobia Report 2015*.

10. All names used in this text are pseudonyms.

11. One form of head covering worn by some female Muslims which covers the face and leaves the eyes exposed.

12. P. Hillyard, *Suspect Community: People's Experience of the Prevention of Terrorism Acts in Britain*, London: Pluto Press, 1993.

13. The term 'guards' is a popular term of reference for the Irish Police service, *An Garda Síochána*.

14. Claire Dwyer, 'Veiled Meanings: Young British Muslim Women and the Negotiation of Differences', *Gender, Place and Culture: A Journal of Feminist Geography*, 6:1, pp. 5–26., p. 7.

15. J. Carr, *European Islamophobia Report 2015: Ireland*, islamophobiaeurope.com/reports/2015/en/EIR_2015_IRELAND.pdf; accessed 1 June 2016.

CHAPTER EIGHTEEN
The Transformative Power of Dialogue
Eamon Rafter

1. A. Camus, quoted in K. Cloke, *Mediating Dangerously: The Frontiers of Conflict Resolution*, San Francisco: Jossey-Bass, 2001.

2. B. Pruitt and P. Thomas, *Democratic Dialogue: A Handbook for Practitioners*, USA: International IDEA, 2007.

3. D. Bohm, *On Dialogue*, London: Routledge, 1996.

4. J.P. Lederach, *The Moral Imagination: The Art and Soul of Building Peace*, Oxford: Oxford University Press, 2005.

5. D. Bohm, *On Dialogue*, London: Routledge, 1996.

CONCLUSION

Patricia Kieran

1. G. Biesta, *The Rediscovering of Teaching*, London: Routledge, 2017.

2. Adherents, adherents.com/; accessed on 10 November 2016. For further details see the Council of Europe, coe.int/en/web/compass/religion-and-belief; accessed 16 October 2017.

3. Julia Ipgrave's chapter outlined the complexity of dialogue in UK school settings. Her work to date has highlighted the possibilities (and also the limitations) of digital technology and social media to enhance dialogue. Julia Ipgrave, Ursula McKenna, Robert Jackson, *Interfaith Dialogue by Email in Primary Schools*, Munster: Waxmann Verlag, 2008.

4. 'Census 2016 Summary Results: Religion', CSO, cso.ie/en/media/csoie/releasespublications/documents/population/2017/Chapter_8_Religion.pdf; accessed 16 December 2017.

5. L.P. Barnes (ed.), *Debates in Religious Education*, London: Routledge, 2012.

6. D. Faas, M. Darmody and B. Sokolowska, 'Religious Diversity in Primary Schools: Reflections from the Republic of Ireland', *British Journal of Religious Education*, 38:1, 2015, pp. 83–98.

7. E. Cassidy, *Ecumenism and Interreligious Dialogue*, New York: Paulist Press, 2005, p. 33. In 2011 after five years of working together, the Pontifical Council for Interreligious Dialogue (PCID) of the Roman Catholic Church, the World Council of Churches (WCC) and the World Evangelical Alliance (WEA) produced a document, *Christian Witness in a Multi-Religious World: Recommendations for Conduct*. This document arose from a need for a code of conduct to move beyond interreligious tensions and difference in religious convictions.

8. R.E. Hassner, and J. Wittenberg, 'Barriers to Entry: Who Builds Fortified Boundaries and Are They Likely to Work?', *International Security*, 40:1, 2015, pp. 157–90. A version of this is available from the 2009 Toronto Meeting Paper, ssrn.com/abstract=1449327; accessed 17 December 2017.

9. Suspicion and mistrust of Muslims was a key theme in Trump's election campaign. Xenophobic remarks about other groups including Mexicans peppered the airwaves. Many voters seemed to like the rhetoric. 'While many were troubled by what he had said about Muslims ... they mentioned his strength, his "straightforward" approach to "bombing the shit" out of them, and "building a wall" to make sure that we take control of who comes into the country. These voters are anxious and feel a loss of control.' M. Kranish and M. Fisher, *Trump Revealed: An American Journey of Ambition, Ego, Money and Power*, New York: Scribner, 2016, p. 319. In 2016, Justin Barrett registered a new far-right political party in Ireland, called the National Party, which has among its aims the desire to deport illegal immigrants, restrict mass immigration, give Irish people priority in employment and restrict Muslims entering Ireland.

10. S.P. Lovett, 'Pope at UAE Interreligious Meeting: Dialogue and Prayer for Peace', *Vatican News*, 4 February 2019, vaticannews. va/ en/pope/news/2019-02/pope-francis-uae-interreligious-meetingdialogue-peace.html; accessed 2 March 2019.

11. 'Religions for Peace', High-level Conversation of the United Nations General Assembly, 6 May 2016, un.org/pga/70/wp-content/uploads/sites/10/2015/08/5-April_High-level-Conversation-on-Religions-for-Peace-5-April-2016.pdf; accessed 17 December 2017.

12. D. Tracy, *Dialogue with the Other: The Interreligious Dialogue*, Louvain: Peters Press, 1990, p. 95.

13. G. Byrne and P. Kieran (eds), *Toward Mutual Ground: Pluralism, Religious Education and Diversity in Irish Schools*, Dublin: Columba Press, 2013, p. 24.

14. M.L. Seeberg, I. Levin and C. Lenz, *The Holocaust as Active Memory: The Past in the Present*, Ashgate, 2013, p. 2.

15. Justin Barrett founded the Irish National Party in 2016, The National Party, nationalparty.ie/; accessed 14 December 2017.

16. *Directory of Migrant Organisations and Support Groups in Dublin*, Dublin: New Communities Partnership, 2012, newcommunities.ie/download/pdf/20130812153718.pdf; accessed 15 December 2017.